SMP interact

Higher
transition

for **AQA, Edexcel** and **OCR two-tier GCSE mathematics**

CAMBRIDGE
UNIVERSITY PRESS

The School Mathematics Project

Writing and editing for this edition   John Ling, Paul Scruton, Susan Shilton, Heather West
SMP design and administration   Melanie Bull, Pam Keetch, Nicky Lake, Cathy Syred, Ann White

The following people contributed to the original edition of SMP Interact for GCSE.

Benjamin Alldred	David Cassell	Spencer Instone	Susan Shilton
Juliette Baldwin	Ian Edney	Pamela Leon	Caroline Starkey
Simon Baxter	Stephen Feller	John Ling	Liz Stewart
Gill Beeney	Rosemary Flower	Carole Martin	Biff Vernon
Roger Beeney	John Gardiner	Lorna Mulhern	Jo Waddingham
Roger Bentote	Colin Goldsmith	Mary Pardoe	Nigel Webb
Sue Briggs	Bob Hartman	Paul Scruton	Heather West

CAMBRIDGE UNIVERSITY PRESS
Cambridge, New York, Melbourne, Madrid, Cape Town, Singapore, São Paulo

Cambridge University Press
The Edinburgh Building, Cambridge CB2 2RU, UK

www.cambridge.org
Information on this title: www.cambridge.org/9780521689953

© The School Mathematics Project 2006

First published 2006

Printed in the United Kingdom at the University Press, Cambridge

A catalogue record for this publication is available from the British Library

ISBN-13   978-0-521-68995-3 paperback
ISBN-10   0-521-68995-3 paperback

Typesetting and technical illustrations by The School Mathematics Project
Other illustrations by Robert Calow and Steve Lach at Eikon Illustration
Photographs by Graham Portlock
Cover design by Angela Ashton
Cover image by Jim Wehtje/Photodisc Green/Getty Images

The authors and publisher are grateful to the following examination boards for permission to reproduce
questions from past examination papers, identified in the text as follows.
AQA   Assessment and Qualifications Alliance
Edexcel   Edexcel Limited
OCR   Oxford, Cambridge and RSA Examinations
WJEC   Welsh Joint Education Committee
The authors, and not the examination boards, are responsible for the method and accuracy of the answers
to examination questions given; these may not necessarily constitute the only possible solutions. The AQA
questions reproduced as I5 and I6 on page 57 and as T3 on page 188 are not from the live examinations for
the specification current at the date of publication of this book; new specifications were introduced in 2003.

Using this book

For Higher tier GCSE there are two main students' books, *Higher 1* and *Higher 2*. This book, *Higher transition*, is for students who have followed any 'core' course in key stage 3 and need to cover or revise the more basic topics before they start *Higher 1*.

To help users identify material that can be omitted by some students – or just dipped into for revision or to check competence – chapter sections estimated to be at national curriculum level 6 (or in a few cases level 5) are marked as such. These levels are also given in the detailed contents list on the next few pages.

At the end of the contents list is a precedence diagram to help those who want to use chapters selectively or in a different order from that of the book.

Each chapter begins with a summary of what it covers and ends with a self-assessment section ('Test yourself').

Topics that can be used as the basis of teacher-led activity or discussion – with the whole class or smaller groups – are marked with this symbol.

There are clear worked examples – and past exam questions, labelled by board, to give the student an idea of the style and standard that may be expected, and to build confidence.

Questions to be done without a calculator are marked with this symbol.

Questions marked with a star are more challenging.

 Suggestions for work on a spreadsheet and for web searches are marked like this.

After every few chapters there is a review section containing a mixture of questions on previous work.

The small number of resource sheets linked to this book can be downloaded in PDF format from www.smpmaths.org.uk and may be printed out for use within the institution purchasing this book.

Practice booklets

There is a practice booklet for each students' book. The practice booklet follows the structure of the students' book, making it easy to organise extra practice, homework and revision. Unlike the students' books, the practice booklets do not contain answers; these can be downloaded in PDF format from www.smpmaths.org.uk

Contents

continues >

The precedence diagram below, showing all the chapters, is designed to help with planning, especially where the teacher wishes to select from the material to meet the needs of particular students or to use chapters in a different order from that of the book. A blue line connecting two chapters indicates that, to a significant extent, working on the later chapter requires competence with topics dealt with in the earlier one.

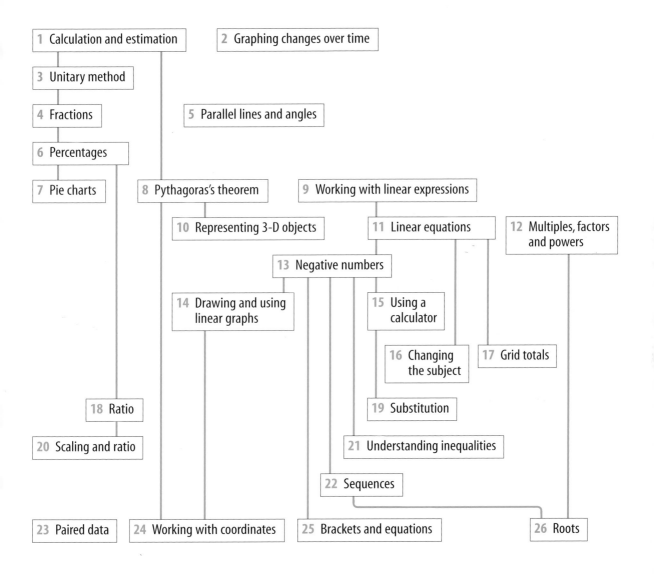

1 Calculation and estimation

You will revise how to

- multiply and divide by a decimal without a calculator
- round numbers to the nearest hundred, thousand, ...
- round numbers to a given number of decimal places

This work will help you

- round to a given number of significant figures
- estimate the result of a calculation by rounding
- give answers to a sensible degree of accuracy

A Decimals and place value   level 5

A1 The '5' in 6.35 represents $\frac{5}{100}$.

What does the 5 represent in each of these numbers?

   (a) 1524.9   (b) 13.52   (c) 5 200 000   (d) 0.015

A2 Put each list of decimals in order, smallest first.

   (a) 0.18, 1.9, 1.27, 0.3   (b) 0.25, 0.4, 0.05, 0.14

   (c) 0.47, 0.4, 0.407, 0.047   (d) 0.902, 0.092, 0.0092, 0.92

When a number is multiplied by 10, the digits all move one place to the left.
For example, $35.72 \times 10 = 357.2$.

When a number is multiplied by 100, the digits all move two places to the left, and so on.

A3 Write the answers to these.

   (a) 6.29×10 (b) 4.851×100 (c) 15.74×100 (d) 2.96×1000

   (e) 0.21×100 (f) 0.04×1000 (g) 0.501×10 (h) 0.0609×1000

When a number is divided by 10, the digits all move one place to the right.
For example, $35.72 \div 10 = 3.572$.

When a number is divided by 100, the digits all move two places to the right, and so on.

A4 Write the answers to these.

   (a) $56.1 \div 10$ (b) $72.31 \div 100$ (c) $6.4 \div 100$ (d) $39.87 \div 1000$

   (e) $3.07 \div 10$ (f) $0.13 \div 100$ (g) $0.095 \div 100$ (h) $24.08 \div 1000$

A5 Write the answers to these.

(a) 3.91×10 (b) $42.5 \div 10$ (c) 8.69×100 (d) $52.63 \div 100$

(e) 5.9×100 (f) $0.3 \div 10$ (g) $1.56 \div 100$ (h) $2.1 \times 10\,000$

B Multiplying by a decimal

For 0.3×50 you could start with 3×50.

$$3 \times 50 = 150$$

$\div 10$ $\div 10$

$$0.3 \times 50 = 15$$

Divide one number by 10. The result will be divided by 10.

For 30×0.05 you could start with 30×5.

$$30 \times 5 = 150$$

$\div 100$ $\div 100$

$$30 \times 0.05 = 1.5$$

Divide one number by 100. The result will be divided by 100.

For 0.3×0.5 you could start with 3×5.

$$3 \times 5 = 15$$

$\div 10$ $\div 10$ $\div 100$

$$0.3 \times 0.5 = 0.15$$

Divide **both** numbers by 10. The result will be divided by 100.

B1 Work these out.

(a) 3×0.4 (b) 0.3×0.4 (c) 30×0.4 (d) 3×0.04 (e) 30×0.04

(f) 80×5 (g) 80×0.5 (h) 0.8×50 (i) 0.08×5 (j) 800×0.5

B2 Show how to arrange these nine cards to make three correct multiplications.

| 50 | × 400 | = 200 | × 50 | 0.4 | = 2000 | 0.5 | × 40 | = 20 |

B3 The number 40 is fed into this chain of machines.

Input 40   ×0.5   + 40   ×0.1   − 20   Output

What is the largest output you can get by changing the order of the machines?

B4 Do the calculation in each box.
Arrange the answers in order of size, smallest first.
The letters will spell a word.

N	H	F	S
0.3×0.3	0.02×30	0.2×0.2	3×0.1

I	D	I	E
0.3×0.4	200×0.04	0.2×0.4	0.1×8

C Dividing by a decimal level 6

You can change division by a decimal to division by a whole number by multiplying 'top and bottom' by 10 or 100 or …

Examples

$$\frac{8}{0.2} \overset{\times 10}{\underset{\times 10}{=}} \frac{80}{2} = 40 \qquad \frac{1.5}{0.03} \overset{\times 100}{\underset{\times 100}{=}} \frac{150}{3} = 50$$

C1 Work these out.

(a) $\dfrac{6}{0.3}$ (b) $\dfrac{12}{0.2}$ (c) $\dfrac{2.4}{0.3}$ (d) $\dfrac{1.4}{0.2}$ (e) $\dfrac{120}{0.4}$

C2 Work these out.

(a) $\dfrac{1.2}{0.03}$ (b) $\dfrac{8}{0.04}$ (c) $\dfrac{16}{0.08}$ (d) $\dfrac{0.15}{0.03}$ (e) $\dfrac{0.8}{0.02}$

C3 Work these out.

(a) $\dfrac{4}{0.2}$ (b) $\dfrac{2}{0.05}$ (c) $\dfrac{2.8}{0.7}$ (d) $\dfrac{3.2}{0.04}$ (e) $\dfrac{0.36}{0.09}$

C4 These three cards | 0.5 | | = 8 | | 4 | can make a division. $\dfrac{4}{0.5}$ = 8

Arrange these six cards to make two correct divisions.

| 0.3 | | = 0.5 | | 1.5 | | 30 | | 15 | | = 5 |

C5 Arrange these six cards to make two correct divisions.

| 0.8 | | 24 | | 2.4 | | 0.08 | | = 3 | | = 300 |

C6 Choose two of the four numbers in the loop to go in the boxes to make a correct division.

(4 0.4 0.8 8) $\dfrac{\square}{\square} = 5$

C7 Do the same as in C6 for each of these.

(a) $\dfrac{\square}{\square} = 30$ (b) $\dfrac{\square}{\square} = 5$ (c) $\dfrac{\square}{\square} = 2.5$ (d) $\dfrac{\square}{\square} = 20$

(12 4 1.2 0.4) (9 4.5 0.45 0.9) (10 0.5 5 0.2) (10 0.05 5 1)

C8 Work these out.

(a) $\dfrac{4.68}{0.2}$ (b) $\dfrac{0.42}{0.3}$ (c) $\dfrac{0.18}{0.6}$ (d) $\dfrac{0.06}{0.3}$ (e) $\dfrac{0.86}{0.05}$

10 1 Calculation and estimation

D Rounding whole numbers level 5

D1 Round 4386 to the nearest   (a) thousand   (b) hundred   (c) ten

D2 Round 2396 to the nearest   (a) thousand   (b) hundred   (c) ten

D3 Round 40 789 to the nearest   (a) ten   (b) hundred   (c) thousand

D4 Round   (a) 32 096 to the nearest ten   (b) 48 607 to the nearest hundred

D5 This table shows the population of Greater London at each census in the early part of the 20th century.

Greater London	
Year	Population
1901	6 586 269
1911	7 225 946
1921	7 488 382
1931	8 215 673

   (a) Round the 1901 population to the nearest

     (i) hundred thousand   (ii) ten thousand

   (b) Round the 1931 population to the nearest

     (i) hundred thousand   (ii) thousand

   (c) Round each of the 1901, 1911, and 1921 populations to the nearest million. Why is it not a good idea to round them like this?

E Rounding decimals level 6

Example

Round 4.2763 to two decimal places.

4.2763 is between 4.27 and 4.28 .

Round up if the digit in the next decimal place is 5 or more. Here it is 6, so round up to **4.28** .

E1 Round each of these numbers to one decimal place (1 d.p.).

   (a) 48.32   (b) 8.754   (c) 0.4503   (d) 23.962   (e) 70.0413

E2 Round each of these numbers to two decimal places.

   (a) 3.9563   (b) 0.087 32   (c) 0.1659   (d) 3.5031   (e) 143.6395

E3 Round   (a) 3.4783 to 1 d.p.   (b) 4.083 12 to 2 d.p.   (c) 8.057 23 to 3 d.p.

         (d) 0.796 21 to 2 d.p.   (e) 0.067 843 to 3 d.p.   (f) 10.8956 to 1 d.p.

E4 Do these on a calculator and round each answer to two decimal places.

   (a) $2.65 \div 3.47$ (b) $4.818 \div 0.357$ (c) 0.159×0.357 (d) 16.77×0.167

   (e) 4.87×0.913 (f) $3.007 \div 27.55$ (g) $0.2619 \div 0.125$ (h) $1.169 \div 0.3894$

E5 (a) Calculate $2.467 \div 6.123$, giving the answer to 3 d.p.

   (b) Calculate 3.348×4.17, giving the answer to 1 d.p.

   (c) Calculate 0.5913^2, giving the answer to 3 d.p.

F Rounding to one significant figure

The first significant figure in a number is the figure with the highest value.

It is the first non-zero figure you come to working along from left to right.

	37 168	2.346	0.004 83
Rounding to one significant figure, we get:	40 000	2	0.005

F1 Round these numbers to one significant figure.

    (a) 278   (b) 11 328   (c) 5418   (d) 863   (e) 304 657

    (f) 5842   (g) 421 987   (h) 27 083   (i) 800 264   (j) 961

F2 Round these numbers to one significant figure.

    (a) 7.537   (b) 0.8851   (c) 0.6763   (d) 0.003 196   (e) 4.0075

    (f) 17.507   (g) 0.010 05   (h) 0.008 089   (i) 2.0775   (j) 0.9858

F3 A coach has 57 seats.
This is how Jack estimates the number of seats in 32 coaches.
Complete his estimate.

> Round the numbers to one significant figure:
> 57 becomes 60.   32 becomes 30.
> So 57 × 32 is roughly

F4 Work out a rough estimate for each of these.

    (a) 78 × 21   (b) 42 × 39   (c) 63 × 22   (d) 48 × 19   (e) 27 × 44

    (f) 291 × 33   (g) 58 × 188   (h) 37 × 487   (i) 81 × 77   (j) 196 × 207

Example

Estimate the answer to 0.364×516.

0.364 × 516	
Round to one significant figure: 0.4 × 500 = **200**	

> 4 × 5 = 20
> 4 × 50 = 200
> 4 × 500 = 2000
> 0.4 × 500 = 200

F5 Estimate the answer to each of these.

    (a) 7.2 × 0.23   (b) 0.48 × 3.13   (c) 0.27 × 0.41   (d) 0.186 × 176   (e) 68.2 × 0.27

    (f) 2.84 × 0.32   (g) 378 × 1.77   (h) 0.471 × 42.7   (i) 8.71 × 0.031   (j) 53.2 × 0.97

F6 Estimate the cost of these.

    (a) 0.475 kg of Stilton

    (b) 0.856 kg of Brie

    (c) 32.5 kg of Cheddar

Stilton £3.88 per kg	Brie £5.15 per kg	Cheddar £1.96 per kg

G Rounding to two or more significant figures

To round to two significant figures, pick out the
first two significant figures.

	2372	0.006 81	4.028

Then round to two significant figures: 2400   0.0068   4.0

G1 Round these numbers to two significant figures.

(a) 4628　　(b) 20 984　　(c) 29 741　　(d) 5381　　(e) 9642

G2 Round these numbers to three significant figures.

(a) 43 209　　(b) 3328　　(c) 28 031　　(d) 600 813　　(e) 10 527

G3 Round these numbers to two significant figures.

(a) 0.053 14　(b) 2.387　　(c) 3.075　　(d) 0.004 284　(e) 0.6696

(f) 0.000 485 1　(g) 51.852　(h) 0.067 52　(i) 6.0238　　(j) 0.000 974

G4 Round these numbers to three significant figures.

(a) 0.023 74　(b) 8.189　　(c) 41.023　　(d) 0.006 414　(e) 0.7791

(f) 0.000 155 8　(g) 254.756　(h) 0.080 284　(i) 12.1238　(j) 0.006 918

H Sensible accuracy

- What would be a sensible degree of accuracy in each of these?

A It takes **8 minutes 55.16 seconds** to walk to the station.

B Tim has been dieting.
He has lost **1.5054 kg** in **2 weeks 5 days 7 hours and 4 minutes**.

C The distance from Amber's house to town is **2 kilometres and 435.54 metres**.

D Helen has a very big dictionary.
It weighs **2.732 kg**.

E Vijay spent **2 hours 44 minutes**
on his homework.

F Tom is going to paint a rectangular wall.
First he measures the wall and calculates its area.

Length 4.125 m
Height 3.452 m

Area = 4.125 × 3.452
     = **14.2395 m²**

H1 Write each of the quantities in bold to a sensible degree of accuracy.
(Some may already be sensible, in which case don't change them!).

> The city of Bunchester is **243.673 km** from the capital. The journey by train takes **2.482** hours.
>
> The population of the city is **148 843**, of whom **21.783%** are over the age of sixty.
>
> Bunchester covers an area of **11.8643 km²**. It is situated on the River Bunn, which at this point is **186.23 m** wide and is **35.271 km** from the point where it flows into the sea.
>
> In the city there are four bridges across the river. The newest of these is a suspension bridge with a span of **144.8 m** and towers of height **58.3 m** above the river bed.
> Each of the main cables of this bridge is **316.6 mm** in diameter.
>
> Bunchester Cathedral dates from **1284** and has a spire of height **87.632 m**. Inside it is a bishop's throne made from solid granite and weighing **18 538.296 kg**.
>
> Bunchester is famous for its open air Rock Music Festival. Last year **184 529** people visited the festival and the final concert by The Maniacs could be heard up to a distance of **6.842 km** away.

H2 Bickerton Rovers and Naggingford United play in a football league.
Teams get 4 points for an away win, 3 for a home win, 2 for an away draw and 1 for a home draw.

So far Bickerton have 26 points from 15 games.
Naggingford have 30 points from 18 games.

Calculate the mean number of points per game for each team, to a sensible degree of accuracy. Which team is doing better?

I Mixed questions

I1 You are told that $364 \div 14 = 26$.

Write down the answers to these.

(a) $\dfrac{36.4}{1.4}$
(b) $\dfrac{3.64}{0.14}$
(c) $\dfrac{36400}{14}$
(d) $\dfrac{364}{1.4}$
(e) $\dfrac{3640}{0.14}$

I2 Given that $17 \times 14 = 238$, write down the answers to these.

(a) 1.7×1.4
(b) 170×1.4
(c) 17×0.14
(d) $238 \div 14$

(e) $2380 \div 14$
(f) $238 \div 17$
(g) $23.8 \div 1.7$
(h) $23.8 \div 0.14$

I3 Put these calculations into groups, so that the calculations in each group have the same answer.

1.8×55	18×550	0.18×550	180×55	0.18×0.55
18×0.55	0.18×55	1.8×5.5	180×0.55	1.8×0.055

I4 Round 2 886 032 to

(a) the nearest million
(b) the nearest ten thousand
(c) one significant figure

15 (a) Estimate the answer to 28×59 by rounding the numbers to one significant figure.

(b) Explain why your estimate must be bigger than the exact answer.

(c) Work out 28×59.

16 Pam works 28 hours a week. She is paid £6.85 per hour.

(a) Estimate how much she earns in a week.

(b) Estimate how much she earns in 31 weeks.

17 A rectangular room measures 31.2 m by 42.3 m.

(a) Estimate the area of the room by rounding the measurements to one significant figure.

(b) Is your estimate bigger or smaller than the actual area? Explain how you can tell.

(c) Calculate the actual area, giving your answer to three significant figures.

A spreadsheet can round values.
How can you control the degree of accuracy it uses?

Does a spreadsheet use the same rule as you have been using to decide whether to round up or down?

Test yourself

T1 Work these out.

(a) 2.63×100 (b) $19.05 \div 1000$ (c) 0.045×1000 (d) $0.803 \div 100$

T2 Work these out.

(a) 0.4×80 (b) 0.4×0.8 (c) 0.4×0.2 (d) 400×0.6 (e) 30×0.07

T3 Given that $63 \times 82 = 5166$, write down the answers to these.

(a) 6.3×0.82 (b) 0.63×8.2 (c) 0.63×820 (d) 0.63×0.82

(e) $51.66 \div 0.63$ (f) $516.6 \div 8.2$ (g) $5166 \div 6.3$ (h) $5166 \div 0.82$

T4 Round 2085.19 to

(a) the nearest hundred   (b) one decimal place

(c) one significant figure   (d) three significant figures

T5 Estimate the answer to each of these.

(a) 27.8×0.93 (b) 0.084×61.1 (c) 0.47×0.31 (d) 8.387×218 (e) 0.962×0.48

T6 (a) Write down 45.3476 correct to three significant figures.

(b) Write down 7462 correct to two significant figures.

WJEC

2 Graphing changes over time

You will draw and interpret graphs in various practical situations where changes take place over time.

A Fairground graphs

At Jeff's stall you can win a goldfish. The goldfish are in different shaped bowls.

Jeff fills the bowls with water before he puts the goldfish in.
He uses a hosepipe, from which water flows at a steady rate.

One type of bowl is shaped like this.

When he fills this bowl with water the graph of the water's height is like this:

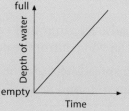

• Draw some different shaped bowls and sketch the corresponding graphs.

A1 Here are three different shaped bowls.

(a) Which description of filling the bowls with water goes with which bowl?

   P   The water level goes up fast at first and then suddenly goes up more slowly.

   Q   The water level goes up slowly at first, then changes to go up more quickly.

   R   The water level starts by going up quickly, but gets slower and slower.

(b) Which graph goes with which bowl?

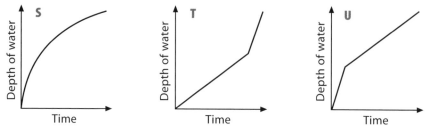

A2 Here are three more bowls.
For each one, sketch a graph showing how it fills up with water.

(a)   (b)   (c)

A3 The graph shows the number of people (customers and workers)
in the fairground one evening.

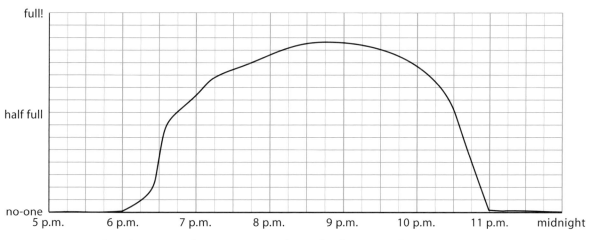

(a) At what time were there most people in the fairground?

(b) When do you think the fair opened?

(c) What time do you think the fair closed?

(d) At what time were most people arriving?

(e) Jeff is happy when the fair is more than half full.
For about how long was Jeff happy this evening?

A4 Look at the graphs at the bottom of the page.
Some of the graphs describe these four situations at the fairground.
Which graph describes which situation?

(Two graphs don't describe any of these!)

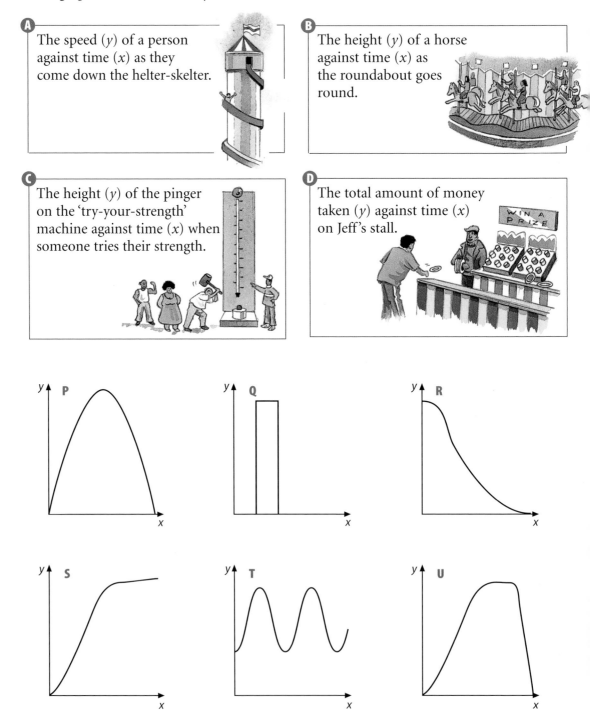

A The speed (y) of a person against time (x) as they come down the helter-skelter.

B The height (y) of a horse against time (x) as the roundabout goes round.

C The height (y) of the pinger on the 'try-your-strength' machine against time (x) when someone tries their strength.

D The total amount of money taken (y) against time (x) on Jeff's stall.

WIN A PRIZE

A5 Sketch a graph for each of these situations.
For each graph, write a short explanation of why it looks as you have drawn it.

(a) A dodgem car is going round the track at constant speed.
(Draw the dodgem car's speed on the y-axis against time on the x-axis.)

(b) A dart is thrown and then hits the dart board, 2 metres away.
(Draw the dart's speed (y) against time (x).)

(c) The big wheel goes round twice at constant speed.
(Draw the height of a person on the wheel (y) against time (x).)

Test yourself

T1 The container below is filled with water flowing at a steady rate.
Sketch a graph showing the height of the water level over time.

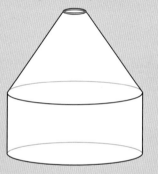

T2 Draw sketch graphs for each of these situations.
For each graph, write a short explanation of why it looks as you have drawn it.

(a) A cyclist who travels at a steady speed, then goes up a steep hill and
stops at the top
(Draw the cyclist's speed (y) against time (x).)

(b) The distance travelled on a motorway by a car going at constant speed
(Draw the car's distance (y) against time (x).)

(c) The temperature of a saucepan of water that is heated up on a stove,
and then left boiling for a short while
(Draw the pan's temperature (y) against time (x).)

3 Unitary method

You will revise using the unitary method to solve problems.

This work will help you cancel common factors to simplify a calculation.

A Problems

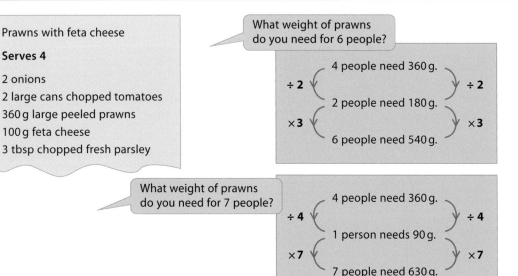

Prawns with feta cheese

Serves 4

2 onions
2 large cans chopped tomatoes
360 g large peeled prawns
100 g feta cheese
3 tbsp chopped fresh parsley

What weight of prawns do you need for 6 people?

4 people need 360 g.

÷ 2   ÷ 2

2 people need 180 g.

× 3   × 3

6 people need 540 g.

What weight of prawns do you need for 7 people?

4 people need 360 g.

÷ 4   ÷ 4

1 person needs 90 g.

× 7   × 7

7 people need 630 g.

A1 For the recipe above, work these out in your head.

(a) How many onions would you need for 2 people?

(b) How many cans of tomatoes would you need for 6 people?

(c) How much feta cheese would you need for 3 people?

(d) How much parsley would you need for 2 people?

A2 Work these out in your head.

(a) The cost of 3 fruit chews is 12p.
Work out the cost of 5 fruit chews.

(b) The cost of 5 metres of ribbon is £1.50.
Find the cost of 3 metres of the same ribbon.

(c) You need 6 slices of bread for marmalade pudding for 4 people.
How many slices would you need for 6 people?

A3 Here are the ingredients for poached apricots.

(a) What weight of apricots would you need to make poached apricots for 2 people?

(b) How many cardamom pods would you need for 7 people?

(c) How much sugar would you need for 8 people?

(d) What weight of pistachios would you need for 5 people?

> Poached apricots
>
> **Serves 6**
>
> 300 g dried apricots
> 60 ml water
> 60 g sugar
> 6 cardamom pods
> 2 teaspoons of lemon juice
> 90 g pistachios

A4 Altogether, 3 identical packing cases weigh 240 kg.
What will 7 of these packing cases weigh?

A5 Jim lays 8 identical drainage pipes end to end.
The total length is 32 m.
Work out the total length of 5 of these pipes.

A6 The weight of 7 identical bolts is 140 g.
What would 11 of these bolts weigh?

A7 In a recipe for buns, 600 ml of milk is needed to make 20 buns.
How much milk would be needed to make 25 of these buns?

A8 The total cost of 3 identical jars of marmalade is £2.94.
How much would I pay for 5 jars?

A9 100 g of sugar is needed to make blackberry fool for 5 people.
How much sugar would be needed for 12 people?

B Cancelling common factors

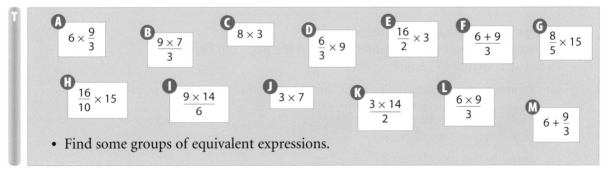

A $6 \times \dfrac{9}{3}$

B $\dfrac{9 \times 7}{3}$

C 8×3

D $\dfrac{6}{3} \times 9$

E $\dfrac{16}{2} \times 3$

F $\dfrac{6+9}{3}$

G $\dfrac{8}{5} \times 15$

H $\dfrac{16}{10} \times 15$

I $\dfrac{9 \times 14}{6}$

J 3×7

K $\dfrac{3 \times 14}{2}$

L $\dfrac{6 \times 9}{3}$

M $6 + \dfrac{9}{3}$

• Find some groups of equivalent expressions.

B1 For each calculation, simplify by cancelling common factors and then evaluate it.

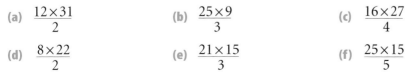

(a) $\dfrac{12 \times 31}{2}$

(b) $\dfrac{25 \times 9}{3}$

(c) $\dfrac{16 \times 27}{4}$

(d) $\dfrac{8 \times 22}{2}$

(e) $\dfrac{21 \times 15}{3}$

(f) $\dfrac{25 \times 15}{5}$

Examples of cancelling common factors

$$\frac{16}{7} \times 14 = \frac{16}{\cancel{7}_1} \times \cancel{14}^{\,2}$$
$$= 16 \times 2$$
$$= 32$$

$$4 \times \frac{13}{8} = \cancel{4}^{\,1} \times \frac{13}{\cancel{8}_2}$$
$$= \frac{13}{2}$$
$$= 6.5$$

$$\frac{93 \times 25}{15} = \frac{93 \times \cancel{25}^{\,5}}{\cancel{15}_3}$$
$$= \frac{\overset{31}{\cancel{93}} \times \cancel{25}^{\,5}}{\cancel{15} \, \cancel{3}_1}$$
$$= 31 \times 5$$
$$= 155$$

B2 For each calculation, simplify by cancelling common factors and then evaluate it.

(a) $\dfrac{24}{5} \times 10$

(b) $\dfrac{13}{3} \times 9$

(c) $30 \times \dfrac{13}{6}$

(d) $45 \times \dfrac{8}{15}$

(e) $\dfrac{36}{14} \times 7$

(f) $12 \times \dfrac{7}{24}$

B3 For each calculation, simplify by cancelling common factors and then evaluate it.

(a) $\dfrac{15 \times 26}{6}$

(b) $\dfrac{25 \times 14}{10}$

(c) $\dfrac{22}{4} \times 14$

(d) $25 \times \dfrac{12}{15}$

(e) $\dfrac{21}{12} \times 6$

(f) $\dfrac{27}{18} \times 3$

B4 Joe has 12 bags of sweets, each holding 36 sweets.
He wants to share the sweets equally between 16 children.

(a) Which of these calculations gives the number of sweets each child gets?

$$\frac{36 \times 16}{12} \qquad \frac{12 \times 36}{16} \qquad \frac{12 \times 16}{36}$$

(b) Simplify this calculation by cancelling.
Work out how many sweets each child gets.

B5 Ms Spence has 15 bags of counters.
She wants to share out the counters between the pupils in her class of 25.
Each bag contains 45 counters.

(a) Which of these calculations gives the number of counters each pupil gets?

$$\frac{25 \times 45}{15} \qquad \frac{15 \times 25}{45} \qquad \frac{45 \times 15}{25}$$

(b) Simplify this calculation by cancelling.
Work out how many counters each pupil gets.

B6 Dee has 14 packs of humbugs, each holding 32 humbugs.
She shares the humbugs equally between 28 children.

How many humbugs does each child get?

C Using cancelling

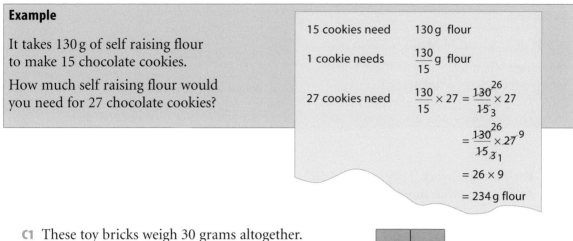

Example

It takes 130 g of self raising flour to make 15 chocolate cookies.

How much self raising flour would you need for 27 chocolate cookies?

15 cookies need   130 g flour

1 cookie needs $\dfrac{130}{15}$ g flour

27 cookies need $\dfrac{130}{15} \times 27 = \dfrac{\overset{26}{130}}{\underset{3}{15}} \times 27$

$= \dfrac{\overset{26}{130}}{\underset{1}{\underset{3}{15}}} \times \overset{9}{27}$

$= 26 \times 9$

$= 234$ g flour

C1 These toy bricks weigh 30 grams altogether.

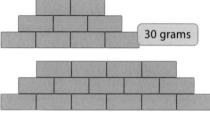

30 grams

(a) Which calculation gives the total weight of the toy bricks on the right?

$\dfrac{30}{9} \times 15$ $\dfrac{30}{15} \times 9$ $\dfrac{9}{30} \times 15$

(b) Simplify this calculation by cancelling. Work out the weight of these bricks.

C2 12 bolts weigh 40 grams.
How much will 15 of these bolts weigh?

C3 21 nails weigh 28 grams.
How much will 27 of these nails weigh?

C4 It takes 150 ml of milk to make 12 scones.
How much milk would you need for 20 scones?

C5 15 sweets weigh 100 grams.
Find the weight of 21 of these sweets.

C6 It takes 450 g of caster sugar to make 36 marbled fudge bars.
How much caster sugar would you need to make 28 fudge bars?

C7 A tray of 24 cookie twists can be made with 100 g of butter.
How much butter would you need for 42 cookie twists?

C8 You need 90 g of sugar to make 64 Neapolitan cookies.
How much sugar would you need for 48 cookies?

Example

A pile of 15 identical books is 38 cm high.

How high will a pile of 35 of these books be?
Give your answer to the nearest cm.

Height of 15 books is 38 cm

Height of 1 book is $\frac{38}{15}$ cm

Height of 35 books is $\frac{38 \times 35}{15}$

= 88.666 666 …

= 89 cm (nearest cm)

D1 For 14 hours' work, Lucy was paid £67.06.
At this rate, what should she be paid for 38 hours' work?

D2 A small aircraft flies 275 km on 110 litres of fuel.
How much fuel is needed for a journey of 400 km?

D3 50 ml of milk contains 60 mg of fat.
How much fat is in 568 ml of milk?
Give your answer correct to the nearest mg.

D4 260 sheets of paper have a total thickness of 3.1 cm.
What would be the thickness of 550 of these sheets of paper, to the nearest 0.1 cm?

D5 A Caesar salad recipe for 6 uses 250 g of diced potatoes.
How much diced potato would you need for a Caesar salad for 11 people?
Give your answer correct to the nearest 5 g.

D6 Hayley bought 250 g of olives for £1.89.
What would 160 g of these olives cost?

D7 A shop charges £4.80 for 3.5 m of wire.
At this rate, what would be the cost of 8.2 m of this wire?

D8

Buy **£20 000** worth of Premium Bonds and on average you'll win **13** prizes a year.

On average, someone with £20 000 in Premium Bonds should win 13 prizes each year.

Flora has £7700 in Premium Bonds.

(a) Work out the number of prizes she should win, on average, each year.

Premium Bonds are sold in multiples of £10.
Rajesh works out that he is likely to win 9 prizes next year.

(b) Work out an estimate for the amount of money Rajesh has in Premium Bonds.

Edexcel

*D9 A 1 kg block of gold is worth £5780 and has a volume of 52 cm^3.

    (a) What is the weight of a 65 cm^3 block of gold?

    (b) What weight of gold, to the nearest kilogram, would be worth £1 million?

    (c) What is the volume of this £1 million block, to the nearest cm^3?

> 52 cm^3 is about the size of a medium bar of chocolate.

E Dealing with units of measure

Example

There are 4.546 litres in one gallon.
Work out the number of gallons in 40 litres, correct to 1 d.p.

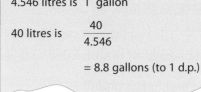

4.546 litres is 1 gallon

1 litre is $\dfrac{1}{4.546}$ gallon

40 litres is $\dfrac{1}{4.546} \times 40$

    = 8.8 gallons (to 1 d.p.)

4.546 litres is 1 gallon

40 litres is $\dfrac{40}{4.546}$

    = 8.8 gallons (to 1 d.p.)

E1 The exchange rate to change Norwegian kroners into pounds is

    12.74 Norwegian kroners = £1

Work out the number of pence in 5.50 Norwegian kroners.
Give your answer to the nearest penny.

E2 1 kilogram is equivalent to about 2.205 pounds.
What is the weight in kilograms of 5 pounds of flour?
Give your answer correct to two decimal places.

E3 One pint is equivalent to about 0.568 litres.
How many pints are equivalent to 3.6 litres?
Give your answer correct to one decimal place.

E4 On average a car travels 100 km on fuel costing £4.40.

    (a) Calculate the cost of fuel for a journey of 720 km.

    (b) The fuel for another journey cost £14.30.
        Calculate the length of this journey.

OCR

E5 A litre is about 0.220 gallons.
A litre of fuel costs 85.9p.
Calculate the cost of 800 gallons of this fuel.

E6 The table shows the amount of foreign currency that can be bought with £1.

Dave has just returned from Hong Kong. He has 940 Hong Kong dollars.

His next trip is to South Korea. He changes his Hong Kong dollars into South Korean won.

Calculate, to the nearest thousand, how many South Korean won he will get.

Far-east currencies £1 will buy	
India	66.65 rupees
Hong Kong	11.03 Hong Kong dollars
Indonesia	13 192.2 rupiahs
South Korea	1816.9 won

Test yourself

T1 The cost of 3 pencils is 72p.
What is the cost of 5 pencils?   Edexcel

T2 It takes 100 g of flour to make 15 shortbread biscuits.

 (a) How many shortbread biscuits can be made from 1 kg of flour?

 (b) Calculate the weight of flour needed to make 24 biscuits.   OCR

T3 Recipe for bread and butter pudding

 6 slices of bread
 2 eggs
 1 pint of milk
 150 g raisins
 10 g margarine

This recipe is enough for 4 people.

 (a) Work out the amounts needed so that there will be enough for 6 people.

There are 450 g in 1 pound. There are 16 ounces in 1 pound.

 (b) Change 150 g into ounces. Give your answer correct to the nearest ounce.   Edexcel

T4 A pile of 12 identical coins is 3.8 cm high.
How high will a pile of 25 of these coins be, correct to the nearest mm?

T5 Asra goes on holiday to Hungary.
The exchange rate is £1 = 397.6 forints.

She changes £250 into forints.

 (a) How many forints should Asra get?

She changes 1450 forints back into pounds.
The exchange rate is the same.

 (b) How much money should she get?
      Give your answer to the nearest penny.

4 Fractions

You will revise

- what is meant by equivalent fractions
- how to express one quantity as a fraction of another
- how to add and subtract fractions

This work will help you

- put fractions in order of size
- multiply a fraction by an integer or by a fraction
- divide a fraction by an integer
- change a decimal to a fraction and a fraction to a decimal

A Fractions review

Fractions from dice

Roll a dice twice (or roll two dice).
The first score is the numerator of a fraction.
The second is the denominator.

This gives
$\frac{3}{5}$

Roll the dice to make a fraction. Is it

- a proper fraction or an improper fraction
- equivalent to a whole number
- a fraction that can be simplified

Challenge

How many different fractions do the dice give?

Repeat for other fractions you can make with the dice.

A1 Copy these and find the missing numbers.

(a) $\frac{2}{3} = \frac{10}{}$ (b) $\frac{5}{6} = \frac{20}{}$ (c) $\frac{5}{7} = \frac{}{35}$ (d) $\frac{4}{9} = \frac{}{36}$ (e) $\frac{7}{12} = \frac{}{60}$

A2 Write each of these fractions in its lowest terms.

(a) $\frac{20}{30}$ (b) $\frac{3}{9}$ (c) $\frac{12}{16}$ (d) $\frac{20}{25}$ (e) $\frac{30}{36}$

(f) $\frac{21}{28}$ (g) $\frac{36}{60}$ (h) $\frac{26}{39}$ (i) $\frac{22}{55}$ (j) $\frac{72}{96}$

A3 Change these mixed numbers to improper fractions.

(a) $1\frac{1}{4}$ (b) $1\frac{2}{3}$ (c) $3\frac{1}{5}$ (d) $1\frac{5}{8}$ (e) $2\frac{1}{10}$

A4 Change these improper fractions to mixed numbers.

(a) $\frac{22}{4}$ (b) $\frac{13}{6}$ (c) $\frac{20}{7}$ (d) $\frac{14}{5}$ (e) $\frac{29}{10}$

A5 In a typical 24-hour period, Karl spends 6 hours working, 8 hours sleeping, 3 hours eating and the rest of the time doing other things.

Write, in its simplest form, the fraction of the time Karl spends

(a) working   (b) sleeping   (c) eating   (d) doing other things

A6 Gert owns 30 acres of land: 12 acres are woodland, 15 are grass and the rest is marsh. Write, in its simplest form, the fraction of Gert's land that is

(a) woodland   (b) grass   (c) marsh

A7 Last season Brockleton United won 18 matches, drew 8 and lost 10. What fraction, in its simplest form, of the matches were

(a) won   (b) drawn   (c) lost

A8 Errol has to calculate three quarters of 52. He knows he has to do something with 3 and 4 but doesn't know what. Explain briefly what he has to do.

A9 Calculate these in your head.

(a) $\frac{1}{7}$ of 28   (b) $\frac{2}{7}$ of 28   (c) $\frac{3}{7}$ of 28   (d) $\frac{1}{9}$ of 72   (e) $\frac{4}{9}$ of 72

(f) $\frac{3}{5}$ of 45   (g) $\frac{4}{5}$ of 30   (h) $\frac{3}{8}$ of 32   (i) $\frac{2}{9}$ of 180   (j) $\frac{5}{6}$ of 420

B Ordering fractions
level 6

Example

Which fraction is greater, $\frac{5}{8}$ or $\frac{7}{12}$?

We need to change $\frac{5}{8}$ and $\frac{7}{12}$ into equivalent fractions with the **same denominator**. The denominator must be a multiple of 8 and also a multiple of 12. So **24** will do.

$$\frac{5}{8} = \frac{15}{24} \qquad \frac{7}{12} = \frac{14}{24}$$

×3   ×2

So $\frac{5}{8}$ is greater than $\frac{7}{12}$.

×3   ×2

B1 Which fraction is greater, $\frac{3}{4}$ or $\frac{17}{20}$? (Change $\frac{3}{4}$ to twentieths.)

B2 Work out which fraction in each pair is greater.

(a) $\frac{1}{3}$, $\frac{5}{12}$ (b) $\frac{11}{16}$, $\frac{3}{4}$ (c) $\frac{19}{30}$, $\frac{7}{10}$ (d) $\frac{2}{5}$, $\frac{7}{20}$ (e) $\frac{3}{8}$, $\frac{11}{24}$

B3 Work out which fraction in each pair is greater.

(a) $\frac{1}{3}$, $\frac{2}{5}$ (b) $\frac{3}{5}$, $\frac{5}{8}$ (c) $\frac{5}{6}$, $\frac{7}{8}$ (d) $\frac{7}{8}$, $\frac{4}{5}$ (e) $\frac{5}{8}$, $\frac{7}{10}$

B4 Work out which fraction in each pair is greater.

(a) $\frac{5}{9}, \frac{3}{5}$ (b) $\frac{4}{7}, \frac{5}{8}$ (c) $\frac{3}{10}, \frac{1}{3}$ (d) $\frac{2}{5}, \frac{3}{7}$ (e) $\frac{3}{8}, \frac{5}{12}$

B5 Write each list of fractions in order, smallest first.

(a) $\frac{4}{5}, \frac{7}{10}, \frac{3}{4}$ (b) $\frac{5}{6}, \frac{7}{10}, \frac{11}{15}$ (c) $\frac{3}{8}, \frac{5}{12}, \frac{1}{3}$

B6 Answer these questions using the fractions in the loop.

(a) Which fraction is smallest?

(b) Which fraction is largest?

(c) Which fraction is nearest to $\frac{3}{4}$?

(d) Which pair of fractions are equivalent?

$\frac{21}{30}$ $\frac{4}{5}$ $\frac{5}{6}$ $\frac{7}{10}$

$\frac{7}{12}$ $\frac{11}{15}$ $\frac{2}{3}$

C Addition and subtraction level 6

C1 Work these out. Simplify the result where possible.

(a) $\frac{3}{5} + \frac{4}{5}$ (b) $\frac{3}{10} + \frac{9}{10}$ (c) $1 - \frac{2}{7}$ (d) $\frac{7}{12} - \frac{5}{12}$ (e) $\frac{5}{8} + \frac{5}{8}$

(f) $2\frac{5}{6} + \frac{5}{6}$ (g) $1\frac{5}{8} - \frac{7}{8}$ (h) $4\frac{1}{4} - 2\frac{3}{4}$ (i) $3\frac{2}{5} + 2\frac{4}{5}$ (j) $5\frac{1}{10} - 3\frac{7}{10}$

Example

Work out $\frac{3}{4} + \frac{1}{6}$.

We need to change $\frac{3}{4}$ and $\frac{1}{6}$ into equivalent fractions with the **same denominator**.
The denominator must be a multiple of 4 and also a multiple of 6. So **12** will do.

$$\overset{\times 3}{\frac{3}{4}} = \underset{\times 3}{\frac{9}{12}} \qquad \overset{\times 2}{\frac{1}{6}} = \underset{\times 2}{\frac{2}{12}}$$

So $\frac{3}{4} + \frac{1}{6}$

$= \frac{9}{12} + \frac{2}{12} = \frac{11}{12}$

C2 Work these out.

(a) $\frac{1}{4} + \frac{1}{3}$ (b) $\frac{2}{3} + \frac{1}{4}$ (c) $\frac{1}{6} + \frac{1}{4}$ (d) $\frac{1}{5} + \frac{2}{3}$ (e) $\frac{2}{5} + \frac{1}{4}$

C3 Work these out.

(a) $\frac{2}{5} - \frac{1}{4}$ (b) $\frac{3}{4} - \frac{1}{6}$ (c) $\frac{2}{3} - \frac{1}{4}$ (d) $\frac{3}{4} - \frac{2}{3}$ (e) $\frac{1}{2} - \frac{2}{5}$

C4 Work these out.

(a) $\frac{2}{5} + \frac{1}{3}$ (b) $\frac{3}{5} - \frac{1}{4}$ (c) $\frac{3}{4} - \frac{2}{5}$ (d) $\frac{1}{8} + \frac{5}{6}$ (e) $\frac{1}{12} + \frac{2}{5}$

C5 Work these out. Write the results as mixed numbers.

(a) $\frac{3}{8} + \frac{2}{3}$ (b) $\frac{11}{12} + \frac{2}{3}$ (c) $1\frac{1}{3} - \frac{1}{8}$ (d) $1\frac{3}{4} + \frac{2}{5}$ (e) $3 - 1\frac{3}{5}$

(f) $2\frac{4}{5} + 1\frac{1}{8}$ (g) $2\frac{2}{5} - 1\frac{1}{4}$ (h) $2\frac{2}{3} + 1\frac{2}{5}$ (i) $4\frac{3}{8} - 2\frac{1}{6}$ (j) $3\frac{2}{7} - 1\frac{1}{2}$

C6 From the fractions in this list find

$\frac{1}{6}$	$\frac{1}{5}$	$\frac{1}{4}$	$\frac{1}{3}$	$\frac{2}{5}$	$\frac{2}{3}$	$\frac{3}{4}$	$\frac{4}{5}$	$\frac{5}{6}$

(a) a pair whose sum is $\frac{9}{20}$ (b) a pair whose sum is $\frac{11}{12}$

(c) a pair whose difference is $\frac{7}{15}$ (d) a pair whose difference is $\frac{2}{3}$

(e) three fractions whose sum is $1\frac{1}{4}$ (f) three fractions whose sum is $1\frac{11}{30}$

*C7 The difference between $\frac{1}{6}$ of a number and $\frac{1}{7}$ of the number is 5.
What is the number?

*C8 Rama, Gavin and Jake share a pizza.
Rama and Gavin together have $\frac{5}{8}$. Gavin and Jake together have $\frac{2}{3}$.
What fraction do Rama and Jake have together?

D Multiplying a fraction by a whole number

This picture shows 7 lots of $\frac{3}{4}$.

21 quarters = 5 whole ones and 1 quarter

$$7 \times \frac{3}{4} = \frac{21}{4} = 5\frac{1}{4}$$

Cancelling common factors

$$8 \times \frac{3}{4} = {}^{2}\cancel{8} \times \frac{3}{\cancel{4}_{1}} = 6 \qquad 12 \times \frac{5}{8} = {}^{3}\cancel{12} \times \frac{5}{\cancel{8}_{2}} = \frac{15}{2} = 7\frac{1}{2}$$

D1 Work these out. The answers are all whole numbers.

(a) $\frac{1}{5} \times 20$ (b) $24 \times \frac{1}{8}$ (c) $\frac{3}{4} \times 8$ (d) $12 \times \frac{2}{3}$ (e) $32 \times \frac{5}{8}$

D2 It takes Prakesh $\frac{3}{4}$ hour to paint a window frame.
How many hours will it take him to paint 5 window frames?

D3 Dylan jogs for $\frac{2}{3}$ mile every day.
How far does he run altogether in 7 days?

D4 Work these out.

(a) $\frac{1}{4} \times 15$ (b) $8 \times \frac{1}{3}$ (c) $\frac{1}{5} \times 12$ (d) $14 \times \frac{1}{8}$ (e) $17 \times \frac{1}{2}$

D5 Work these out.

(a) $\frac{3}{4} \times 9$ (b) $10 \times \frac{2}{3}$ (c) $\frac{4}{5} \times 6$ (d) $6 \times \frac{3}{8}$ (e) $5 \times \frac{4}{5}$

D6 Copy and complete these multiplications.

(a) $\frac{1}{10} \times \blacksquare = \frac{1}{2}$ (b) $\blacksquare \times 5 = \frac{1}{3}$ (c) $\blacksquare \times 6 = 4$

$\frac{1}{2}$ of 8 = 4 $\frac{1}{2} \times 8 = 4$	of and $\times$ give the same result	$\frac{3}{4}$ of 12 = 9 $\frac{3}{4} \times 12 = 9$

D7 Put the given digits in the boxes to make each calculation correct.

(a) $\dfrac{\square}{\square} \times \square = \square$ 2, 3, 4, 6

(b) $\square\square \times \dfrac{\square}{\square} = \square$ 0, 1, 2, 4, 5

(c) $\dfrac{\square}{\square}$ of $\square\square = \square$ 0, 1, 4, 5, 8

(d) $\dfrac{\square}{\square}$ of $\square\square = \square\square$ 0, 1, 2, 3, 4, 5

D8 Use the fact that $\frac{2}{3}$ of 8 = $\frac{2}{3} \times 8$ to work out $\frac{2}{3}$ of 8. Write the answer as a mixed number.

D9 Work these out.   (a) $\frac{1}{4}$ of 7   (b) $\frac{3}{4}$ of 15   (c) $\frac{2}{3}$ of 10   (d) $\frac{2}{5}$ of 14

E Dividing a fraction by a whole number

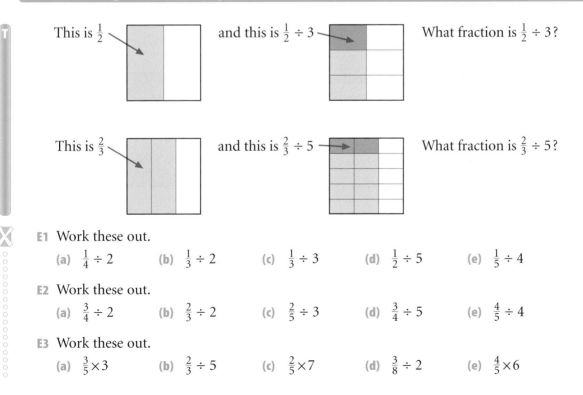

This is $\frac{1}{2}$ and this is $\frac{1}{2} \div 3$ What fraction is $\frac{1}{2} \div 3$?

This is $\frac{2}{3}$ and this is $\frac{2}{3} \div 5$ What fraction is $\frac{2}{3} \div 5$?

E1 Work these out.

(a) $\frac{1}{4} \div 2$ (b) $\frac{1}{3} \div 2$ (c) $\frac{1}{3} \div 3$ (d) $\frac{1}{2} \div 5$ (e) $\frac{1}{5} \div 4$

E2 Work these out.

(a) $\frac{3}{4} \div 2$ (b) $\frac{2}{3} \div 2$ (c) $\frac{2}{5} \div 3$ (d) $\frac{3}{4} \div 5$ (e) $\frac{4}{5} \div 4$

E3 Work these out.

(a) $\frac{3}{5} \times 3$ (b) $\frac{2}{3} \div 5$ (c) $\frac{2}{5} \times 7$ (d) $\frac{3}{8} \div 2$ (e) $\frac{4}{5} \times 6$

F Fractions of fractions

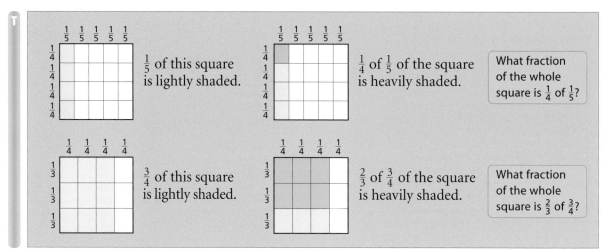

$\frac{1}{5}$ of this square is lightly shaded.

$\frac{1}{4}$ of $\frac{1}{5}$ of the square is heavily shaded.

What fraction of the whole square is $\frac{1}{4}$ of $\frac{1}{5}$?

$\frac{3}{4}$ of this square is lightly shaded.

$\frac{2}{3}$ of $\frac{3}{4}$ of the square is heavily shaded.

What fraction of the whole square is $\frac{2}{3}$ of $\frac{3}{4}$?

F1 What does each of these diagrams show?

(a)   (b)   (c)

$\frac{2}{3}$ of $\frac{5}{6}$ = ... of ... = ... of ... = ...

F2 Draw this diagram.

By light and dark shading, show some different fractions of fractions (at least three).

Here is one to start you off.

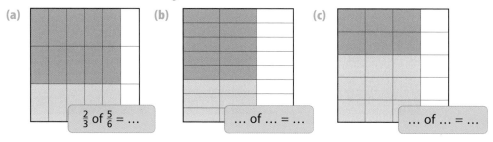

$\frac{1}{3}$ of $\frac{4}{5}$ = ...

F3 Draw a diagram to show that $\frac{2}{3}$ of $\frac{4}{5}$ is the same as $\frac{4}{5}$ of $\frac{2}{3}$.

F4 Work these out without drawing diagrams.

(a) $\frac{1}{2}$ of $\frac{1}{4}$ (b) $\frac{1}{3}$ of $\frac{1}{7}$ (c) $\frac{1}{8}$ of $\frac{1}{10}$ (d) $\frac{1}{4}$ of $\frac{1}{9}$

F5 Work these out without drawing diagrams. Give each result in its simplest form.

(a) $\frac{3}{4}$ of $\frac{1}{2}$ (b) $\frac{2}{3}$ of $\frac{1}{5}$ (c) $\frac{2}{5}$ of $\frac{2}{3}$ (d) $\frac{3}{5}$ of $\frac{2}{7}$

(e) $\frac{3}{4}$ of $\frac{2}{7}$ (f) $\frac{2}{9}$ of $\frac{3}{5}$ (g) $\frac{4}{5}$ of $\frac{1}{8}$ (h) $\frac{5}{8}$ of $\frac{3}{10}$

G Multiplying fractions together

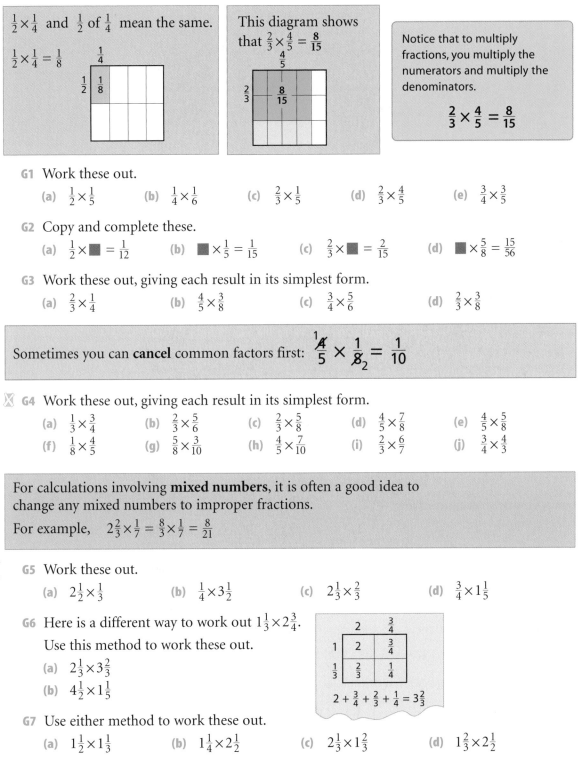

$\frac{1}{2} \times \frac{1}{4}$ and $\frac{1}{2}$ of $\frac{1}{4}$ mean the same.

$\frac{1}{2} \times \frac{1}{4} = \frac{1}{8}$

This diagram shows that $\frac{2}{3} \times \frac{4}{5} = \frac{8}{15}$

Notice that to multiply fractions, you multiply the numerators and multiply the denominators.

$$\frac{2}{3} \times \frac{4}{5} = \frac{8}{15}$$

G1 Work these out.

(a) $\frac{1}{2} \times \frac{1}{5}$ (b) $\frac{1}{4} \times \frac{1}{6}$ (c) $\frac{2}{3} \times \frac{1}{5}$ (d) $\frac{2}{3} \times \frac{4}{5}$ (e) $\frac{3}{4} \times \frac{3}{5}$

G2 Copy and complete these.

(a) $\frac{1}{2} \times \blacksquare = \frac{1}{12}$ (b) $\blacksquare \times \frac{1}{5} = \frac{1}{15}$ (c) $\frac{2}{3} \times \blacksquare = \frac{2}{15}$ (d) $\blacksquare \times \frac{5}{8} = \frac{15}{56}$

G3 Work these out, giving each result in its simplest form.

(a) $\frac{2}{3} \times \frac{1}{4}$ (b) $\frac{4}{5} \times \frac{3}{8}$ (c) $\frac{3}{4} \times \frac{5}{6}$ (d) $\frac{2}{3} \times \frac{3}{8}$

Sometimes you can **cancel** common factors first: $\frac{\overset{1}{\cancel{4}}}{5} \times \frac{1}{\underset{2}{\cancel{8}}} = \frac{1}{10}$

G4 Work these out, giving each result in its simplest form.

(a) $\frac{1}{3} \times \frac{3}{4}$ (b) $\frac{2}{3} \times \frac{5}{6}$ (c) $\frac{2}{3} \times \frac{5}{8}$ (d) $\frac{4}{5} \times \frac{7}{8}$ (e) $\frac{4}{5} \times \frac{5}{8}$

(f) $\frac{1}{8} \times \frac{4}{5}$ (g) $\frac{5}{8} \times \frac{3}{10}$ (h) $\frac{4}{5} \times \frac{7}{10}$ (i) $\frac{2}{3} \times \frac{6}{7}$ (j) $\frac{3}{4} \times \frac{4}{3}$

For calculations involving **mixed numbers**, it is often a good idea to change any mixed numbers to improper fractions.

For example, $2\frac{2}{3} \times \frac{1}{7} = \frac{8}{3} \times \frac{1}{7} = \frac{8}{21}$

G5 Work these out.

(a) $2\frac{1}{2} \times \frac{1}{3}$ (b) $\frac{1}{4} \times 3\frac{1}{2}$ (c) $2\frac{1}{3} \times \frac{2}{3}$ (d) $\frac{3}{4} \times 1\frac{1}{5}$

G6 Here is a different way to work out $1\frac{1}{3} \times 2\frac{3}{4}$.

Use this method to work these out.

(a) $2\frac{1}{3} \times 3\frac{2}{3}$

(b) $4\frac{1}{2} \times 1\frac{1}{5}$

	2	$\frac{3}{4}$
1	2	$\frac{3}{4}$
$\frac{1}{3}$	$\frac{2}{3}$	$\frac{1}{4}$

$2 + \frac{3}{4} + \frac{2}{3} + \frac{1}{4} = 3\frac{2}{3}$

G7 Use either method to work these out.

(a) $1\frac{1}{2} \times 1\frac{1}{3}$ (b) $1\frac{1}{4} \times 2\frac{1}{2}$ (c) $2\frac{1}{3} \times 1\frac{2}{3}$ (d) $1\frac{2}{3} \times 2\frac{1}{2}$

Example

Change each of these decimals to a fraction in its lowest terms.   (a) 0.32   (b) 0.275

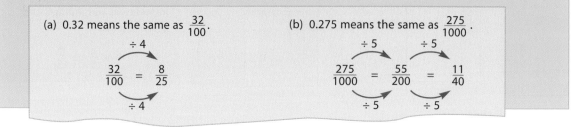

(a) 0.32 means the same as $\frac{32}{100}$.

$$\frac{32}{100} = \frac{8}{25}$$

(b) 0.275 means the same as $\frac{275}{1000}$.

$$\frac{275}{1000} = \frac{55}{200} = \frac{11}{40}$$

H1 Change each of these decimals to a fraction in its lowest terms.

(a) 0.6   (b) 0.64   (c) 0.625   (d) 0.35   (e) 0.08

(f) 0.825   (g) 0.035   (h) 0.72   (i) 0.004   (j) 0.152

Example

Change $\frac{3}{8}$ to a decimal.

You need to divide 3 by 8.
To allow for decimal places, write 3 as 3.00…

$$\begin{array}{r} 0.375 \\ 8\overline{)3.0^60^40} \end{array}$$

$\frac{3}{8} = 0.375$

H2 Change each of these fractions to a decimal.

(a) $\frac{1}{8}$ (b) $\frac{5}{8}$ (c) $\frac{7}{8}$ (d) $\frac{1}{16}$ (e) $\frac{5}{16}$

Fractions with denominator 50, 20 or 25 can be changed to decimals using equivalent fractions.

$$\frac{9}{50} = \frac{18}{100} = 0.18 \qquad \frac{7}{20} = \frac{35}{100} = 0.35 \qquad \frac{6}{25} = \frac{24}{100} = 0.24$$

H3 Write each of these lists in order, smallest first.

(a) 0.6, $\frac{5}{8}$, $\frac{13}{20}$, 0.59   (b) $\frac{37}{50}$, 0.7, $\frac{4}{5}$, 0.77   (c) $\frac{3}{10}$, 0.35, $\frac{9}{20}$, 0.4

(d) 0.25, $\frac{3}{8}$, 0.3, $\frac{7}{20}$ (e) 0.4, 0.405, $\frac{9}{20}$, 0.5   (f) $\frac{7}{8}$, $\frac{3}{4}$, 0.85, 0.8

H4 Decode this message. Rewrite the letters in the order of the numbers, smallest first.

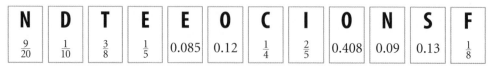

N	D	T	E	E	O	C	I	O	N	S	F
$\frac{9}{20}$	$\frac{1}{10}$	$\frac{3}{8}$	$\frac{1}{5}$	0.085	0.12	$\frac{1}{4}$	$\frac{2}{5}$	0.408	0.09	0.13	$\frac{1}{8}$

$$\frac{1}{3} = ? \qquad \frac{1}{6} = ? \qquad \frac{1}{11} = ? \qquad \frac{1}{7} = ?$$

I1 Change these fractions to decimals.

(a) $\frac{2}{3}$ (b) $\frac{1}{9}$ (c) $\frac{2}{9}$ (d) $\frac{4}{9}$ (e) $\frac{7}{9}$

I2 Change each of these fractions to recurring decimals.
What do you notice about the results?

(a) $\frac{1}{7}$ (b) $\frac{2}{7}$ (c) $\frac{3}{7}$ (d) $\frac{4}{7}$ (e) $\frac{5}{7}$ (f) $\frac{6}{7}$

I3 Change each of these fractions to decimals.

(a) $\frac{5}{6}$ (b) $\frac{2}{11}$ (c) $\frac{3}{11}$ (d) $\frac{1}{12}$ (e) $\frac{1}{13}$

Investigation

How can you tell when a fraction will give a recurring decimal?

Which of these fractions will be recurring? $\frac{1}{15} \quad \frac{1}{16} \quad \frac{1}{17} \quad \frac{1}{30} \quad \frac{1}{40}$

J Mixed questions

J1 Write each of these as a fraction in its lowest terms.

(a) £2.00 out of £2.50 (b) £2.50 out of £7.50 (c) £2.40 out of £3.00

J2 Marty has a jug which holds $1\frac{1}{4}$ litres. He finds that 7 jugfuls will just fill his fish tank. How many litres does his fish tank hold?

J3 Work these out.

(a) $9 \times \frac{3}{4}$ (b) $\frac{1}{3}$ of 20 (c) $\frac{2}{3} \times 10$ (d) $\frac{3}{4}$ of 22 (e) $7 \times \frac{2}{5}$

J4 Jill eats $\frac{1}{3}$ of a bar of chocolate. Morven eats $\frac{1}{4}$ of what's left.
What fraction of the whole bar has Morven eaten?

J5 Work these out.

(a) $\frac{1}{3} \div 2$ (b) $\frac{1}{2} \div 4$ (c) $\frac{2}{3} \div 3$ (d) $\frac{3}{4} \div 3$ (e) $\frac{3}{5} \div 6$

J6 Rosie, Alex and Dan share a bar of chocolate.
Rosie eats $\frac{3}{8}$ of the chocolate, Alex eats $\frac{1}{3}$ and Dan eats the rest.
What fraction of the chocolate does Dan eat?

J7 Copy and complete this addition table.

+	$\frac{1}{4}$	$\frac{3}{10}$
$\frac{1}{2}$	$\frac{3}{4}$	
		$\frac{11}{30}$

J8 Work these out.

(a) $1\frac{1}{3} + \frac{3}{4}$ (b) $1\frac{1}{5} \times \frac{2}{3}$ (c) $2\frac{2}{3} - 1\frac{3}{5}$ (d) $\left(\frac{4}{5}\right)^2$ (e) $\left(1\frac{3}{4}\right)^2$

J9 Dawn and Eve run a race. After Dawn has covered $\frac{3}{5}$ of the distance, Eve has covered $\frac{2}{3}$ and is 50 metres ahead of Dawn.
How many metres does Eve still have to run?

J10 Copy and complete this multiplication table.

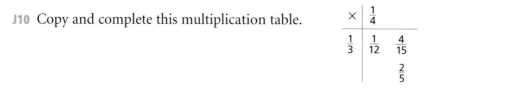

$\times$	$\frac{1}{4}$	
$\frac{1}{3}$	$\frac{1}{12}$	$\frac{4}{15}$
	$\frac{2}{5}$	

Test yourself

T1 Jim said 'I've got three quarters of a tin of paint'.
Mary said 'I've got four sixths of a tin of paint and my tin of paint is the same size as yours'.
Who has the most paint, Mary or Jim? Explain your answer.

Edexcel

T2 Fabia planted 80 lettuce seeds but only 25 of them grew into plants.
What fraction of the seeds grew? Write it in its lowest terms.

T3 A landowner died. In his will the land was to be shared between his three children.
The eldest inherited $\frac{2}{5}$ of the land and the second child inherited $\frac{1}{3}$.
What fraction did the youngest inherit?

T4 Work these out, giving each result in its simplest form.

(a) $3\frac{1}{3} + 1\frac{5}{6}$ (b) $4\frac{3}{10} - 2\frac{5}{6}$ (c) $2\frac{1}{5} \times 1\frac{1}{4}$ (d) $\frac{3}{8} \div 6$

T5 Write each list in order, starting with the smallest value.

(a) $0.04,\ \frac{3}{20},\ 0.1,\ \frac{1}{50}$ (b) $\frac{7}{8},\ 0.9,\ \frac{17}{20},\ 0.86$

T6 Two rods are fastened together.
The total length is $3\frac{1}{3}$ inches.
The length of rod B is $1\frac{3}{4}$ inches.
Find the length of rod A.

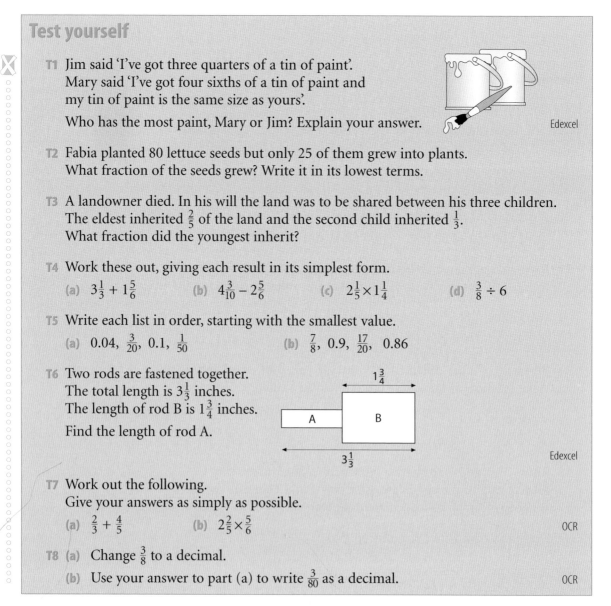

Edexcel

T7 Work out the following.
Give your answers as simply as possible.

(a) $\frac{2}{3} + \frac{4}{5}$ (b) $2\frac{2}{5} \times \frac{5}{6}$

OCR

T8 (a) Change $\frac{3}{8}$ to a decimal.

(b) Use your answer to part (a) to write $\frac{3}{80}$ as a decimal.

OCR

5 Parallel lines and angles

You will revise vertically opposite angles and angles made with parallel lines.

This work will help you work out angles and explain your reasoning.

A Angles from parallel lines crossing

T Draw two sets of parallel lines like this.

Mark two **different-sized** angles on your diagram and label them p and q.

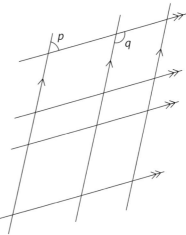

- Mark with a p every angle that equals angle p.
- Mark with a q every angle that equals angle q.
- If you know the size of p, how do you work out q?

A1 Here are two more sets of parallel lines.
If this angle is 50°, what will each angle marked with a letter be?

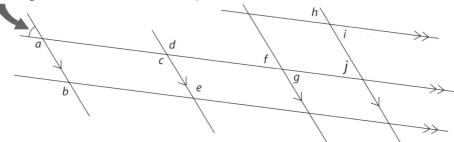

A2 Here are another two sets of parallel lines.
If this angle is 110°, what will each angle marked with a letter be?

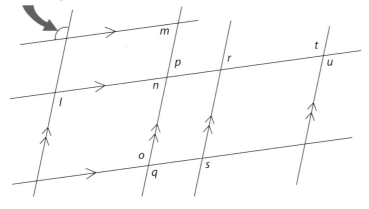

5 Parallel lines and angles 37

Vertically opposite angles are equal angles like this 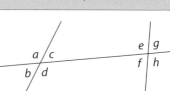 or this.

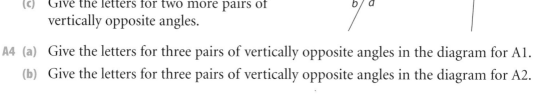

A3 (a) Which angle is vertically opposite to angle *g*?

(b) Which angle is vertically opposite to angle *b*?

(c) Give the letters for two more pairs of vertically opposite angles.

A4 (a) Give the letters for three pairs of vertically opposite angles in the diagram for A1.

(b) Give the letters for three pairs of vertically opposite angles in the diagram for A2.

A5 Use vertically opposite angles to find the angles marked with letters here.

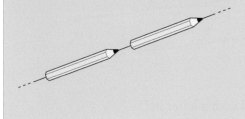

Corresponding angles are equal angles like these.

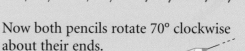

You can trace an F or a reverse F over them.

To see how corresponding angles work, think of two pencils in a straight line.

Now both pencils rotate 70° clockwise about their ends.

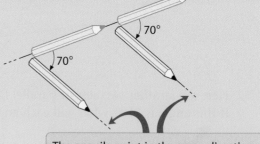

The pencils point in the same direction, so these lines are parallel.

A6 Give the missing letters for these.

(a) Angles *p* and ___ are corresponding angles.

(b) Angles ___ and *t* are corresponding angles.

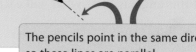

A7 (a) Give the letters for four pairs of corresponding angles in the diagram for A1.

(b) Give the letters for four pairs of corresponding angles in the diagram for A2.

A8 Use corresponding angles to find the angles marked with letters here.

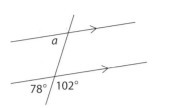

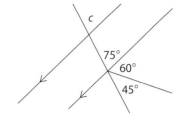

A9 Give the missing letters for these.

(a) Angles *a* and ____ are corresponding angles.

(b) Angles *h* and ____ are corresponding angles.

(c) Angles ____ and *i* are corresponding angles.

(d) Angles ____ and *j* are corresponding angles.

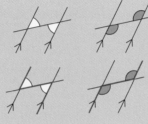

Alternate angles are equal angles like these.

You can trace a Z or a reverse Z over them.

To understand alternate angles, think of one pencil.

It rotates 70° clockwise about its end …

… then 70° anticlockwise about its point.

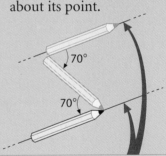

The pencil points in its original direction, so these lines are parallel.

A10 Give the missing letters for these.

(a) Angles *c* and ____ are alternate angles.

(b) Angles *f* and ____ are alternate angles.

(c) Angles ____ and *h* are alternate angles.

(d) Angles ____ and *a* are alternate angles.

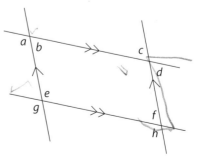

A11 Use alternate angles to find the angles marked with letters here.

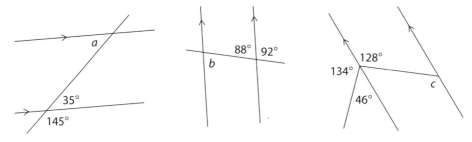

A12 Find four pairs of alternate angles in this diagram.
Give their letters.

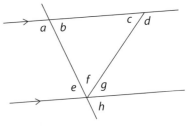

Supplementary angles add up to 180°.

You get supplementary angles on a straight line

or between parallel lines like this   or this.

A13 **(a)** Give the missing letters for these.

   (i) Angles ____ and *d* are supplementary angles
   on a straight line.

   (ii) Angles *g* and ____ are supplementary angles
   between parallel lines.

 (b) Find one more pair of supplementary angles
   on a straight line. Give their letters.

 (c) Find one more pair of supplementary angles
   between parallel lines. Give their letters.

A14 Find three pairs of supplementary angles in this diagram.
Give their letters.

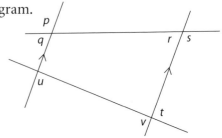

A15 Use supplementary angles to find the angles marked with letters here.

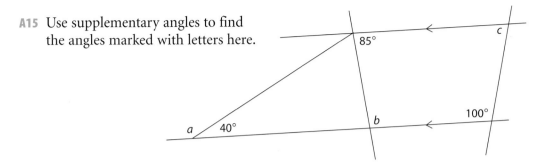

A16 Describe each of these pairs of angles. Choose from these boxes.

(a) Angles *b* and *d*

(b) Angles *b* and *f*

(c) Angles *c* and *g*

(d) Angles *a* and *b*

(e) Angles *e* and *f*

(f) Angles *c* and *e*

(g) Angles *e* and *g*

(h) Angles *a* and *e*

(i) Angles *d* and *g*

Vertically opposite angles

Corresponding angles (F)

Alternate angles (Z)

Supplementary angles on a straight line

Supplementary angles between parallel lines

A17 Give the value of each lettered angle and the reason you know the angle.
(Choose each reason from one of the boxes in A16.)

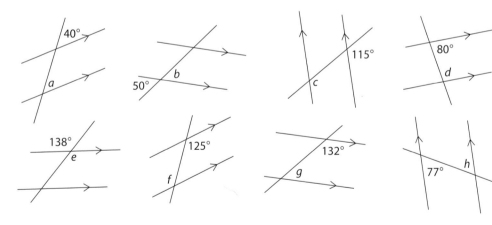

A18 Find the size of each lettered angle, giving a reason.

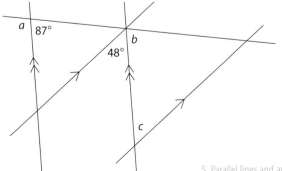

Even if lines have 'stopped' you still get related angles.

Corresponding   Alternate   Supplementary between parallels

You can think of the lines as extended if it helps.

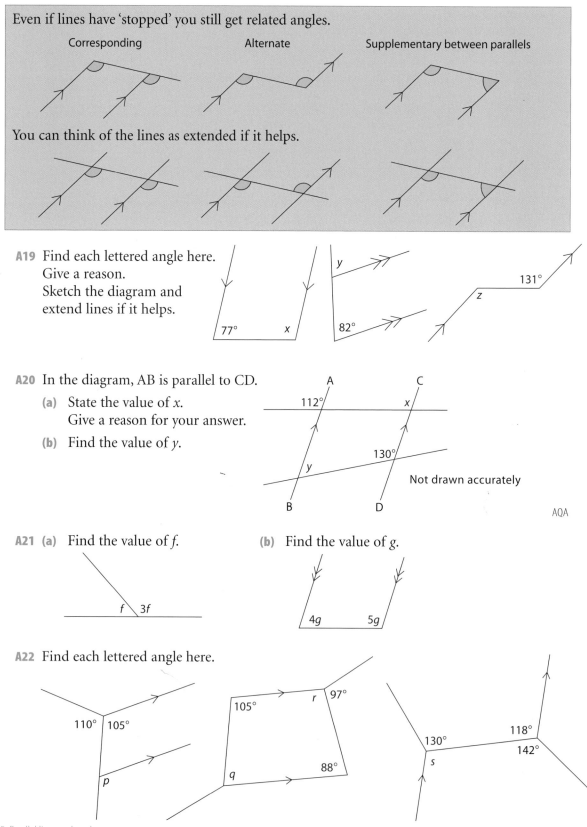

A19 Find each lettered angle here.
Give a reason.
Sketch the diagram and
extend lines if it helps.

77°   x   82°   y   z   131°

A20 In the diagram, AB is parallel to CD.

(a) State the value of x.
Give a reason for your answer.

(b) Find the value of y.

A   C
112°   x
y   130°

Not drawn accurately

B   D

AQA

A21 (a) Find the value of f.

f   3f

(b) Find the value of g.

4g   5g

A22 Find each lettered angle here.

110°   105°

p

105°   r   97°

q   88°

130°   118°
s   142°

Labelling points with capital letters helps when explaining how you have found angles.

'Angle DAB' means the angle with A at its vertex and
D and B along its arms.
You can also write ∠DAB or D̂AB.

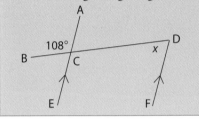

Example

Work out angle x, giving reasons.

∠ACD = 180° − 108° = 72° (supplementary on straight line BD)
∠CDF = ∠ACD = 72° (alternate), so x = 72°

OR

∠BCE = 180° − 108° = 72° (supplementary on straight line AE)
∠CDF = ∠BCE = 72° (corresponding), so x = 72°

B1 Work out the angles marked in blue, explaining your reasoning.

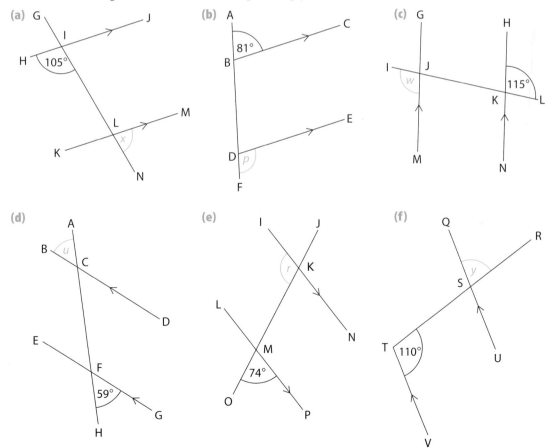

B2 Write down the values of *a* and *b*.

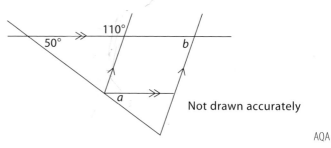

Not drawn accurately

When solving angle problems you may need to know the following facts as well as those you have just been using.

- The sum of the angles of a triangle is 180°.
- The sum of the angles round a point is 360°.

B3 ABCE is a trapezium.
Work out the angles *x* and *y*, explaining your reasoning.

B4 FGHJ is a parallelogram.
Work out the angles *p*, *q* and *r*, explaining your reasoning.

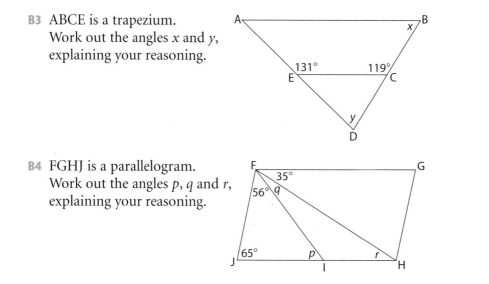

B5 Work out the angles marked in blue, explaining your reasoning.

(a)

(b)

(c)

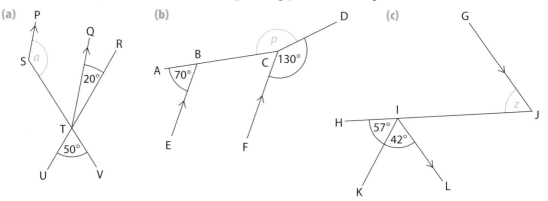

44   5 Parallel lines and angles

B6 Work out the angles marked in blue.
If you need to, copy the diagram and draw any extra lines you need.
Explain your reasoning.

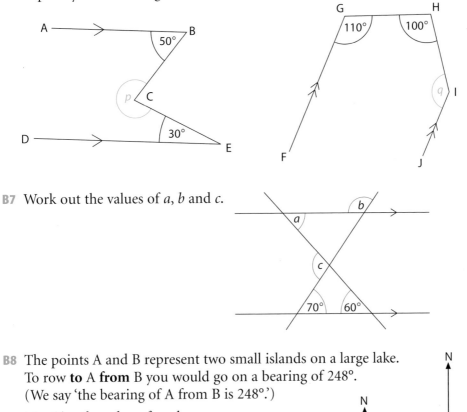

B7 Work out the values of a, b and c.

B8 The points A and B represent two small islands on a large lake.
To row **to** A **from** B you would go on a bearing of 248°.
(We say 'the bearing of A from B is 248°.')

   (a) Give the value of angle x.

   (b) What is the bearing of B from A?

B9 C and D are two lighthouses. The bearing of D from C is 112°.
Draw a sketch of the situation and use it to find the bearing of C from D.

B10 P and Q are two points on flat ground.
The bearing of Q from P is $x°$.

   (a) Write an expression for the angle coloured orange.

   (b) Hence write an expression for the bearing of P from Q.

   (c) If P and Q are any two points on flat ground, does this
expression always give you the bearing of P from Q
when $x°$ is the bearing of Q from P?

Test yourself

T1 Find four pairs of alternate angles in this diagram. Give their letters.

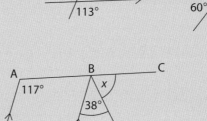

T2 Write down the values of the lettered angles. Give a reason for each.

T3 Work out the angle marked x, explaining your reasons.

T4 In the diagram, the lines AB and CD are parallel.
CRQ is a straight line.
Angle CRS = 94°.
Angle QRB = 56°.
Angle RSC = x°.

Find the value of x.

Diagram NOT accurately drawn.

Edexcel

T5 PQRS is a parallelogram.
Angle QSP = 47°
Angle QSR = 24°
PST is a straight line.

(a) (i) Find the size of the angle marked x.
(ii) Give a reason for your answer.
(b) (i) Work out the size of angle PQS.
(ii) Give a reason for your answer.

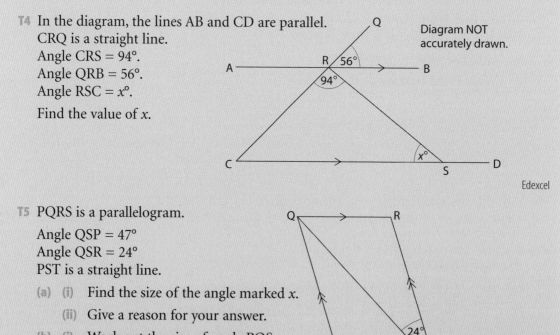

Edexcel

6 Percentages

You will revise how to

- change between fractions, decimals and percentages
- find a percentage of a quantity
- write one quantity as percentage of another

This work will help you

- calculate an amount after a percentage increase or decrease
- calculate a percentage increase or decrease

A Percentages, decimals and fractions
level 6

$$\frac{4}{5} = 4 \div 5 = 0.8 = 80\%$$

$$28\% = 0.28 = \frac{28}{100} = \frac{7}{25}$$

$$\frac{6}{40} = \frac{3}{20} = \frac{15}{100} = 15\%$$

A1

A	D	E	I	J	K	L	M	N	O	R	S	T	V	W
$\frac{1}{2}$	$\frac{4}{100}$	40%	0.75	45%	$\frac{1}{5}$	6%	0.01	0.8	$\frac{5}{100}$	$\frac{1}{3}$	$\frac{1}{4}$	60%	0.3	10%

Use this code to find a letter for each fraction, decimal or percentage below.
Rearrange each set of letters to spell a mountain.

(a) 25% $\frac{4}{10}$ $\frac{2}{5}$ 0.4   0.6   0.333 333...   30%

(b) 80%   0.1 $\frac{8}{10}$ 4%   0.25   5% $\frac{1}{20}$

(c) $\frac{4}{5}$ 1%   75%   20%   50% $\frac{3}{4}$ 0.06   0.45   0.5 $33\frac{1}{3}\%$ 0.05

A2 Write these percentages as decimals.

(a) 99%   (b) 3%   (c) 70%   (d) 49.5%   (e) $12\frac{1}{2}\%$

A3 Write these percentages as fractions, simplifying where possible.

(a) 60%   (b) 35%   (c) 48%   (d) 8%   (e) 33%

A4 Write these fractions as percentages.

(a) $\frac{11}{25}$ (b) $\frac{17}{20}$ (c) $\frac{18}{40}$ (d) $\frac{27}{30}$ (e) $\frac{64}{200}$ (f) $\frac{1}{8}$

A5 Write these decimals as percentages.

(a) 0.55   (b) 0.07   (c) 0.8   (d) 0.375   (e) 0.015

A6 Put each set of decimals, percentages and fractions in order, smallest first.

(a) 0.5 $\frac{1}{10}$ 49% $\frac{1}{4}$ 20%   (b) $\frac{4}{5}$ 76%   0.9   0.08   5%

(c) $\frac{1}{3}$ $\frac{2}{5}$ 45%   33%   0.03   (d) $\frac{1}{5}$ 5%   0.4   4%   51%

B Percentage of a quantity

To find a percentage of a quantity, you can change the percentage into a decimal and then multiply.

$23\% = \frac{23}{100} = 0.23$

Find 23% of £140.

$0.23 \times 140 = 32.2$

So 23% of £140 = £32.20

B1 Work these out.

(a) 34% of 86   (b) 62% of 140   (c) 57% of 230

(d) 8% of 4500   (e) 12% of 32.5   (f) 90% of 3725

B2 82% of UK teenagers are worried about exams.
52% of UK teenagers worry about skin problems.

Out of a year group of 180, how many would you expect to

(a) worry about exams   (b) worry about skin problems

B3 In many countries cattle or donkeys are used in harness for pulling ploughs or carts. This table shows the number of cattle and donkeys and the percentage used for work in harness, in various African countries.

Country	Cattle		Donkeys	
	Total number	% used in harness	Total number	% used in harness
Angola	3 100 000	10%	5000	100%
Botswana	2 616 000	14%	152 000	92%
Mali	5 000 000	5%	550 000	27%
Senegal	2 740 000	5%	310 000	50%

(a) How many cattle work in harness in Mali?

(b) Which country uses the largest number of cattle in harness? Show how you decided on your answer.

(c) Which country uses the largest number of donkeys in harness?

(d) Which country uses in harness more donkeys than cattle?

B4 In a town of 15 000 only 1.4% of the population cycle to work.

(a) Write 1.4% as a decimal.

(b) How many people in this town cycle to work?

B5 Work these out.

(a) 17.6% of £850   (b) 60.8% of 600 kg   (c) $3\frac{1}{2}$% of £5000

B6 Amanda has to pay a deposit of 2.25% on a car costing £13 500. How much deposit does she have to pay?

Example

Out of a class of 30 students, 6 of them don't eat breakfast. What percentage don't eat breakfast?

$$\overset{\div 6}{\overbrace{}} \quad \overset{\times 20}{\overbrace{}}$$
$$\frac{6}{30} = \frac{1}{5} = \frac{20}{100} = 20\%$$
$$\underset{\div 6}{\underbrace{}} \quad \underset{\times 20}{\underbrace{}}$$

C1 Out of a total of 20 people, 18 of them said they felt happier in the summer than in the winter. What percentage is this?

C2 In a survey, 24 out of 40 people chose chicken tikka massala as their favourite meal. What percentage is this?

C3 This bag contains some different sweets.

(a) What percentage of the sweets are

    (i) Mintos   (ii) Toffees   (iii) Humbugs

(b) The Toffees and Choccos are wrapped in red paper. What percentage of the sweets are wrapped in red?

(c) Freda doesn't like Munchos. What percentage of the sweets does she like?

(d) Dean only likes Mintos and Munchos. What percentage does he like?

12 MINTOS
18 TOFFEES
15 MUNCHOS
12 CHOCCOS
3 HUMBUGS

Example

Rose earns £320 each week.
One week, she spent £65 on food.
What percentage of her earnings went on food?

> Round your answer to one decimal place if necessary.

$$\frac{65}{320} = 65 \div 320 = 0.203\,125$$
$$0.203\,125 \times 100 = 20.3125$$
So 20.3% of Rose's earnings went on food.

C4 In a school 115 of the 250 pupils in year 10 own a bicycle. What percentage is this?

C5 In Kenya there are 420 000 motor vehicles and 32 000 of these are motorbikes. What percentage of the motor vehicles in Kenya are motorbikes?

C6 In 1996, there were the following motor vehicles in the UK.

- 21 172 000 passenger vehicles
- 3 011 000 commercial vehicles
- 609 000 motorbikes

(a) How many motor vehicles were there in total in the UK in 1996?

(b) What percentage were passenger vehicles?

C7 This table shows the estimated number of donkeys in North Africa in 1996.

North African country	Number of donkeys (thousands)
Algeria	230
Egypt	1690
Libya	55
Morocco	880
Tunisia	230
Total	3085

(a) How many donkeys were there in Egypt?

(b) What percentage of North African donkeys were in Egypt?

(c) What percentage were found in Tunisia?

(d) Is it true that about 18% of North African donkeys were in Libya?

D Percentage increase and decrease   level 6

D1 David has a discount card for his local outdoor shop.
It gives him a 10% reduction on the price of everything in the shop.
How much will he pay for a pair of boots that cost £60?

D2 Peter weighed 4 kg at birth.
After six weeks his weight had increased by 25%.
What was his new weight?

D3 A bar of chocolate weighs 200 g.
A special offer bar is advertised as having 15% extra free.
What is the weight of the special offer bar of chocolate?

D4 Joe weighed 80 kg.
He was ill for a while and lost 20% of his body weight.
What was his weight after his illness?

D5 An engineering company employs 5000 people.
It wins a new contract and increases the number of employees by 15%.
How many people are employed after the increase?

D6 1 litre of orange juice is enough to fill 5 cups.

(a) How many litres of orange juice are needed to fill 60 cups for a school concert?

The total cost of orange juice for 60 cups is £15.00.
40% is added to the cost of the juice when it is sold at the concert.

(b) Work out the price at which each cup of juice is sold.

E Increasing using a multiplier

Gas prices to rise by 15%

Pensioners will be hit hard this winter as gas companies are expected to increase prices by 15%. The elderly spend a higher proportion of their income on

If prices go up by 15%, this means 15% of the old price is added on to make the new price.

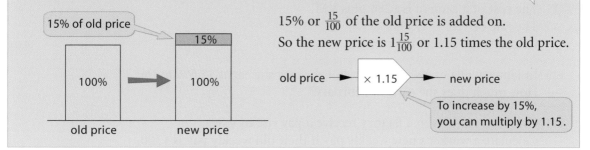

15% or $\frac{15}{100}$ of the old price is added on.

So the new price is $1\frac{15}{100}$ or 1.15 times the old price.

To increase by 15%, you can multiply by 1.15.

E1 Calculate the new price after a 15% increase for each of these old prices.

(a) £42   (b) £25.60   (c) £36.80   (d) £15   (e) £17.80

E2 If bus fares go up by 12%, what number should you multiply by to get the new fare?

E3 To the nearest penny, calculate the new fare after a 12% increase on these old fares.

(a) £2.90   (b) £38.60   (c) £60   (d) £15.90   (e) £36.75

E4 A shop buys coffee for £2.50 per kilogram.
It adds 55% on when it sells the coffee.
What is the selling price of one kilogram of coffee in this shop?

E5 At the start of 2005, Mary had 140 budgies.
During the year the number of budgies went up by 35%.
How many budgies did Mary have at the end of the year?

E6 A population in a town is expected to rise by 8%.

(a) Tina says you should multiply the present population by 1.8.
Tim says you should multiply by 1.08.
Who is right?

(b) If the present population is 56 000, what will the population be after a rise of 8%?

E7 The puffin population on a small island is estimated to be 1500 birds.
One year the population is expected to rise by 6%.
What would the new puffin population be after a rise of 6%?

E8 In 1997 Mrs Patel earned £16 640 for a 52-week year.
At the start of 1998 she was given a rise of 3%.
Calculate how much she will earn **per week** in 1998?

OCR

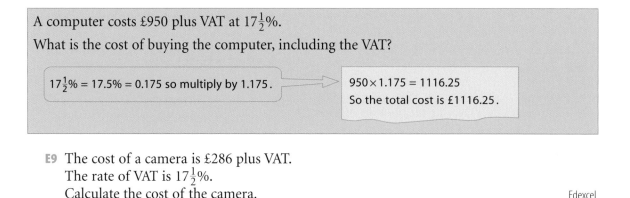

A computer costs £950 plus VAT at $17\frac{1}{2}$%.

What is the cost of buying the computer, including the VAT?

$17\frac{1}{2}$% = 17.5% = 0.175 so multiply by 1.175.

950 × 1.175 = 1116.25
So the total cost is £1116.25.

E9 The cost of a camera is £286 plus VAT.
The rate of VAT is $17\frac{1}{2}$%.
Calculate the cost of the camera.   Edexcel

E10 In January Ella earns £1250 but in February she earns 15.6% more.
How much does she earn in February?

E11 One year, workers in a factory receive a pay rise of 4.8%.
Calculate a worker's new weekly pay if their old weekly pay is £300.

E12 (a) Increase £540 by 12.2%   (b) Increase £600 by 68.4%

  (c) Increase £15 by 2.5%   (d) Increase £3.60 by 6.7%

F Decreasing using a multiplier

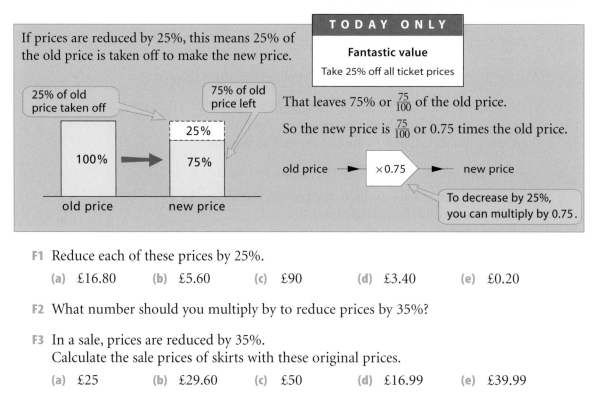

If prices are reduced by 25%, this means 25% of
the old price is taken off to make the new price.

TODAY ONLY

Fantastic value

Take 25% off all ticket prices

25% of old
price taken off

75% of old
price left

That leaves 75% or $\frac{75}{100}$ of the old price.

So the new price is $\frac{75}{100}$ or 0.75 times the old price.

25%

100%   75%

old price → ×0.75 → new price

old price   new price

To decrease by 25%,
you can multiply by 0.75.

F1 Reduce each of these prices by 25%.
  (a) £16.80   (b) £5.60   (c) £90   (d) £3.40   (e) £0.20

F2 What number should you multiply by to reduce prices by 35%?

F3 In a sale, prices are reduced by 35%.
Calculate the sale prices of skirts with these original prices.
  (a) £25   (b) £29.60   (c) £50   (d) £16.99   (e) £39.99

F4 Reduce each of these prices by 16%.

    (a) £4.80   (b) £6.30   (c) £19.99   (d) £35.50   (e) £280

F5 What number should you multiply by to reduce prices by 9%?

F6 Reduce each of these prices by 9%.

    (a) £1240   (b) £680   (c) £9.50   (d) £0.64   (e) £14.70

F7 What should you multiply by to reduce prices by these percentages?

    (a) 72%   (b) 23%   (c) 30%   (d) 5%   (e) 2%

F8 Reduce

    (a) £240 by 13%   (b) £620 by 82%   (c) £2.95 by 22%   (d) £430 by 8%

F9 Sally is interested in buying a car that is priced at £6200.
She is offered a 7% reduction in the price if she pays cash.
How much would the car cost her?

F10 Every percentage increase or decrease corresponds to a multiplier.
Match these percentage changes to their multipliers.

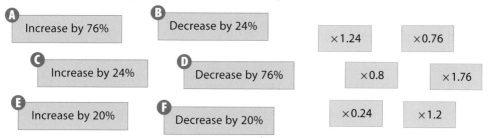

F11 Since last year the price of houses has increased by 9% on average.
How much would you expect to pay this year for a house that cost £110 000 last year?

F12 The value of a car decreased by 18% over the last year.
The car was worth £4500 a year ago.
How much is the car worth now?

F13 Between the ages of five and ten years, Mike's weight increased by 66%.
When he was five years old he weighed 18 kg.
How heavy was he when he was ten, correct to the nearest kg?

F14 Between 2000 and 2005, the number of school age children in a town
went down by 23%.
The number of children in this town in 2000 was 9560.
How many children were living in this town in 2005, correct to the nearest 10?

G Finding an increase as a percentage

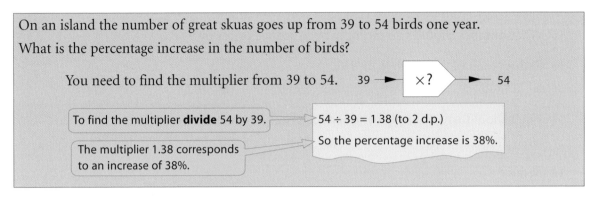

On an island the number of great skuas goes up from 39 to 54 birds one year.
What is the percentage increase in the number of birds?

You need to find the multiplier from 39 to 54.   39 → ×? → 54

To find the multiplier **divide** 54 by 39. → 54 ÷ 39 = 1.38 (to 2 d.p.)

The multiplier 1.38 corresponds to an increase of 38%. → So the percentage increase is 38%.

G1 The price of a camera goes up from £250 to £270.
Calculate the percentage increase.

G2 Calculate the percentage increase in each case below.

(a) From £25 to £28.50

(b) From £150 to £247.50

(c) From 69 kg to 117.3 kg

(d) From 2 metres to 2.14 metres

G3 Jake buys a painting for £400 and sells it for £520.
By what percentage has its value increased?

G4 Meena sells a book for £22.20 that she bought for only £12.
By what percentage has its price increased?

G5 From 1975 to 1994, the number of UK public libraries increased from 3714 to 4499.
What was the percentage increase in the number of libraries, correct to the nearest 1%?

G6 In 1994 the number of registered heroin addicts in the UK was 22 313.
In 1992 the number was 16 964.
Find the percentage increase in the number of registered addicts between 1992 and 1994.

G7 The table shows the average price of a
UK dwelling in 1985, 1990 and 1995.

Find the percentage increase in price between

(a) 1985 and 1990   (b) 1990 and 1995

1985	1990	1995
£31 103	£59 785	£65 079

G8 The table shows the populations of England and
Scotland in 1931 and 1991.
From 1931 to 1991, find the percentage
increase in the population in each country.

	1931	1991
England	37 358 000	48 209 000
Scotland	4 843 000	5 100 000

G9 In 1980 there were 2556 km of motorway in the UK.
By 1994 there were 3168 km of motorway.
Find the percentage increase, correct to one decimal place.

H Finding a decrease as a percentage

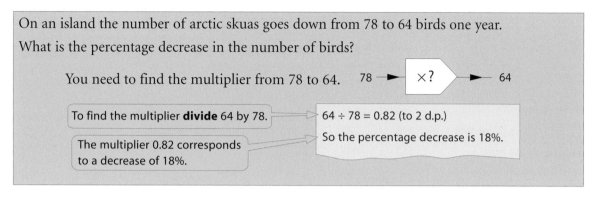

On an island the number of arctic skuas goes down from 78 to 64 birds one year.
What is the percentage decrease in the number of birds?

You need to find the multiplier from 78 to 64.   78 → ×? → 64

To find the multiplier **divide** 64 by 78. → 64 ÷ 78 = 0.82 (to 2 d.p.)

The multiplier 0.82 corresponds to a decrease of 18%. → So the percentage decrease is 18%.

H1 In a sale, the price of a jumper is cut from £42 to £27.30.
Calculate the percentage decrease in the price.

H2 Calculate the percentage decrease in each case below.

(a) From £75 to £57   (b) From £8.50 to £3.23

(c) From 84 kg to 58.8 kg   (d) From 6.5 metres to 6.24 metres

H3 Between 1981 and 1991, the population of Sheffield fell from 538 000 to 503 000.
What was the percentage decrease in the population, correct to the nearest 1%?

H4 Sanjay is buying a car that is priced at £6450.
The saleswoman reduces the price to £5700 as Sanjay is paying cash.
What percentage discount is this?

H5 In 1984 the number of deaths through road accidents in the UK was 5599.
In 1994 the number of deaths had gone down to 3650.
Find the percentage decrease in the number of deaths between 1984 and 1994.

H6 Calculate the percentage change in each case below, correct to the nearest 1%.
Say whether it is an increase or a decrease.

(a) From £560 to £476   (b) From 20 kg to 28.6 kg

(c) From 58 kg to 75.2 kg   (d) From 82 m to 60 m

(e) From £150 to £90   (f) From 40 kg to 43.6 kg

(g) From 1200 to 1176   (h) From 60 to 64

H7 The table shows the numbers of men and women in employment in the UK in 1970 and 1995.

Between 1970 and 1995, what was the percentage change in the number employed in the UK for

	Men	Women
1970	13 952 000	8 450 000
1995	11 047 000	10 842 000

(a) men   (b) women

Say whether it is an increase or decrease each time.

H8 Copy and complete this table to show estimates of the percentage changes in our consumption of different foodstuffs between 1965 and 1994.

Estimated consumption in grams per person per week			
	1965	1994	% change
Cheese	91	106	16% increase
Beef and veal	229	131	
Fish	164	145	
Fresh green veg	406	245	
Fresh fruit	533	645	
Instant coffee	7	13	

Just show the first and last columns in your answer.

I Mixed questions

I1 This table shows data on the use of the Channel Tunnel in 1996.

Use of the Channel Tunnel in 1996		
Purpose	UK residents (thousands)	Non-residents (thousands)
Holiday	1910	1458
Business	666	481
Visiting friends and relatives	299	498
Other	583	271
Total	3458	2708

(a) How many UK residents used the Channel Tunnel in 1996?

(b) What percentage of UK residents using the tunnel were going on holiday?

(c) What percentage of people not resident in the UK used the tunnel for a business trip?

(d) What percentage of all users of the tunnel were visiting friends and relatives?

I2 An electricity company makes a standing charge of £11.50 each quarter and charges customers 7.2p for every unit of electricity they use.
VAT is charged on the whole amount at 5%.

Ann uses 545 units of electricity in a particular quarter.

(a) Calculate the cost of the units Ann has used.

(b) Add on the standing charge.

(c) Work out the VAT to the nearest penny on the total in (b) and add it on to get the amount Ann has to pay.

13 A health club puts up its annual subscription from £480 to £495.
At the time, the rate of inflation is 2.8%.
Is the increase more or less than the rate of inflation?

14 Sam wants to buy a Hooper washing machine.
Hooper washing machines are sold in three different shops.

Washing Power

$\frac{1}{4}$ OFF
usual price
of £330

Whytes

20% OFF
usual price
of £320

Clean Up

£210
plus VAT
at $17\frac{1}{2}$%

(a) Work out the cost of the washing machine in the Washing Power shop.

(b) Work out the cost of the washing machine in the Whytes shop.

(c) Work out the cost of the washing machine in the Clean Up shop.   Edexcel

15
London – Paris by plane

Normal price: £91

Special offer: 15% discount

An airline company has flights from London to Paris for £91.
They offer a 15% discount.
Calculate the cost of the flight after the discount.   AQA

16 Tom buys 200 tomato plants at a total cost of £40 to sell at a school fair.
He sells $\frac{3}{4}$ of them at 50p each.
He then reduces the price of the remaining plants to 40p.
At the end of the day there are 18 plants left which have **not** been sold.

(a) How much money does he receive from selling the tomato plants at the school fair?

(b) Find the percentage profit which Tom made on these plants.   AQA

17 In 1981 there were 855 000 tonnes of cod in the North Sea.
By 1996, this had fallen to 438 000 tonnes.
Calculate the percentage decrease in the cod stocks.

18 Aisha works in a clothes shop.
She is paid at a basic rate of £4.65 per hour plus 6% of the value of her sales.
In one week she worked for 32 hours and sold clothes to the value of £1750.

Calculate her total earnings for the week.   OCR

*19 A bedspread is a square 2.5 m by 2.5 m.
After washing, its length and breadth have both shrunk by 15%.
Calculate the percentage reduction in the area of the bedspread.

Test yourself

T1 A group of 40 women applied to go on an art trip.
Only 80% of all the women who applied went on the trip.
How many women went on the trip?

T2 Out of a year group of 180 students, 25% walk to school.
How many of these students walk to school?

T3 In 1974 the number of students in a college was 5000.
This year the number of students is 5750.
What is the percentage increase in the number of students in the college?   AQA

T4 There are 3270 students at a university.
At this university 1962 students have a part-time job.
What percentage of the students have a part-time job?

T5 A carriage in a train has 60 seats.
Only one of these is reserved for disabled passengers.
What percentage of seats are reserved for disabled passengers?

T6 In 1995 police carried out a total of 702.7 thousand breath tests.
13% of them were positive. How many was this, correct to the nearest thousand?

T7 In one year a plant's height increased by 24%.
It was 1.75 m tall at the beginning of the year.
How tall was it at the end of the year?

T8 323 child pedestrians died in road accidents in 1985.
Between 1985 and 1995, the number of child pedestrians
killed in road accidents decreased by 59%.
How many child pedestrians died in road accidents in 1995?

T9 Between 1950 and 1995, the number of self-employed people in the UK
rose by 80.5%. In 1950, there were 1 802 000 self-employed people.
How many self-employed people were there in 1995, correct to
the nearest thousand?

T10 A shop increases the price of a television from £480 to £648.
What is the percentage increase in price?

T11 Rana chooses a new car. It has a cash price of £9750.
The credit terms are shown below.

> Deposit 27% of the cash price
> Plus 24 monthly instalments of £325.50

How much more is the credit price than the cash price?   OCR

7 Pie charts

Pie charts can be a useful way of displaying information.
You may find them helpful in your GCSE coursework.

This work will help you draw and interpret a pie chart.

Pie charts are often labelled with
the percentage for each category.

Computer programs that draw pie charts
can usually be made to show percentages.

This pie chart shows the school uniform
colour choice of 28 students in a class.

The number who chose blue was
29% of 28 = 0.29×28 = 8.12 so 8 students.

- How many students chose each other colour?

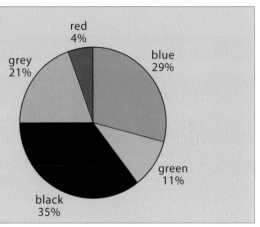

A1 A group of 80 students were asked what was the main
carbohydrate in their evening meal main last night.
This pie chart shows the results.

(a) How many of the students said chips?

(b) How many students said pizza?

(c) How many students had something
other than chips or potatoes?

(d) Approximately what fraction of the
students had chips?

A2 The 55 students in a school year group each
entered a piece for a local art exhibition.
The pieces that were exhibited were awarded
commendation, merit or distinction certificates.
This pie chart shows what happened.

(a) Use a pie chart scale to find the percentage
of students whose work was not exhibited.

(b) How many students gained a distinction?

(c) What fraction of the students gained a merit?

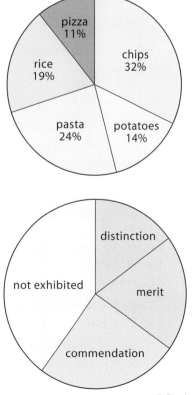

A3 Josh asked a group of 120 students who watched more TV – they or their parents. He has drawn this pie chart using angles. He wants to show the percentage for each answer on his chart, correct to 1 d.p.

(a) Calculate the percentages who said

    (i) parents   (ii) students

    (iii) about the same

(b) How many of these students thought they watched more TV than their parents?

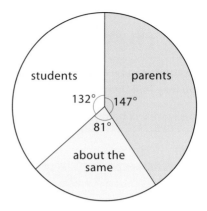

B Drawing a pie chart using angles

Are you a veggie?

Sarah asks a sample of people about the kinds of foods they eat.
This table shows her results.

She thinks that a pie chart is the best way to show her results.

Reply	Tally	Frequency
Vegan	//	2
Vegetarian	⅃𝘏𝘛 ⅃𝘏𝘛 //	12
Vegetarian – but eat fish	⅃𝘏𝘛 ///	8
Meat eater	⅃𝘏𝘛 ⅃𝘏𝘛 ⅃𝘏𝘛 ⅃𝘏𝘛	20
Total		42

First she works out what angle is used to show a single person.

$\div 42$ (42 people are shown by $360°$

1 person is shown by $8.571\,428\,571\ldots°$) $\div 42$ This is an example of the unitary method.

$8.571\,428\,571\ldots$ could be rounded but it is more accurate to store it in full in your calculator memory to use each time.

So the angle in the pie chart needed for vegan is
$2 \times 8.571\,428\,571\ldots° = 17.14\ldots° \approx 17°$

• Work out the angles for the other responses.
(Check that your angles add up to $360°$.)
Use them to draw a pie chart.

Reply	Frequency	Angle
Vegan	2	17°
Vegetarian		

B1 In a survey, the eye colour of 270 children was recorded.
The table shows the information.

Draw a pie chart to show this information.
Label the size of each angle in degrees.

Eye colour	Number of children
Green	24
Blue	75
Grey	66
Brown	105
Total	270

B2 A council is looking at the causes
of road accidents in its area last year.
This table shows the data collected.

Draw a pie chart to illustrate these results.
Label the size of each angle in degrees.

Cause of accident	Number of accidents
Speeding	101
Driver error	79
Weather conditions	44
Mechanical failure	32
Other	28
Total	284

C Drawing a pie chart using a percentage scale

This table shows the results of a survey of 125
students on what they think of school uniform.

To find the percentage who said 'should be
compulsory', work out

$36 \div 125$
$= 0.288$

which is the decimal equivalent of 28.8%.

Response	Frequency
Should be compulsory	36
Compulsory but more choice	50
Should not be compulsory	25
Don't know	14
Total	125

- What percentage of the students gave each of
  the other responses?
  (Check that your percentages add up to 100%.)

A percentage pie chart scale can be used to draw the pie chart.

C1 A school canteen sells 150 packets of crisps one lunchtime.
The table shows the number of each flavour sold.

Flavour	Plain	Salt and vinegar	Cheese and onion	Other
Packets sold	21	57	66	6

(a) What percentage of the crisps sold were plain?

(b) Draw a pie chart to show the sales of the different flavours of crisps.

C2 Canoeists taking a survival test can achieve
a gold, silver or bronze award.
Last year 253 canoeists took the test.
The results are shown in the table.

Draw a pie chart to illustrate this information.
Label each sector with its percentage,
correct to 1 d.p.

Award	Number of canoeists
Gold	42
Silver	63
Bronze	126
Failed	22
Total	253

Sometimes rounding gives a set of percentages for a pie chart that add up to, say, 99% or 101% instead of 100%.

Working correct to 1 d.p. usually avoids this problem.
Draw each pie chart using an angle measurer or pie chart scale.

D1 In a survey, a total of 2975 families with dependent children were asked who looked after the children.
Here are the results.

Main carers	Number of families
Couple	2352
Widowed, divorced or separated mother	357
Single mother	208
Lone father	58

(a) Draw a pie chart to show these results.

(b) Approximately what fraction of these families have a couple looking after the children?

D2 In a survey, a total of 9128 people were asked what type of home they lived in.
Here are the results.

Type of home	Frequency
Detached house	1922
Semi-detached house	2928
Terraced house	2457
Flat or maisonette	1821

(a) Draw a pie chart to show these results.

(b) Approximately what fraction of these people lived in a detached or semi-detached house?

D3 This table shows some information about the weight of aluminium cans recycled in the UK.

Explain why a pie chart would not be an appropriate way to display this information.

Year	Weight of cans recycled (tonnes)
1990	4000
1992	11 700
1994	25 440
1996	23 900
1998	24 740
2000	34 400

D4 This data is about the total number of people killed in road accidents in the UK.

Number of people killed				
	Pedestrians	Cyclists	Motor cyclists	All other road users
1950	2251	805	1129	827
2000	857	127	605	1820

(a) Draw pie charts to show the data.

(b) Susie concludes from the data that it was more dangerous to be a cyclist in 1950 than it was in 2000.
Comment on her conclusion.

Test yourself

T1 This pie chart gives information about the readers of a magazine.

The magazine has about 7000 readers.

(a) About how many men aged under 25 read the magazine?

(b) About how many women read the magazine?

(c) About how many people aged 25 or more read the magazine?

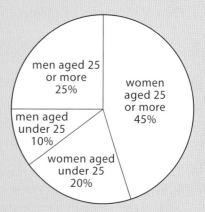

T2 The table shows information about government spending in the UK in 1930 and 1990.

Government spending in the UK (billions of £s)					
	Defence	Education	Health and social services	Debt interest	Other
1930	0.12	0.11	0.32	0.29	0.31
1990	22.91	26.72	91.69	18.75	55.52

(a) Draw pie charts to show the data.

(b) Sean concludes from his charts that the amount of money spent on defence was about the same in both years.
Comment on his conclusion.

(c) Briefly compare the data for the two years.

Review 1

1 Out of 30 students, 9 walk to school.
  What percentage of the students walk to school?

2 Which fraction is greater, $\frac{9}{16}$ or $\frac{13}{24}$?

3 Find the area of each rectangle in m^2.

  (a)   0.4 m

         0.3 m

  (b)   3.45 m

         0.2 m

4 What is the exact value of $\frac{5}{9}$ written as a decimal?

5 How many pieces of ribbon 0.7 m long could be cut from a roll of ribbon 28 m long?

6 Work these out, giving each answer in its simplest form.

  (a) $84 \times \frac{3}{4}$ (b) $17 \times \frac{2}{3}$ (c) $\frac{1}{6} \div 4$ (d) $\frac{3}{4} \div 9$ (e) $\frac{3}{5} \times \frac{5}{6}$

  (f) $\frac{2}{3} + \frac{4}{5}$ (g) $1\frac{2}{9} - \frac{3}{4}$ (h) $\frac{4}{5}$ of $3\frac{1}{8}$ (i) $1\frac{4}{11} \times 2\frac{1}{3}$ (j) $4\frac{1}{6} \div 5$

7 Given that $12 \times 23 = 276$, work out the answers to

  (a) 1.2×2.3 (b) 230×0.012 (c) $27.6 \div 1.2$ (d) $2.76 \div 0.0023$

8 There are 30 students in a class.
  40% of the students are boys.
  20% of the students wear glasses.
  2 girls wear glasses.
  What fraction of the boys do not wear glasses?

9 Joan is paid £201.24 for $19\frac{1}{2}$ hours' work.

  (a) (i) By rounding to one significant figure, find an estimate for her hourly
           rate of pay.

      (ii) Without doing any more calculation, decide if your estimate is more
           or less than her actual hourly rate. Explain how you decided.

  (b) Use a calculator to calculate her exact pay for 25 hours' work at the same rate.

10 The cost of a laser printer is £250 plus VAT.
   The rate of VAT is $17\frac{1}{2}$%.
   Calculate the cost of the printer.

11 The instructions for some soluble lawn food say
   '450 grams of lawn food is enough to feed 100 m^2 of lawn'.
   How much lawn food, to the nearest 10 g, is needed for a rectangular
   lawn 18 m by 16 m?

12 The membership of a badminton club falls from 58 to 47 members over a year. What is the percentage decrease in the number of members, correct to 1 d.p.?

13 This diagram shows a design for a square patchwork cushion.

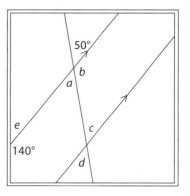

(a) Copy and complete:

Angles *a* and ____ are alternate angles.

(b) Work out the size of each lettered angle. Give a reason each time.

14 A factory producing computers recorded this information over several weeks.

Week number	1	2	3	4	5	6
Number of computers made	2030	2289	3982	2847	4021	3109
Number of computers faulty	124	109	154	61	62	47

(a) Use percentages to comment on whether the quality of production is improving or getting worse.

(b) The managers plan to produce 3700 computers in week 7 and want at least 99% of them to be fault-free. How many fault-free computers is that?

15 ABCD is a trapezium with AB parallel to DC. Work out the size of angle *x*, explaining your reasons.

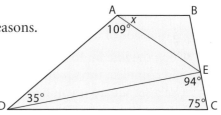

16 A pint is approximately 0.57 of a litre. A supermarket sells milk at 78p for a two-pint carton. How much is this per litre?

17 The table gives some information about the ages of people in the UK in 2005.

Age range (years)	0–14	15–64	65+
Number of people	10 720 283	40 185 134	9 536 040

(a) How many people were aged 65 years or over, correct to the nearest million.

(b) How many people were aged 15–64, correct to three significant figures?

(c) What percentage of the population were aged 0–14 years?

(d) Draw a pie chart to show the information in the table.

8 Pythagoras's theorem

You will revise square roots.

This work will help you

- find the length of one side of a right-angled triangle if you know the lengths of the other two sides
- solve problems involving the lengths of sides of right-angled triangles

A The area of a tilted square

To get the area of a tilted square …

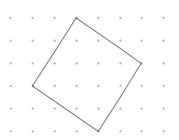

… find the area of a surrounding square, then subtract the area of the triangles …

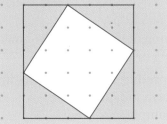

… **or** divide the square up like this and find the area of the parts.

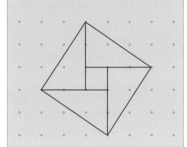

A1 This is one side of a tilted square.

    (a) Copy the line on to square dotty paper and complete the square.
Use a set square if you need to.

    (b) Work out the area of the square.

A2 Each of these is the side of a tilted square.
Draw each square and work out its area.

    (a)   **(b)**   **(c)**

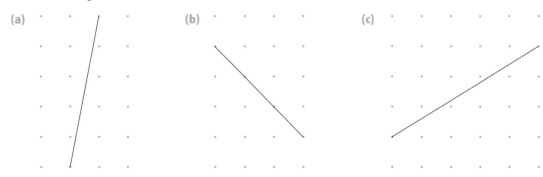

B Squares on right-angled triangles

The three squares Q, R and S are drawn on
the sides of a right-angled triangle.

Copy the drawing on to dotty paper.
Find and record the area of each square.

Repeat this process for different right-angled triangles.
You could do this in a group, sharing out the work.

Square S must be on the side opposite the right angle.
Record your results in a table.

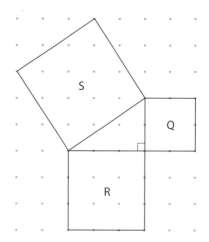

Area of square Q	Area of square R	Area of square S

What do you notice about the areas?

B1 Find the missing areas of the squares on these right-angled triangles.

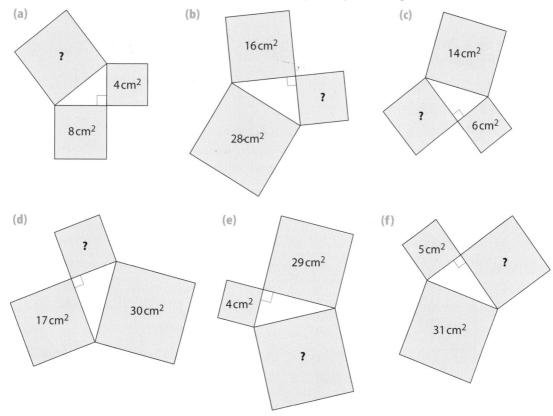

(a) ? 4 cm² 8 cm²

(b) 16 cm² ? 28 cm²

(c) 14 cm² ? 6 cm²

(d) ? 17 cm² 30 cm²

(e) 29 cm² 4 cm² ?

(f) 5 cm² ? 31 cm²

Pythagoras's theorem

In a right-angled triangle the side opposite the right angle
is called the **hypotenuse.**

You have found that the area of the square on the hypotenuse
equals the total of the areas of the squares on the other two sides.

Here, Area C = Area A + Area B

This is known as Pythagoras's theorem (or 'Pythagoras' for short).
Pythagoras was a Greek mathematician and mystic.
A theorem is a statement that can be proved true.

Using Pythagoras's theorem you can work with the
lengths of sides as well as the areas of squares on them.

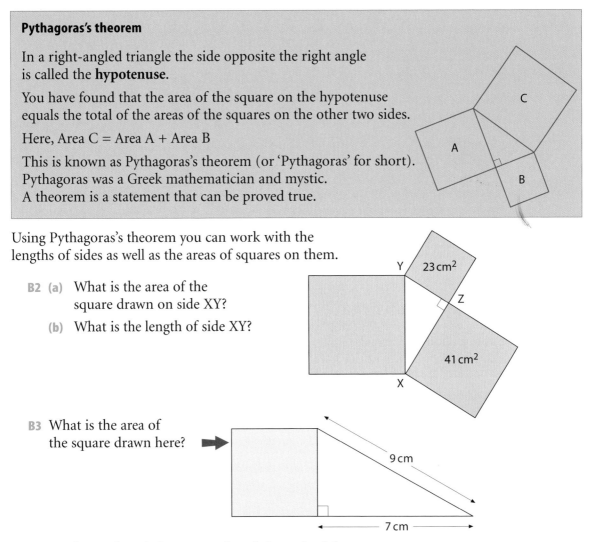

B2 (a) What is the area of the
square drawn on side XY?

(b) What is the length of side XY?

B3 What is the area of
the square drawn here?

B4 Work out the missing area or length in each of these.

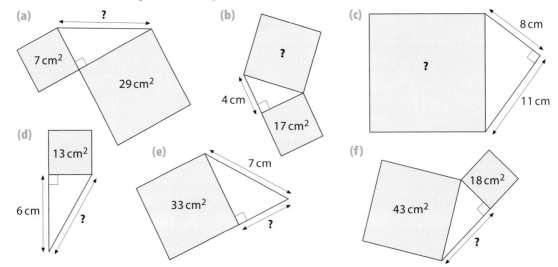

(a) ? 7 cm² 29 cm²

(b) ? 4 cm 17 cm²

(c) 8 cm ? 11 cm

(d) 13 cm² 6 cm ?

(e) 7 cm 33 cm² ?

(f) 18 cm² 43 cm² ?

B5 Work out the missing area or length in each of these.

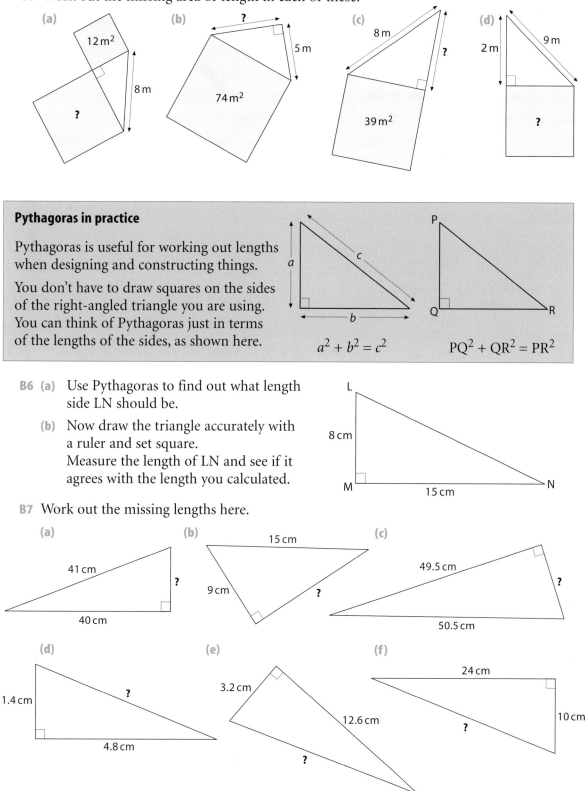

(a) 12 m² | 8 m | ?

(b) ? | 5 m | 74 m²

(c) 8 m | ? | 39 m²

(d) 2 m | 9 m | ?

Pythagoras in practice

Pythagoras is useful for working out lengths when designing and constructing things.

You don't have to draw squares on the sides of the right-angled triangle you are using. You can think of Pythagoras just in terms of the lengths of the sides, as shown here.

$a^2 + b^2 = c^2$ $PQ^2 + QR^2 = PR^2$

B6 (a) Use Pythagoras to find out what length side LN should be.

(b) Now draw the triangle accurately with a ruler and set square.
Measure the length of LN and see if it agrees with the length you calculated.

L | 8 cm | M | 15 cm | N

B7 Work out the missing lengths here.

(a) 41 cm | 40 cm | ?

(b) 15 cm | 9 cm | ?

(c) 49.5 cm | 50.5 cm | ?

(d) 1.4 cm | 4.8 cm | ?

(e) 3.2 cm | 12.6 cm | ?

(f) 24 cm | 10 cm | ?

B8 People marking out sports pitches need to mark lines at right angles.

They sometimes use a rope divided into 12 equal spaces to form a 3, 4, 5 triangle.

Use Pythagoras to check that this produces a right angle. Show your working.

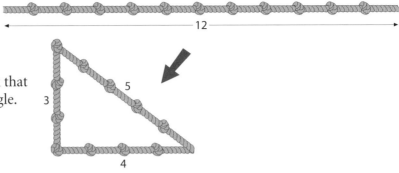

If a square has an area of $16\,\text{cm}^2$, you know the length of its side is $4\,\text{cm}$ because 4^2 is 16.

Remember that 4 is the **square root** of 16.

C1 Copy and complete this table.

Number	Square root
1	
4	
	3
	4
25	
36	
	7

C2 What is the square root of each of these numbers?

(a) 81   (b) 100   (c) 121   (d) 400

We use the symbol $\sqrt{}$ to mean square root.

So $\sqrt{16}$ means the square root of 16.

C3 Work out the value of these.

(a) $\sqrt{49}$ (b) $\sqrt{9}$ (c) $\sqrt{144}$ (d) $\sqrt{169}$

C4 For each of these square roots,

   (i) first write down a rough answer

   (ii) find the value to two decimal places on a calculator

(a) $\sqrt{10}$ (b) $\sqrt{2.5}$ (c) $\sqrt{150}$ (d) $\sqrt{15}$

(e) $\sqrt{200}$ (f) $\sqrt{20}$ (g) $\sqrt{42}$ (h) $\sqrt{420}$

(i) $\sqrt{85}$ (j) $\sqrt{8.5}$ (k) $\sqrt{805}$ (l) $\sqrt{50}$

(m) $\sqrt{500}$ (n) $\sqrt{5}$ (o) $\sqrt{0.5}$ (p) $\sqrt{5000}$

C5 Use the square root key on your calculator to work out the missing lengths here.
Give your answers to one decimal place.

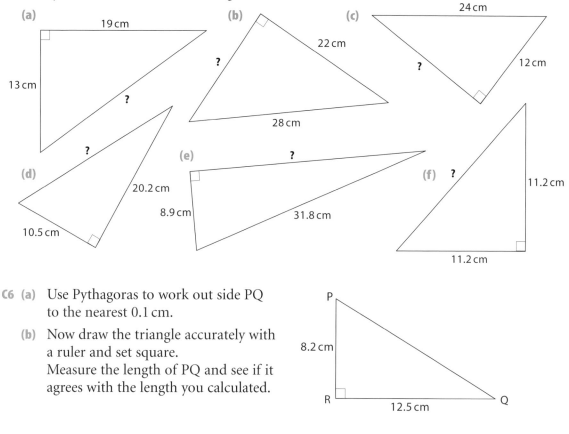

(a) 19 cm, 13 cm, ?

(b) ? , 22 cm, 28 cm

(c) 24 cm, ? , 12 cm

(d) 20.2 cm, ? , 10.5 cm

(e) 8.9 cm, ? , 31.8 cm

(f) ? , 11.2 cm, 11.2 cm

C6 (a) Use Pythagoras to work out side PQ
to the nearest 0.1 cm.

(b) Now draw the triangle accurately with
a ruler and set square.
Measure the length of PQ and see if it
agrees with the length you calculated.

P, 8.2 cm, R, 12.5 cm, Q

D Using Pythagoras

D1 A certain exercise book is 14.0 cm wide by 20.0 cm high.

(a) How long is the longest straight line you can draw on a single page of the book?

(b) How long is the longest straight line you can draw on a double page?

D2 Measure the height and width of your own exercise book.
Repeat the calculations in D1 for your own book.
Measure to check your answers.

D3 This is the plan of a rectangular field.
There is a footpath across the field from A to C.

How much shorter is it to use the footpath
than to walk from A to B and then to C?

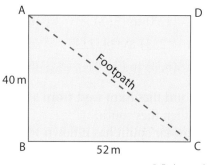

A, D, 40 m, Footpath, B, 52 m, C

D4 Points A and B are plotted on a grid on centimetre squared paper.

(a) How far is it in a straight line from A to B?

(b) How long would a straight line from (2, 2) to (14, 7) be? (Draw them on a grid or make a sketch if you need to.)

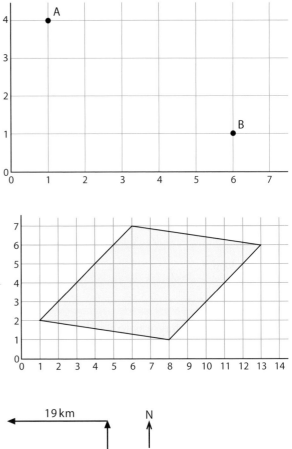

D5 (a) Calculate the lengths of the sides of this quadrilateral.

(b) Use your working to say whether it is exactly a rhombus.

D6 A helicopter flies 26 km north from a heliport, then 19 km west.

How far is it from the heliport now?

19 km

N

26 km

H

D7 How long is a straight line joining each pair of points if they are plotted on a centimetre squared grid? Give your answers to one decimal place.

(a) (1, 3) to (5, 7)

(b) (2, 4) to (8, 1)

(c) (5, 0) to (7, ⁻3)

(d) (⁻2, 3) to (⁻4, 1)

(e) (⁻2, 6) to (2, 8)

(f) (3, 1) to (⁻6, 4)

(g) (6, 3) to (4, ⁻4)

(h) (11, ⁻1) to (8, 3)

(i) (⁻7, 5) to (⁻4, ⁻5)

D8 A bird flies 8 km west from a lighthouse.
It then flies south.
How far south has it flown when it is 22 km from the lighthouse?

D9 In these isosceles triangles the equal angles are shown coloured. Calculate the lengths marked with letters.

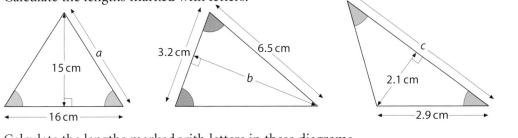

D10 Calculate the lengths marked with letters in these diagrams.

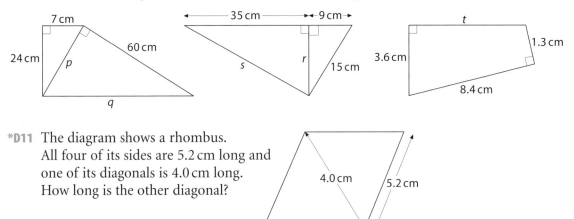

*D11 The diagram shows a rhombus. All four of its sides are 5.2 cm long and one of its diagonals is 4.0 cm long. How long is the other diagonal?

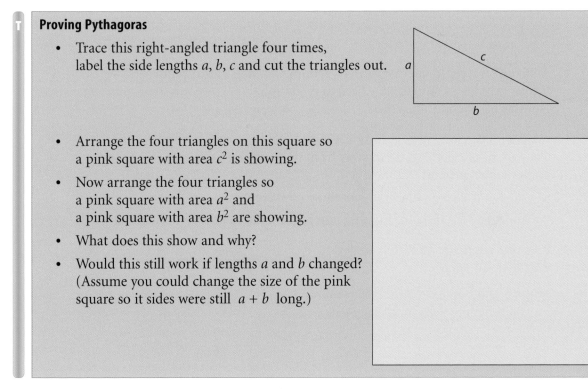

Proving Pythagoras

- Trace this right-angled triangle four times, label the side lengths a, b, c and cut the triangles out.

- Arrange the four triangles on this square so a pink square with area c^2 is showing.

- Now arrange the four triangles so a pink square with area a^2 and a pink square with area b^2 are showing.

- What does this show and why?

- Would this still work if lengths a and b changed? (Assume you could change the size of the pink square so it sides were still $a + b$ long.)

A **proof** is a step-by-step argument that establishes beyond doubt that a statement is true. There are many different proofs of Pythagoras's theorem.

The activity on the previous page will work with any right-angled triangle. It amounts to a proof of Pythagoras's theorem, even though it is informal and visual.

Test yourself

T1 Find the missing areas.

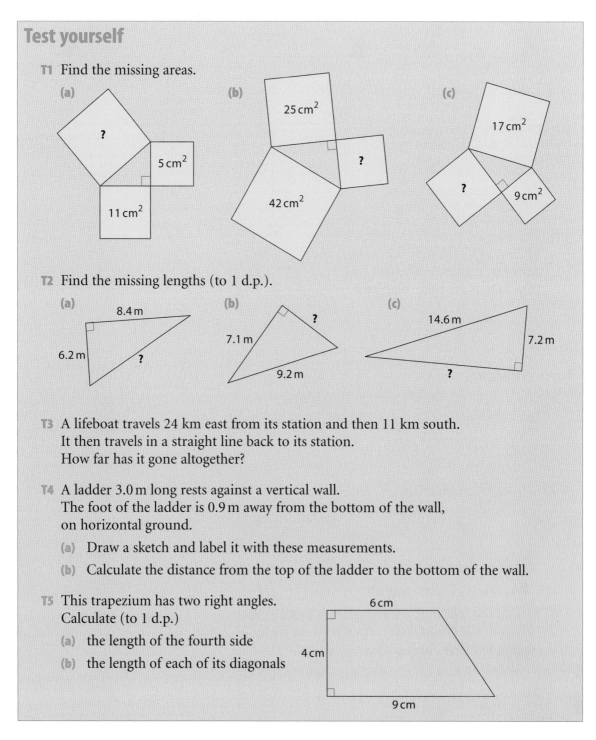

(a)

?   5 cm²   11 cm²

(b)

25 cm²   ?   42 cm²

(c)

17 cm²   ?   9 cm²

T2 Find the missing lengths (to 1 d.p.).

(a) 8.4 m   6.2 m   ?

(b) 7.1 m   ?   9.2 m

(c) 14.6 m   7.2 m   ?

T3 A lifeboat travels 24 km east from its station and then 11 km south.
It then travels in a straight line back to its station.
How far has it gone altogether?

T4 A ladder 3.0 m long rests against a vertical wall.
The foot of the ladder is 0.9 m away from the bottom of the wall,
on horizontal ground.

(a) Draw a sketch and label it with these measurements.

(b) Calculate the distance from the top of the ladder to the bottom of the wall.

T5 This trapezium has two right angles.
Calculate (to 1 d.p.)

(a) the length of the fourth side

(b) the length of each of its diagonals

6 cm   4 cm   9 cm

9 Working with linear expressions

You should know

- how to evaluate expressions such as $2 - 7 + 3$ and $7 - 2 \times 3$
- that $6n$ means $6 \times n$ and $\frac{12a}{4}$ means $12a \div 4$

This work will help you

- substitute into simple linear expressions
- simplify expressions such as $4n \times 6$ and $\frac{8n}{2}$
- simplify expressions such as $2x + 1 + 3x - 7$ and $3 - 6x + 4x$
- multiply out brackets in expressions such as $4(6n + 1)$
- simplify expressions such as $\frac{8n - 4}{2}$
- use algebra to prove general statements like 'The result for this puzzle will always be 2.'

A Substitution

level 5

- Evaluate any expressions in brackets first.
- Then work out any multiplications and divisions.
- Then work out any additions and subtractions.

Examples

Find the value of
$2x + 5$ when $x = 3$.

$$2x + 5 = 2 \times 3 + 5$$
$$= 6 + 5$$
$$= 11$$

Find the value of
$3(x - 1)$ when $x = 5$.

$$3(x - 1) = 3 \times (5 - 1)$$
$$= 3 \times 4$$
$$= 12$$

Find the value of
$\frac{14 - 3h}{2}$ when $h = 2$.

$$\frac{14 - 3h}{2} = \frac{14 - 3 \times 2}{2}$$
$$= \frac{14 - 6}{2}$$
$$= \frac{8}{2}$$
$$= 4$$

A1

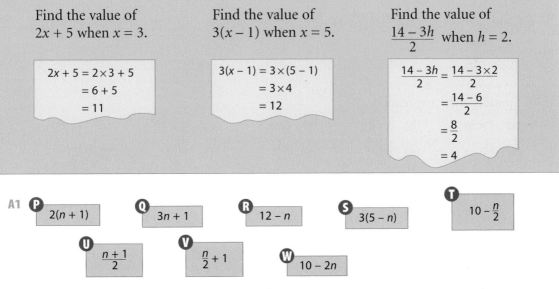

P $2(n + 1)$

Q $3n + 1$

R $12 - n$

S $3(5 - n)$

T $10 - \frac{n}{2}$

U $\frac{n + 1}{2}$

V $\frac{n}{2} + 1$

W $10 - 2n$

(a) Find the value of each expression when $n = 4$.

(b) Which expressions have a value of 0 when $n = 5$?

(c) Which expression has the greatest value when $n = 3$?

(d) Which expression has the lowest value when $n = 1$?

A2 Find the value of the following expressions when $a = 10$.

(a) $2a - 3$
(b) $15 - a$
(c) $30 - 2a$
(d) $2(a + 7)$

(e) $3(2a - 5)$
(f) $\dfrac{2a - 5}{3}$
(g) $\dfrac{2a + 4}{6}$
(h) $10 - \dfrac{3a}{5}$

A3 Each expression in the diagram stands for the length of a side in centimetres.

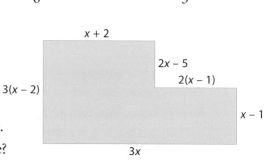

(a) What is the length of the longest side when $x = 3$?

(b) (i) Work out the length of each side when $x = 3$ and draw the shape.

(ii) What is the perimeter of your shape?

(c) What is the perimeter of the shape when $x = 5$?

B Simplifying

level 6

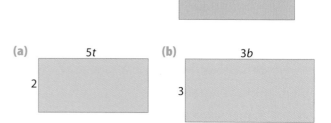

So $2n \times 3 = 6n$

So $\dfrac{8n}{4} = 2n$

B1 Simplify these expressions.

(a) $2 \times 5n$
(b) $3 \times 2y$
(c) $6a \times 5$
(d) $4 \times 7b$
(e) $4x \times 9$

(f) $\dfrac{4n}{2}$
(g) $\dfrac{6a}{3}$
(h) $\dfrac{15y}{5}$
(i) $\dfrac{20x}{4}$
(j) $\dfrac{36b}{9}$

B2 Which of these is an expression for the area of this rectangle?

$\boxed{4 + 2a}$ $\boxed{8a}$ $\boxed{6a}$

2a

4

B3 Write an expression for the area of each of these rectangles.

(a) 5t

2

(b) 3b

3

76 9 Working with linear expressions

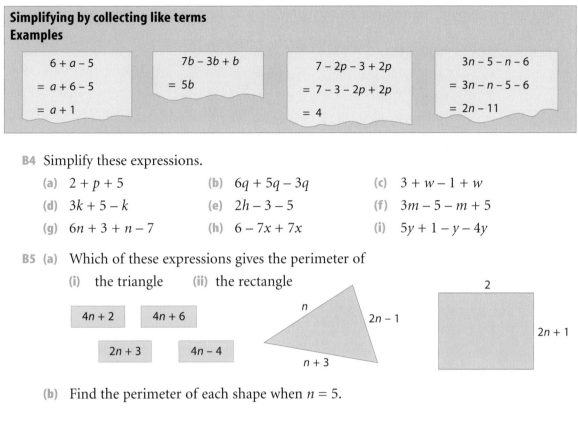

Simplifying by collecting like terms
Examples

$6 + a - 5$

$= a + 6 - 5$

$= a + 1$

$7b - 3b + b$

$= 5b$

$7 - 2p - 3 + 2p$

$= 7 - 3 - 2p + 2p$

$= 4$

$3n - 5 - n - 6$

$= 3n - n - 5 - 6$

$= 2n - 11$

B4 Simplify these expressions.

(a) $2 + p + 5$

(b) $6q + 5q - 3q$

(c) $3 + w - 1 + w$

(d) $3k + 5 - k$

(e) $2h - 3 - 5$

(f) $3m - 5 - m + 5$

(g) $6n + 3 + n - 7$

(h) $6 - 7x + 7x$

(i) $5y + 1 - y - 4y$

B5 (a) Which of these expressions gives the perimeter of

(i) the triangle

(ii) the rectangle

$4n + 2$ $4n + 6$

$2n + 3$ $4n - 4$

n

$2n - 1$

$n + 3$

2

$2n + 1$

(b) Find the perimeter of each shape when $n = 5$.

Simplifying by collecting like terms
Examples

$9 + 2a - 3 - 7a$

$= 9 - 3 + 2a - 7a$

$= 6 - 5a$

$1 - 9n + 10 + 4n$

$= 1 + 10 - 9n + 4n$

$= 11 - 5n$

$8 - 3n - 5 - 4n - 1$

$= 8 - 5 - 1 - 3n - 4n$

$= 2 - 7n$

B6 Simplify these expressions.

(a) $5 + 3m + 2 - 5m$

(b) $7n - 1 - 4n - 3$

(c) $12 + 4p + 2 - 9p$

(d) $3q + 10 - 7q + 2$

(e) $2 - 8v + 3v - 1$

(f) $8 + w - 3 - 3w - w$

(g) $6 - 3g + 3 - 8g - 2$

(h) $4 - 2h - 3 - h$

(i) $4 - 7k + 5 - 4k + 2k$

B7 (a) Find and simplify an expression for the perimeter of this triangle.

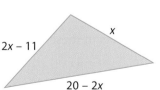

$2x - 11$

x

$20 - 2x$

(b) What is the perimeter of the triangle when $x = 7$?

B8 Find and simplify expressions for the perimeters of these shapes.

(a)

50 – 3x

x

x

50 – 3x

(b)

x

40 – 2x

x

40 – 2x

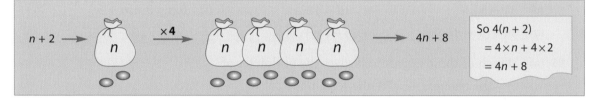

$n + 2$ → n ×**4** n n n n → $4n + 8$

So $4(n + 2)$
$= 4 \times n + 4 \times 2$
$= 4n + 8$

$4(n + 2)$ and $4n + 8$ are **equivalent expressions**.

For example when $n = 3$,

$$4(n + 2) \qquad\qquad 4n + 8$$
$$= 4(3 + 2) \qquad\quad = 4 \times 3 + 8$$
$$= 4 \times 5 \qquad\qquad = 12 + 8$$

20

This works for any value of n.

Examples $8(p - 3) = 8 \times p - 8 \times 3 = 8p - 24$

$2(5x - 1) = 2 \times 5x - 2 \times 1 = 10x - 2$

$3(5 + 2n) = 3 \times 5 + 3 \times 2n = 15 + 6n$

C1 Find four pairs of equivalent expressions.

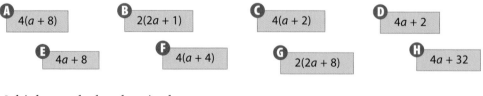

A $4(a + 8)$ **B** $2(2a + 1)$ **C** $4(a + 2)$ **D** $4a + 2$

E $4a + 8$ **F** $4(a + 4)$ **G** $2(2a + 8)$ **H** $4a + 32$

C2 Multiply out the brackets in these.

(a) $6(n + 1)$ (b) $5(m - 4)$ (c) $3(5 + k)$ (d) $5(2c + 1)$ (e) $4(3h - 2)$

(f) $2(5a + 3)$ (g) $6(2w - 3)$ (h) $5(3 - p)$ (i) $4(3 - 8x)$ (j) $7(3c + 4)$

C3 (a) Which of these expressions gives
the area of rectangle A?

$8 + f$ $8 + 4f$ $2 + 4f$

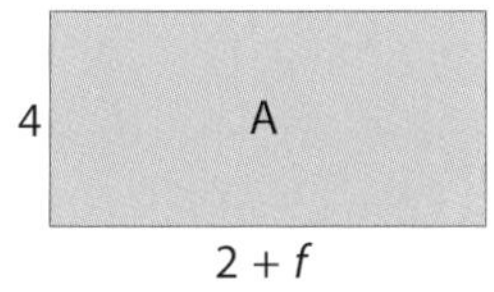

4 | A
$2 + f$

(b) Which of these expressions gives
the area of rectangle B?

$14x - 3$ $2x - 21$ $14x - 21$

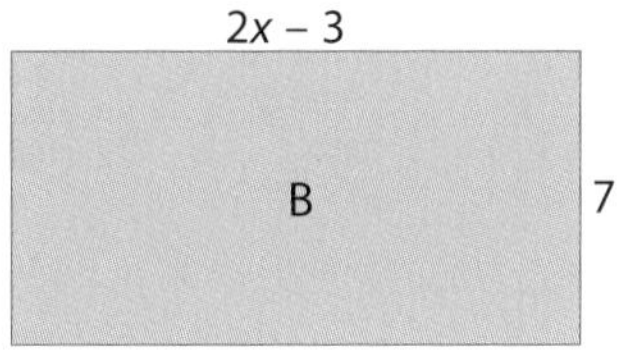

$2x - 3$
B   7

C4 For each shape, write expressions for the missing lengths.

(a) $2p + 1$
Rectangle
?
Area = $6p + 3$

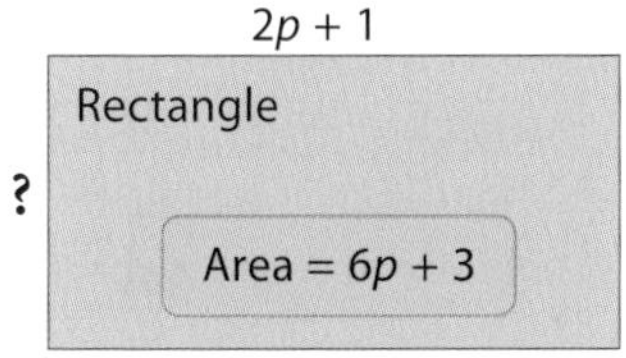

(b)   ?
Rectangle
2
Area = $10b - 4$

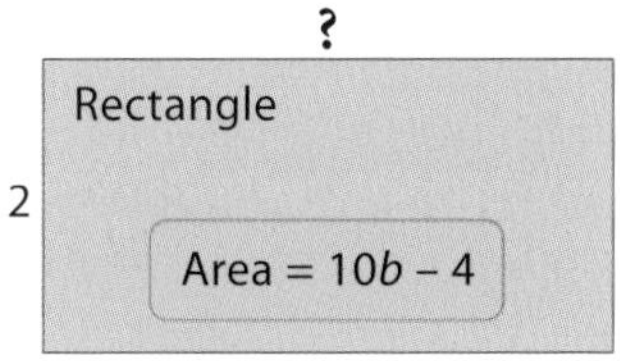

C5 Copy and complete these.

(a) $3(\blacksquare + 5) = 6n + 15$ **(b)** $4(\blacksquare - p) = 8 - 4p$

(c) $5(\blacksquare - 3) = 20m - \blacksquare$ **(d)** $2(\blacksquare + \blacksquare) = 10x + 20$

C6 Ken and Fiona have £x each. They are each given £5.
Which expressions tell you the amount of money they have altogether?

$5 + x$ $2x + 5$ $2(x + 10)$ $2(x + 5)$ $2x + 10$

C7 Jo has three orchards, each with n apple trees.
Two trees in each field are blown down.
Find an expression for the total number of trees left.

C8 Sketch each shape and write expressions for the missing lengths.

(a)   ?
Isosceles
triangle   5
?   Perimeter
= $8m + 5$

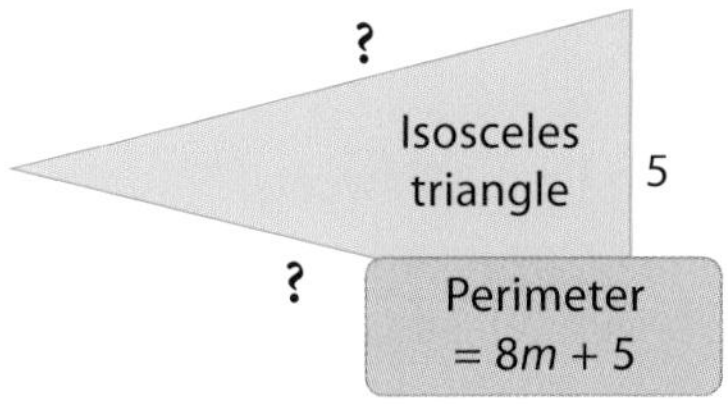

(b)   ?
Perimeter = $6a + 6$
a
Rectangle   ?
?

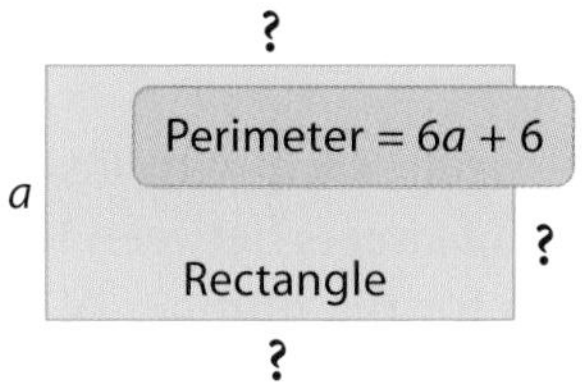

(c)   ?   ?
Kite   Perimeter
= $6k + 8$
$k + 1$?

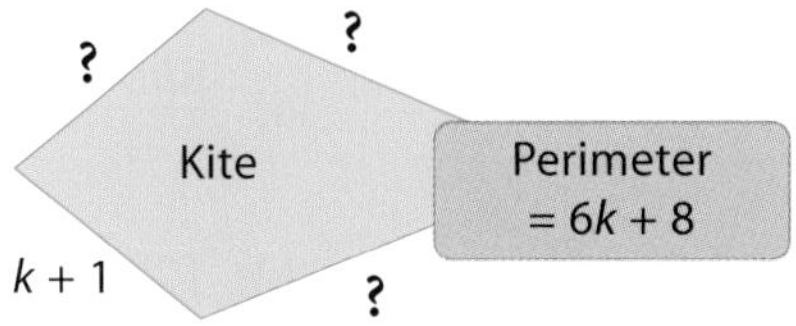

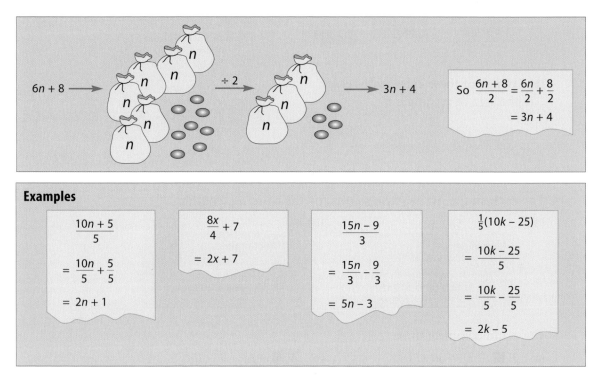

Examples

$$\frac{10n + 5}{5}$$

$$= \frac{10n}{5} + \frac{5}{5}$$

$$= 2n + 1$$

$$\frac{8x}{4} + 7$$

$$= 2x + 7$$

$$\frac{15n - 9}{3}$$

$$= \frac{15n}{3} - \frac{9}{3}$$

$$= 5n - 3$$

$$\frac{1}{5}(10k - 25)$$

$$= \frac{10k - 25}{5}$$

$$= \frac{10k}{5} - \frac{25}{5}$$

$$= 2k - 5$$

D1 I have four bags of sweets, each with n sweets in them. I also have 10 loose sweets.

I share these sweets between two people.
Write an expression for the number of sweets each person has.

D2 Simplify these.

(a) $\dfrac{15n + 10}{5}$

(b) $\dfrac{7m}{7} + 3$

(c) $4 + \dfrac{18k}{6}$

(d) $\dfrac{12h}{3} + 2$

(e) $\dfrac{5p + 10}{5}$

(f) $\dfrac{4c + 6}{2}$

(g) $\dfrac{21y}{7} + 7$

(h) $\dfrac{18 + 12w}{3}$

D3 I have six bags of sweets, each with n sweets in them. I eat 18 sweets.
I share the remaining sweets between three people.
Write an expression for the number of sweets each person has.

D4 Simplify these.

(a) $\dfrac{3a - 6}{3}$

(b) $\dfrac{12b - 16}{4}$

(c) $\dfrac{5k}{5} - 10$

(d) $\dfrac{8h - 4}{4}$

(e) $\dfrac{12d - 18}{6}$

(f) $\dfrac{20g - 30}{10}$

(g) $\dfrac{15 - 5m}{5}$

(h) $12 - \dfrac{20n}{4}$

D5 Copy and complete these.

(a) $\dfrac{2m + \blacksquare}{2} = m + 7$ (b) $\dfrac{\blacksquare - 9}{3} = 2c - 3$ (c) $\dfrac{24 + 18y}{\blacksquare} = 4 + 3y$

D6 Copy and complete this. $\dfrac{1}{3}(6n + 12) = \dfrac{6n + 12}{3} = 2n + \blacksquare$

D7 Simplify these.

(a) $\dfrac{1}{2}(6n + 12)$ (b) $\dfrac{1}{3}(9x - 6)$ (c) $\dfrac{1}{4}(8k + 20)$ (d) $\dfrac{1}{5}(5p - 10)$

D8 Solve the puzzle on sheet HT–1.

*__D9__ Find an expression for the area of each triangle.

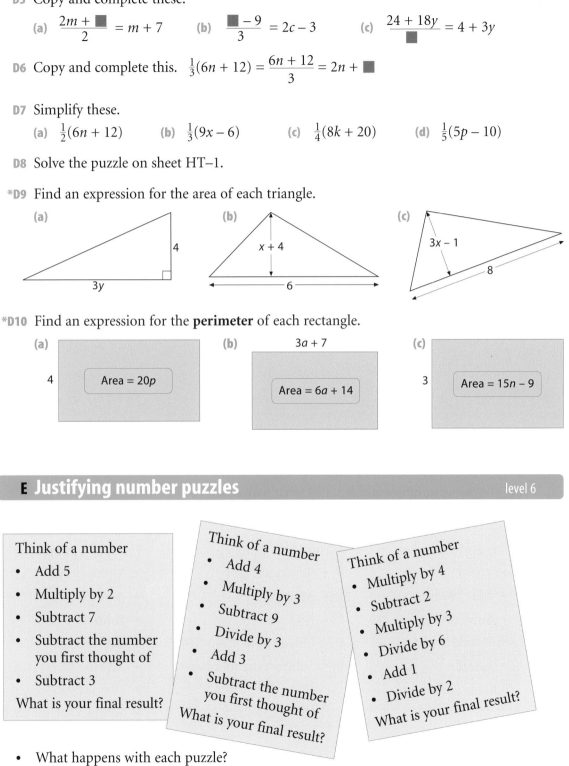

(a)

4

3y

(b)

x + 4

6

(c)

3x – 1

8

*__D10__ Find an expression for the **perimeter** of each rectangle.

(a)

4

Area = 20p

(b)

3a + 7

Area = 6a + 14

(c)

3

Area = 15n – 9

E Justifying number puzzles

level 6

Think of a number
• Add 5
• Multiply by 2
• Subtract 7
• Subtract the number you first thought of
• Subtract 3
What is your final result?

Think of a number
• Add 4
• Multiply by 3
• Subtract 9
• Divide by 3
• Add 3
• Subtract the number you first thought of
What is your final result?

Think of a number
• Multiply by 4
• Subtract 2
• Multiply by 3
• Divide by 6
• Add 1
• Divide by 2
What is your final result?

• What happens with each puzzle?
• Can you use algebra to explain this?

E1 **(a)** Try some numbers for this puzzle and describe what happens.

(b) Copy and complete the algebra box to explain how the puzzle works.

Puzzle

Think of a number

• Multiply by 6

• Add 3

• Divide by 3

• Subtract 1

• Divide by 2

What is the result?

Algebra

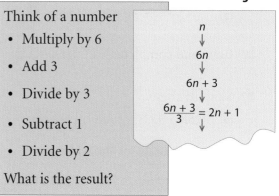

$$n$$
$$\downarrow$$
$$6n$$
$$\downarrow$$
$$6n + 3$$
$$\downarrow$$
$$\frac{6n + 3}{3} = 2n + 1$$
$$\downarrow$$

E2 **(a)** Try some numbers for this puzzle and describe what happens.

(b) Copy and complete the algebra box to explain how the puzzle works.

Puzzle

Think of a number

• Add 6

• Multiply by 3

• Subtract 12

• Divide by 3

• Subtract the number you first thought of

What is the result?

Algebra

$$n$$
$$\downarrow$$
$$n + 6$$
$$\downarrow$$
$$3(n + 6) = 3n + 18$$
$$\downarrow$$

E3 Follow these steps for each puzzle below.

(a) Try some numbers and describe what happens.

(b) Use algebra to explain how the puzzle works.

A

Think of a number

• Add 1

• Multiply by 3

• Subtract 9

• Divide by 3

• Add 2

What is the result?

B

Think of a number

• Subtract 2

• Multiply by 4

• Add 8

• Divide by 4

• Subtract the number you first thought of

What is the result?

C

Think of a number

• Multiply by 6

• Add 15

• Subtract 3

• Divide by 3

• Add 6

• Divide by 2

• Subtract the number you first thought of

What is the result?

*E4 Try to make up your own puzzles like these.

Test yourself

T1 Find the value of the following expressions when $n = 6$.

  (a) $4n - 5$ (b) $5(n - 2)$ (c) $3(2n + 1)$ (d) $\dfrac{2n + 3}{5}$ (e) $10 - \dfrac{n}{2}$

T2 Multiply out the brackets in these expressions.

  (a) $3(b + 6)$ (b) $2(5 - h)$ (c) $5(2a - 3)$ (d) $4(3x + 10)$

T3 Hal and Dwayne have n sweets each. They are each given 3 sweets.
Which expressions give the number of sweets they have altogether?

$3 + n$	$2n + 3$	$2(n + 3)$	$2(n + 6)$	$2n + 6$

T4 Find an expression for the
missing length in the rectangle.

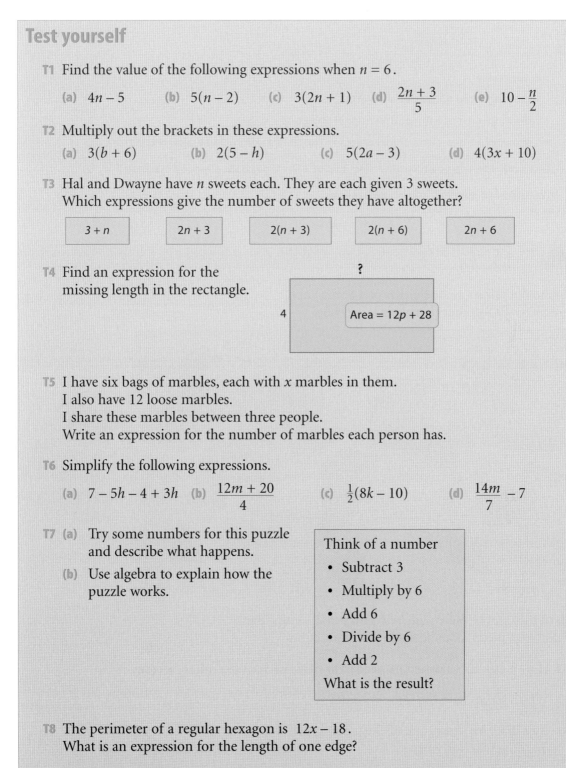

                                       ?

                        4   Area = $12p + 28$

T5 I have six bags of marbles, each with x marbles in them.
I also have 12 loose marbles.
I share these marbles between three people.
Write an expression for the number of marbles each person has.

T6 Simplify the following expressions.

  (a) $7 - 5h - 4 + 3h$ (b) $\dfrac{12m + 20}{4}$ (c) $\frac{1}{2}(8k - 10)$ (d) $\dfrac{14m}{7} - 7$

T7 (a) Try some numbers for this puzzle
     and describe what happens.

   (b) Use algebra to explain how the
     puzzle works.

> Think of a number
> - Subtract 3
> - Multiply by 6
> - Add 6
> - Divide by 6
> - Add 2
>
> What is the result?

T8 The perimeter of a regular hexagon is $12x - 18$.
What is an expression for the length of one edge?

T9 An expression for the length of one edge of a regular octagon is $3x + 5$.
What is the perimeter of this octagon?

10 Representing 3-D objects

You will revise

● drawing three-dimensional objects

● drawing a net of a three-dimensional object

● showing a three-dimensional object in two dimensions using a plan and elevations

This work will help you identify reflections of 3-D shapes and reflection symmetry in 3D.

You will need multilink cubes and a mirror.

A The Soma cube

This photograph shows the pieces of a Soma cube.
These pieces fit together to make a large cube.

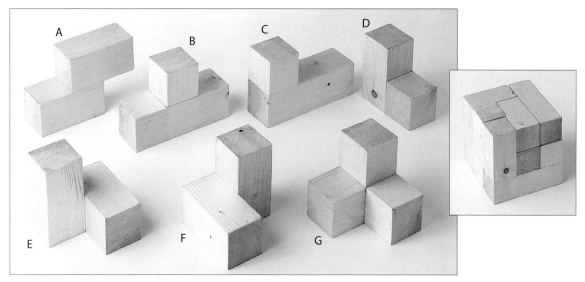

Each of these seven pieces can be constructed using cubes.
For example, piece A can be made with four cubes.

A1 How many cubes would be needed to make each of the other pieces?

A2 Which pieces have the same volume?

A3 This diagram shows one of the pieces drawn
on triangular dotty paper.

• Draw the rest of the pieces on triangular dotty paper.

• Shade sides that face the same direction in the
same way, to help show the object more clearly.

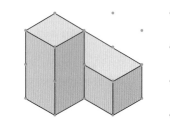

The Soma cube

The Soma cube puzzle was devised by the Danish mathematician Piet Hein in 1929.

It's worth trying the puzzle. It is sold by puzzle shops and educational suppliers.
The one in the photographs was home-made from 50 mm square cross-section wood.

Soma was a stimulant drug in ancient Indo-Iranian culture. The word was
also used for a happiness drug in Aldous Huxley's novel *Brave New World*.
The puzzle seems to have earned this name because people become obsessed by it.

 Do a web search for Soma cube.
There are puzzles and other activities, some of them interactive.

B Nets
level 6

A two-dimensional pattern that folds up to form the surface
of a three-dimensional shape is called a **net** for that shape.
This is a net for a cube.

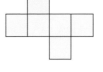

B1 Which of these are possible nets for a cube?

A 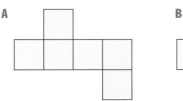   B 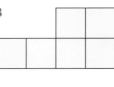   C

B2 There are 11 possible different nets of a cube.
Draw 4 of them on squared paper.

B3 This is a regular tetrahedron.
All of the triangular faces are equilateral.
Use triangular dotty paper to draw a net for this tetrahedron.

What different nets for a tetrahedron can you find?

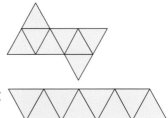

B4 This is a net for a regular octahedron.
It has eight faces all of which are equilateral triangles.

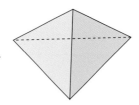

Which of these are nets for an octahedron?

A 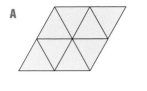   B 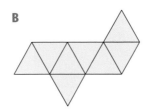   C

B5 The diagram shows a pyramid with a square base.
The base of the pyramid is a square with edges of length 6 cm.
The length of each sloping edge of the pyramid is 5 cm.

   (a) Make a sketch of a suitable net for the pyramid.

   (b) Make an accurate full size drawing of one of
the triangular faces of the pyramid.

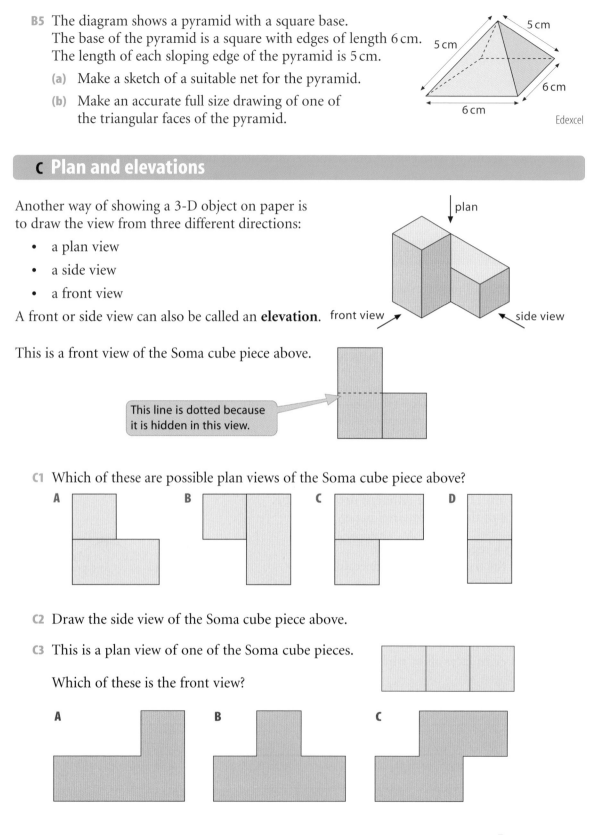

Edexcel

C Plan and elevations

Another way of showing a 3-D object on paper is
to draw the view from three different directions:

- a plan view
- a side view
- a front view

A front or side view can also be called an **elevation**.

This is a front view of the Soma cube piece above.

This line is dotted because
it is hidden in this view.

C1 Which of these are possible plan views of the Soma cube piece above?

   A   B   C   D

C2 Draw the side view of the Soma cube piece above.

C3 This is a plan view of one of the Soma cube pieces.

   Which of these is the front view?

   A   B   C

C4 Look at the photo of the Soma cube pieces on page 84
The plan view for one piece needs to show a hidden edge.

(a) Which piece is it?

(b) Draw the plan view, using a dotted line for the hidden edge.

C5 Choose another Soma cube piece and draw the three views of it.

C6 This object has been made from seven centimetre cubes.
Draw full-size on centimetre squared paper

(a) a plan view

(b) a side view

(c) a front view

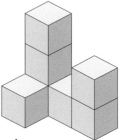

C7 This net makes a 3-D object that stands on the face marked 'base'.
Draw a plan and two elevations of the 3-D object.

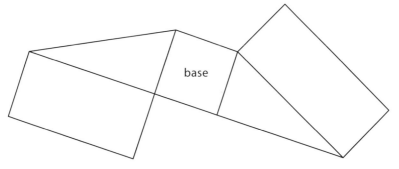

base

C8 (a) Draw a full-size plan view of this shape.

(b) Draw a full-size side view of this shape
from direction S.
Show any hidden edges with dotted lines.

(c) Use your drawings to measure the length
of the sloping edge AB.

(d) Show how to use Pythagoras's theorem
to check your answer to part (c).

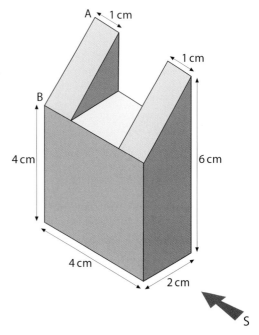

T

Mirror images

This shape is made from five multilink cubes.

What would the reflection of this shape in
the mirror look like?
Can you make the shape that is the reflection?

Make some different shapes using five multilink cubes.
Ask a partner to make the reflection of your shape.
Check with a mirror.

Are any of the reflections identical to the original shape?

Do you get a different shape if you put the mirror in
a different position?

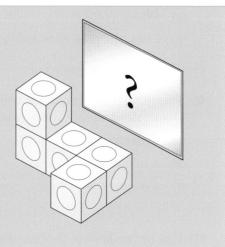

D1 This shape is made from five multilink cubes.
Which of the shapes below is a mirror
image of this shape?

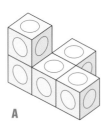

A

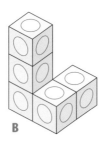

B

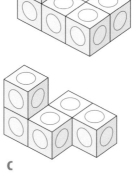

C

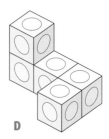

D

D2 Match each of these shapes to its mirror image.

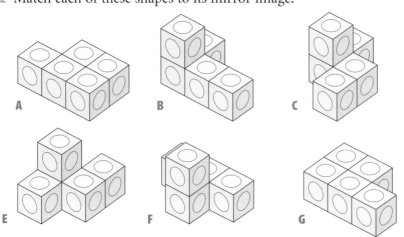

A

B

C

D

E

F

G

H

T This Soma cube piece has been cut in half and placed against a mirror.

The reflection makes the piece look whole again.
This whole shape has **reflection symmetry.**

Is there any other way this Soma piece could be cut so that half placed against a mirror gives the whole shape?

In a situation like this, the position of the mirror is called a **plane of symmetry** of the whole 3-D shape.

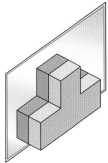

D3 Each of these is a 'half-shape' against a mirror.
Draw each whole shape on triangular dotty paper.

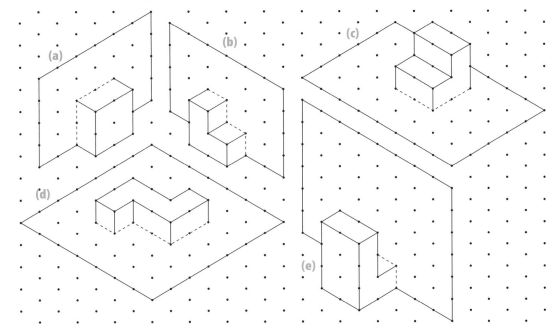

(a) (b) (c) (d) (e)

D4 How many planes of symmetry does each of these Soma cube pieces have?

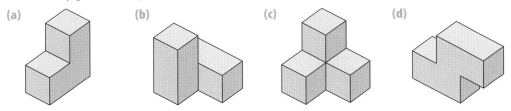

(a)　　　　(b)　　　　(c)　　　　(d)

D5 This shape has been made from multilink cubes.
It has no planes of symmetry.

(a) Make this shape from multilink cubes.

(b) Add one cube to give it reflection symmetry.

(c) Sketch your shape on triangular dotty paper.

Make up some puzzles like these to try on a partner.

*D6 This is a cube made up from 27 small cubes.

    (a) How many planes of symmetry does it have?
(Take care not to count the same one twice!)

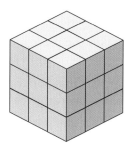

    (b) How many planes of symmetry will it have if you remove

        (i) one cube at the corner **(ii)** a column in the middle **(iii)** 9 cubes from one face

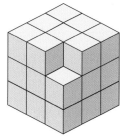 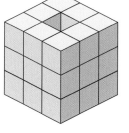 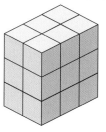

*D7 Describe two shapes that each have six planes of symmetry.

Test yourself

T1 (a) Which of the shapes drawn below are nets of the
cuboid on the right?

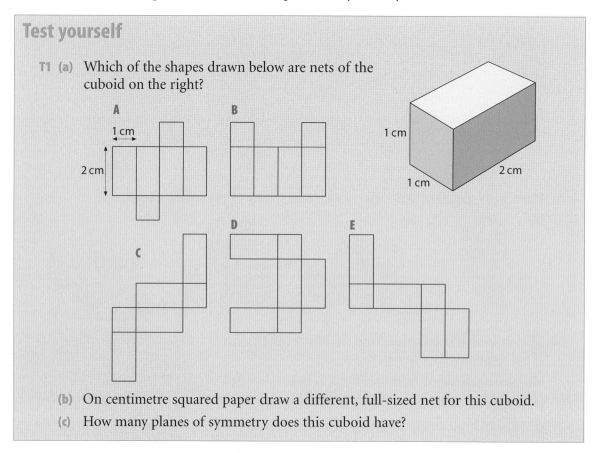

    (b) On centimetre squared paper draw a different, full-sized net for this cuboid.

    (c) How many planes of symmetry does this cuboid have?

T2 The diagram shows a cuboid with a prism removed.
The measurements are in centimetres.

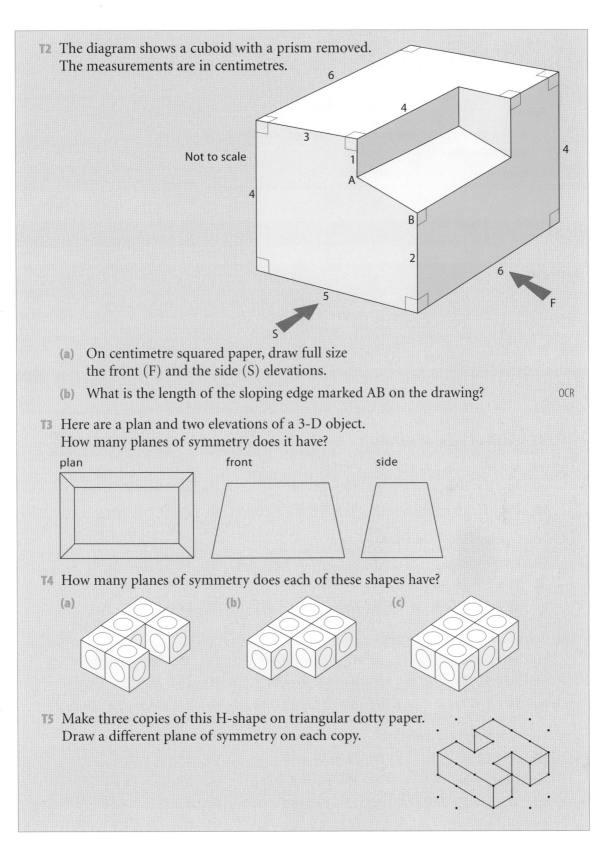

Not to scale

(a) On centimetre squared paper, draw full size
the front (F) and the side (S) elevations.

(b) What is the length of the sloping edge marked AB on the drawing? OCR

T3 Here are a plan and two elevations of a 3-D object.
How many planes of symmetry does it have?

plan   front   side

T4 How many planes of symmetry does each of these shapes have?

(a)   (b)   (c)

T5 Make three copies of this H-shape on triangular dotty paper.
Draw a different plane of symmetry on each copy.

11 Linear equations

You should know that, for example, $3(x + 4) = 3x + 12$

You will

- solve a variety of linear equations, including those where you need to expand brackets first

- form equations to solve problems

A Solving equations

level 6

Examples

Each operation in brackets shows what is done to **both** sides to get the next line.

$3x - 5 = 13$ [+ 5]
$3x = 18$ [÷ 3]
$x = 6$

$3x - 1 = x + 13$ [+ 1]
$3x = x + 14$ [− x]
$2x = 14$ [÷ 2]
$x = 7$

$20 - 5x = 5 - 2x$ [+ 5x]
$20 = 5 + 3x$ [− 5]
$15 = 3x$ [÷ 3]
$5 = x$ or $x = 5$

A1 Solve each of these equations.

(a) $5x = 35$
(b) $4z + 9 = 21$
(c) $10h - 3 = 47$
(d) $40 - y = 30$
(e) $10 - 3g = 4$
(f) $20 - 6n = 2$
(g) $2m + 3 = 4$
(h) $6p - 4 = 5$
(i) $3 - 2t = 0$

A2 Solve each of these equations.

(a) $x + 9 = 4x$
(b) $x + 5 = 2x + 4$
(c) $4x + 3 = 2x + 13$
(d) $3x + 5 = 7x - 3$
(e) $4x + 6 = 8x - 6$
(f) $5x - 9 = 3x - 1$
(g) $2x + 5 = 6x - 1$
(h) $6x + 5 = 2x + 7$
(i) $2x - 1 = 4x - 6$

A3 Solve each of these equations.

(a) $3n + 6 = 10 - n$
(b) $12 - 2n = 3n + 2$
(c) $15 - 3n = 4n - 6$
(d) $2n - 5 = 15 - 3n$
(e) $8 - n = 15 - 2n$
(f) $15 - 2n = 20 - 3n$
(g) $3n + 1 = 7 - n$
(h) $6n - 13 = 12 - 4n$
(i) $3 - n = 5 - 5n$

A4 Solve each of these equations.

(a) $4k = 27$
(b) $5k + 17 = 40$
(c) $8k - 3 = 10$
(d) $3 = 20 - 5k$
(e) $17k + 5 = 8 + k$
(f) $5 + 3k = 7k - 2$
(g) $10 + k = 25 - 3k$
(h) $15 - 8k = 0$
(i) $6 - 7k = 2 + 3k$
(j) $2k - 0.5 = 0.3$
(k) $0.2 - k = 0.5 - 4k$
(l) $0.4 - 2k = 1.5 - 10k$

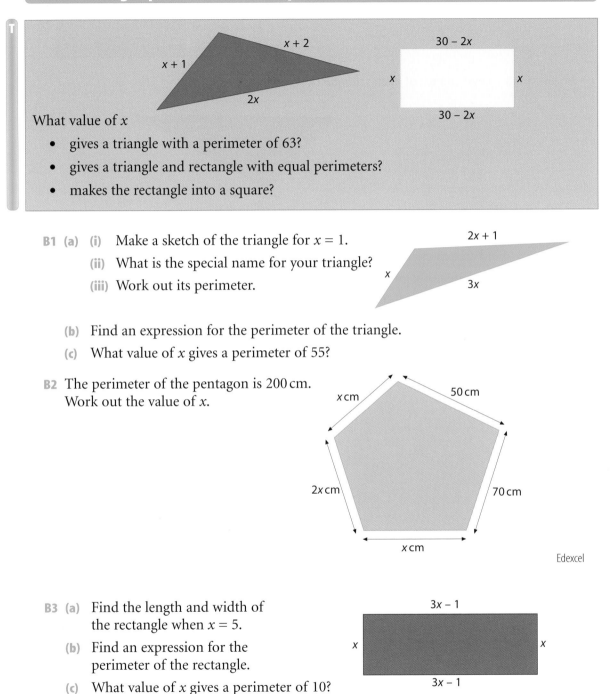

What value of x

- gives a triangle with a perimeter of 63?
- gives a triangle and rectangle with equal perimeters?
- makes the rectangle into a square?

B1 (a) (i) Make a sketch of the triangle for $x = 1$.

    (ii) What is the special name for your triangle?

    (iii) Work out its perimeter.

    (b) Find an expression for the perimeter of the triangle.

    (c) What value of x gives a perimeter of 55?

B2 The perimeter of the pentagon is 200 cm.
Work out the value of x.

Edexcel

B3 (a) Find the length and width of
the rectangle when $x = 5$.

    (b) Find an expression for the
perimeter of the rectangle.

    (c) What value of x gives a perimeter of 10?

    (d) What value of x gives a square?

B4 (a) Find an expression for the perimeter of the rectangle.

(b) What value of x gives a perimeter of 48?

(c) What value of x gives a square?

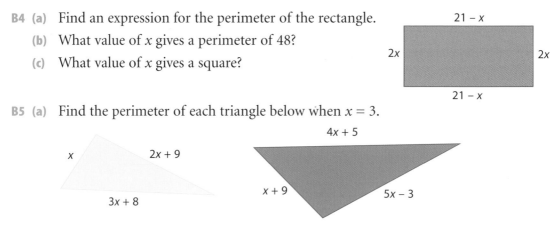

B5 (a) Find the perimeter of each triangle below when $x = 3$.

(b) (i) Find an expression for the perimeter of the yellow triangle.

(ii) What value of x gives a yellow triangle with a perimeter of 143?

(c) (i) Find an expression for the perimeter of the blue triangle.

(ii) What value of x gives a blue triangle with a perimeter of 50?

(d) What value of x gives both triangles the same perimeter?

C Solving equations that involve brackets

• Can you solve each of these equations?

A $2(n + 3) = 10$

B $6(2n - 1) = 10n$

C $3(n + 4) = 6(n - 1)$

C1 Solve each of these equations.

(a) $2(m + 3) = 40$
(b) $3(n + 10) = 9n$
(c) $4(p + 9) = 10p$

(d) $3(2g - 1) = 24$
(e) $5(2h - 3) = 5h + 10$
(f) $4(3k - 7) = 2(3k - 2)$

(g) $2(x + 15) = 3(x + 1)$
(h) $4(y + 9) = 12y - 4$
(i) $5(z - 3) = 7(z - 5)$

(j) $2(a + 5) = 4a + 7$
(k) $3(2b - 2) = 2(b + 2)$
(l) $4(c - 2) = 5(2c - 7)$

C2 Solve these.

(a) $4(10 - n) = 24$
(b) $3(2 - p) = p - 14$
(c) $5(20 - 3q) = 10$

(d) $6(8 - u) = 3(2u - 4)$
(e) $5(10 - 3a) = 4(2a + 1)$
(f) $10(w + 3) = 18(4 - w)$

(g) $3(5 - 2v) = 9(2 - v)$
(h) $4(10 - z) = 3(11 - z)$
(i) $2(11 - 2h) = 3(14 - 3h)$

C3 Solve these.

(a) $12k - 1 = 20$
(b) $2k + 25 = 37k + 4$
(c) $2(k - 1) = 10(k - 2)$

(d) $6(12 - k) = 8(k + 2)$
(e) $6(2k - 5) = 5 + 4k$
(f) $6(k + 2) = 6(5 - 3k)$

(g) $13(k - 2) = 17 - 3k$
(h) $11(4k - 5) = 0$
(i) $2(11 - 4k) = 7 - 2k$

(j) $12 - 19k = 6 - 4k$
(k) $3(2 - k) = 8(k - 2)$
(l) $9(1 + k) = 4(11 - 4k)$

Solving harder equations

Example

$6(x + 2) = 3(13 − x)$ [multiply out brackets]

It is often a good idea to multiply to get rid of brackets as soon as you can.

$6x + 12 = 39 − 3x$ [+ 3x]

$9x + 12 = 39$ [− 12]

$9x = 27$ [÷ 9]

$x = 3$

D Solving number puzzles

D1 **(a)** Kate thinks of a number.
She multiplies it by 2 and adds 7.
Her answer is 15.
What is the number she was thinking of?

(b) Gordon thinks of a number.
He multiplies it by 6 and subtracts 1.
His answer is 2.
What was he thinking of?

D2 **(a)** Which of the equations on the right corresponds to this number puzzle?

I think of a number.
I multiply it by 2.
I add 12.
My answer is three times my starting number.
What number did I start with?

$2n + 12 = 3$ $12n + 2 = 3n$ $2n + 12 = 3n$

(b) Use the correct equation to solve the number puzzle.
Check your solution works.

D3 Solve each of these number puzzles.
In each part, let n stand for the number I start with.

(a)
I think of a number.
I multiply it by 3.
I take off 20.
My answer is twice my starting number.
What was my number?

(b)
I think of a number.
I double it and add 3.
My answer is 10 more than the number I started with.
What was my number?

(c)
I think of a number.
I multiply it by 4.
I add 6.
My answer is 8 times my starting number.
What was my number?

D4 Abby and Becky both think of the same number.
Abby doubles her number and adds 20.
Becky multiplies her number by 5 and takes away 4.
They both get the same answer.
What number did both of them start with?

D5

> I think of a number.
> I take off 5.
> I multiply the result by 3.
> My answer is 21.
> What was my number?

Choose the equation below that you would use to solve this number puzzle.
Then solve the puzzle using the equation.

$$3n - 5 = 21 \qquad 3(n - 5) = 21 \qquad n - 5 \times 3 = 21$$

D6 Solve each of these number puzzles.
In each part, let n stand for the number I start with.

(a)
> I think of a number.
> I add 7.
> I multiply the result by 2.
> My answer is 40.
> What was my number?

(b)
> I think of a number.
> I take off 9.
> I multiply the result by 3.
> My answer is double the number I started with.
> What was my number?

(c)
> I think of a number.
> I take off 6.
> I multiply the result by 5.
> My answer is 2 more than the number I started with.
> What was my number?

Test yourself

T1 Solve these equations.
  (a) $4x + 1 = 13$ (b) $5x - 2 = 3x + 9$ OCR

T2 Solve these equations.
  (a) $5x + 1 = 7x - 3$ (b) $4x + 1 = 10 - 2x$ (c) $10 - 2x = 16 - 5x$

T3 Solve the equation $3x - 14 = 5(6 - x)$ WJEC

T4 Solve these equations.
  (a) $4a + 3 = 9$ (b) $5b - 7 = 2b + 5$ (c) $3(c - 6) = 10 - 2c$ Edexcel

T5 (a) Find an expression for the perimeter of this rectangle.
  (b) What value of n gives a perimeter of 41?

$15 - n$

$2n$

T6 Solve these equations.
  (a) $6(k + 5) = 36$ (b) $4(11 - 2k) = 12$ (c) $3(2k - 5) = k$
  (d) $2(k + 1) = 10(k - 1)$ (e) $7 + k = 4(8 - k)$ (f) $2(3 - k) = 2(7 - 9k)$

T7 I think of a number.
I subtract 3 and multiply by 4.
My answer is the same as the number I started with.
What was my number?

12 Multiples, factors and powers

This work will help you

- work out factors, multiples, prime numbers and powers

- use index notation and the rules for multiplying powers of the same number

- find and use prime factorisations, for example to work out lowest common multiples and highest common factors

A Multiples, factors and primes

Cell 23

Lock up

A prison has 25 prisoners (one in each cell) and 25 jailers.
The cells are numbered 1 to 25.

The jailers all go to a party one night and return very merry!

- The first jailer unlocks every cell.

- The second jailer locks every cell whose number is a multiple of 2.

- The third jailer turns his key in the lock for cells whose numbers are multiples of 3. (He locks or unlocks these cells).

- The fourth jailer turns his key in the lock for cells whose numbers are multiples of 4 … and so on till the twenty-fifth jailer.

All the jailers then fall asleep and the prison is silent.

The prisoners all try their doors – which ones escape?

Multiples

Multiples of 7 are numbers that can be divided exactly by 7.
Examples are 42, 84, 14, 21 and 7 itself.
Multiples of 3 are numbers that can be divided exactly by 3. Examples are 6, 21, 30, 63.

Common multiples of 3 and 7 are numbers that can be divided exactly by 3 **and** by 7.
Some common multiples of 3 and 7 are 42, 21, 63 and 105.

21 is the **lowest common multiple** of 3 and 7.

A1 Write down

   (a) five multiples of 4   (b) five multiples of 3   (c) a common multiple of 4 and 3

A2 (a) Write down a common multiple of 6 and 7 that is greater than 50.
     Is this the lowest common multiple?

   (b) Write down a common multiple of 2 and 8 that is less than 10.
     Is this the lowest common multiple?

A3 What is the lowest common multiple of

(a) 5 and 2   (b) 4 and 8   (c) 12 and 8   (d) 4 and 9

Factors

A factor of a number is a number that divides it exactly.

Factors of 20 are 1, 2, 4, 5, 10 and 20.
Factors of 8 are 1, 2, 4 and 8.

Common factors of 8 and 20 are numbers that divide exactly into 8 **and** 20.
They are 1, 2 and 4.

4 is the **highest common factor** of 8 and 20.

A4 Write down all the factors of 60.

A5 Write down two common factors of 12 and 20.

A6 (a) Find all the common factors of 18 and 45.

(b) What is the highest common factor of 18 and 45?

A7 What is the highest common factor of

(a) 35 and 20   (b) 5 and 9   (c) 10 and 20   (d) 24 and 54

Primes

Prime numbers are numbers with **exactly two** factors.

For example,
17 is a prime number as it has two factors (1 and 17).

8 is not a prime number as it has more than two factors (1, 2, 4 and 8).
1 is not a prime number as it only has one factor (1).

A8 Which of the following numbers are not prime?

2, 6, 14, 19, 11, 9, 13, 21, 10, 15, 5

A9 List all the prime numbers between 20 and 40.

A10 Both 3 and 11 are prime numbers.

Find the highest common factor of 3 and 11.
Find the lowest common multiple of 3 and 11.

Repeat for some other pairs of prime numbers.
Comment on your results.

*A11 Find a rule that links the lowest common multiple and highest common factor
of **any** pair of numbers.

B Powers

Ice cream

Toni sells two flavours of ice cream, strawberry and vanilla.

Here are some different ice creams that each have three scoops.

- How many different ice creams can Toni make with three scoops?
- Investigate for two scoops, one scoop, four scoops, …

Rosa sells three flavours of ice cream, strawberry, vanilla and chocolate.

- How many different ice creams can Rosa make with one scoop, two scoops, … ?

In an expression like 2^5, the raised number 5 is called the index.

Indices (more than one index) are used as a mathematical shorthand.

Examples

$$2\times2\times2\times2\times2 = 2^5 \qquad 3\times3\times3\times3 = 3^4 \qquad \text{The value of } 5^3 \text{ is } 5\times5\times5 = 125$$

We say 3^4 as 'three to the power four'.

Powers of three can be written as $\quad 3^1, \quad 3^2, \quad 3^3, \quad 3^4, \dots$

$$\text{or} \quad 3, \quad 9, \quad 27, \quad 81, \dots$$

B1 Write these in shorthand form using indices.

(a) $2\times2\times2\times2\times2\times2\times2\times2$

(b) $4\times4\times4\times4\times4\times4\times4\times4\times4\times4\times4$

B2 Find the value of these.

(a) 2^4 (b) 4^3 (c) 3^5 (d) 7^2 (e) 5^3

B3 (a) List all the powers of two between 10 and 50.

(b) What is the value of 'three to the power two'?

B4 There is one cell in a flask in a laboratory.
The number of cells doubles every 15 minutes.

(a) How many cells are there after 2 hours?

(b) How long does it take the number of cells to increase to 2^{10}?

B5 Decide whether the following statements are true or false.

(a) $5^2 = 5\times2$ (b) $3^2 > 2^3$ (c) $2^6 < 5^2$ (d) $3^4 < 6^2$

B6 Choose the correct symbol, $<$, $>$ or $=$, for each box below.

(a) $4^3 \blacksquare 3^4$ (b) $7^2 \blacksquare 2^7$ (c) $2^5 \blacksquare 5^2$ (d) $9^1 \blacksquare 1^9$

B7 Find the missing numbers in these statements

(a) $2^\blacksquare = 64$ (b) $8^\blacksquare = 8$ (c) $9^\blacksquare = 81$ (d) $\blacksquare^3 = 1$

B8 Most calculators have a special key for working out powers.

Find this key on your calculator.

(It might look like x^y or $\wedge$.)

(a) Use this key on your calculator to work out

    (i) 2^3 (ii) 10^4 (iii) 3^6

    Check your answers are correct without using this key.

(b) Arrange the following numbers in order of size, smallest first.

    2^{31}, 7^{10}, 3^{20}, 16^6, 100^2

B9 Which do you think will be larger, 2^{25} or 25^4?
Check with your calculator.

B10 What is the smallest whole number value of n so that $3^n > 1000$?

B11 What is the smallest power of two that is greater than a million?

B12 Solve the following equations.

    (a) $x^7 = 823\,543$ (b) $x^8 = 6561$ (c) $x^9 = 262\,144$ (d) $6^x = 10\,077\,696$

B13 Copy and complete this cross number puzzle.

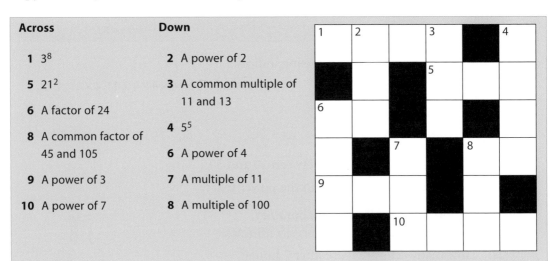

Across	Down
1 3^8	**2** A power of 2
5 21^2	**3** A common multiple of 11 and 13
6 A factor of 24	
8 A common factor of 45 and 105	**4** 5^5
	6 A power of 4
9 A power of 3	**7** A multiple of 11
10 A power of 7	**8** A multiple of 100

B14

'As I was going to St Ives I met a man with seven wives;
each wife had seven sacks; each sack had seven cats and
each cat had seven kittens.'

If each kitten caught one mouse each day and each cat
caught seven mice each day, how many mice would the
cats and kittens catch in seven weeks?

*B15 The last digit of 3^4 is 1 because $3^4 = 81$.

(a) Copy and complete this table.

n	1	2	3	4	5	6	7	8	9	10
Last digit of 3^n	3	9		1						

(b) What are the last digits of   (i) 3^{36} (ii) 3^{101} (iii) 3^{199}

*B16 (a) Investigate the last digits of powers of the form n^5, for example $1^5, 2^5, 3^5, \ldots$

(b) What are the last digits of   (i) 299^5 (ii) 305^5 (iii) 411^5

*B17 Find the last digit of each of these. Give reasons for each answer.

(a) 2^{100} (b) 9^{999} (c) 5^{432} (d) 4^{120} (e) $6^{1\,000\,000}$

C Multiplying powers

C1 Find the missing numbers in these calculations.

(a) $2^3 \times 2^2 = (2 \times 2 \times 2) \times (2 \times 2) = 2^\blacksquare$

(b) $5^3 \times 5^6 = (5 \times 5 \times 5) \times (5 \times 5 \times 5 \times 5 \times 5 \times 5) = 5^\blacksquare$

(c) $7^5 \times 7^4 = (7 \times 7 \times 7 \times 7 \times 7) \times (7 \times 7 \times 7 \times 7) = 7^\blacksquare$

(d) $3^5 \times 3 = 3 \times 3 \times 3 \times 3 \times 3 \times 3 = 3^\blacksquare$

C2 Write down the numbers missing from these calculations.

(a) $3^2 \times 3^3 = 3^\blacksquare$ (b) $4^2 \times 4^4 = 4^\blacksquare$ (c) $8 \times 8^7 = 8^\blacksquare$

(d) $6^3 \times 6^9 = 6^\blacksquare$ (e) $2^\blacksquare \times 2^5 = 2^{11}$ (f) $7^5 \times 7^\blacksquare = 7^6$

C3 (a) Write down a rule for multiplying powers of the same number. Explain why your rule works.

(b) Using your rule, copy and complete $2^{12} \times 2^5 = 2^\blacksquare$

C4 Find three pairs of equivalent expressions.

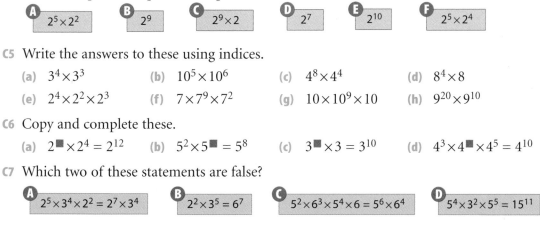

C5 Write the answers to these using indices.

(a) $3^4 \times 3^3$ (b) $10^5 \times 10^6$ (c) $4^8 \times 4^4$ (d) $8^4 \times 8$

(e) $2^4 \times 2^2 \times 2^3$ (f) $7 \times 7^9 \times 7^2$ (g) $10 \times 10^9 \times 10$ (h) $9^{20} \times 9^{10}$

C6 Copy and complete these.

(a) $2^\blacksquare \times 2^4 = 2^{12}$ (b) $5^2 \times 5^\blacksquare = 5^8$ (c) $3^\blacksquare \times 3 = 3^{10}$ (d) $4^3 \times 4^\blacksquare \times 4^5 = 4^{10}$

C7 Which two of these statements are false?

> **A** $2^5 \times 3^4 \times 2^2 = 2^7 \times 3^4$ **B** $2^2 \times 3^5 = 6^7$ **C** $5^2 \times 6^3 \times 5^4 \times 6 = 5^6 \times 6^4$ **D** $5^4 \times 3^2 \times 5^5 = 15^{11}$

C8 Copy and complete these.

(a) $3^2 \times 5^3 \times 5^4 \times 3^6 = 3^{\blacksquare} \times 5^{\blacksquare}$

(b) $2 \times 9^2 \times 2^5 \times 9^3 = 2^{\blacksquare} \times 9^{\blacksquare}$

(c) $4^7 \times 3^{\blacksquare} \times 4 \times 3^2 = 3^{10} \times 4^{\blacksquare}$

(d) $3^4 \times 11^{\blacksquare} \times 3^{\blacksquare} \times 11^5 = 3^5 \times 11^8$

C9 Simplify these.

(a) $10^2 \times 3^4 \times 10^3 \times 3^5$

(b) $2^2 \times 5^3 \times 2^9$

(c) $5^9 \times 7 \times 7^6 \times 5$

To **multiply** powers of the same number, **add** the indices ($a^m \times a^n = a^{m+n}$).

Example

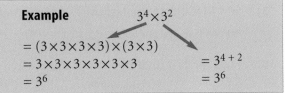

$$= (3 \times 3 \times 3 \times 3) \times (3 \times 3)$$
$$= 3 \times 3 \times 3 \times 3 \times 3 \times 3$$
$$= 3^6$$

$$= 3^{4+2}$$
$$= 3^6$$

D Prime factorisation

There are many ways to write 84 as a product of factors.

For example,
$$84 = 4 \times 21$$
$$84 = 12 \times 7$$
$$84 = 2 \times 6 \times 7$$
$$84 = 2 \times 2 \times 3 \times 7$$

$2 \times 2 \times 3 \times 7$ is called the **product of prime factors** or **prime factorisation** of 84.
We can use index notation to write it as $2^2 \times 3 \times 7$.

We can work out that 96 is $2 \times 2 \times 2 \times 2 \times 2 \times 3$ (or $2^5 \times 3$) in different ways.

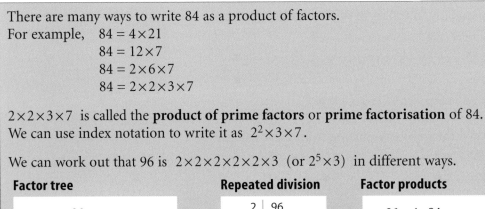

Factor tree

Repeated division

Factor products

D1 Match each number to its prime factorisation.

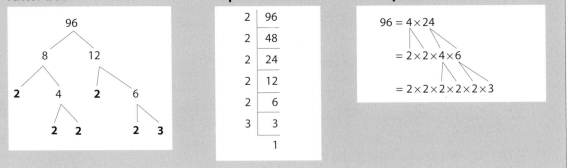

A 120   B 990   C 240   D 7425

E $3^3 \times 5^2 \times 11$ F $2 \times 3^2 \times 5 \times 11$ G $2^4 \times 3 \times 5$ H $2^3 \times 3 \times 5$

D2 Find the prime factorisation of each of these numbers and write it using index notation.

(a) 45   (b) 150   (c) 48   (d) 126   (e) 243

D3 The prime factorisation of 462 is $2 \times 3 \times 7 \times 11$.

(a) Without doing any calculating, decide which of these are factors of 462. Explain how you decided.

| 2 | 3 | 13 | 7 | 4 | 6 | 10 | 14 | 55 |

(b) Check your answers by calculating.

D4 The prime factorisation of 875 is $5 \times 5 \times 5 \times 7$.

(a) Without doing any calculating, decide which of these are factors of 875. Explain how you decided.

| 2 | 3 | 5 | 7 | 20 | 25 | 35 | 45 | 125 |

(b) Check your answers by calculating.

D5 The prime factorisation of 315 is $3 \times 3 \times 5 \times 7$.
The prime factorisation of 3465 is $3 \times 3 \times 5 \times 7 \times 11$.

Without doing any calculating, decide whether 3465 is a multiple of 315.
Explain how you decided.

D6 The prime factorisation of 1155 is $3 \times 5 \times 7 \times 11$.
The prime factorisation of 5005 is $5 \times 7 \times 11 \times 13$.

Without doing any calculating, decide whether 5005 is a multiple of 1155.
Explain how you decided.

D7 The prime factorisation of 24 is $2^3 \times 3$.

(a) Without doing any calculating, decide which of these are multiples of 24.

| $2^3 \times 3 \times 5$ | $2^3 \times 3 \times 7^2$ | $2^3 \times 5$ | $2^4 \times 3$ | $2^3 \times 3^2$ | $2^2 \times 3 \times 5$ |

(b) Check your answers by calculating.

D8 The prime factorisation of 189 is $3^3 \times 7$.

(a) Without doing any calculating, decide which of these are factors of 189.

| 5 | 7 | $3^3 \times 7^2$ | 3×7 | 3×7^3 | $3^2 \times 7$ |

(b) Check your answers by calculating.

D9 The prime factorisation of 275 is $5^2 \times 11$.
The prime factorisation of 1155 is $3 \times 5 \times 7 \times 11$.

Without calculating, decide which of these are **common factors** of 275 and 1155.

| 5 | 3 | 11 | 5×3 | 5×11 | 5^2 | $5^2 \times 11$ |

D10 The prime factorisation of 36 is $2^2 \times 3^2$.

The prime factorisation of 126 is $2 \times 3^2 \times 7$.

Without calculating, decide which of these are **common multiples** of 36 and 126.

| 2×3^2 | $2^3 \times 3^2 \times 7$ | $2^2 \times 3^7 \times 7$ | $2^2 \times 3^2 \times 7 \times 13$ | 2×3 | $2 \times 3^2 \times 7^2$ |

E Highest common factor and lowest common multiple

Example

Find the HCF (highest common factor) of 84 and 120.

• Write each number as a product of prime factors.

$$84 = \underline{2} \times \underline{2} \times \underline{3} \times 7$$
$$120 = \underline{2} \times \underline{2} \times 2 \times \underline{3} \times 5$$

• Look for <u>common</u> prime factors.

The factors 2, 2 and 3 are common to both products (underlined).

So the highest number which is a factor of 84 **and** a factor of 120 is $2 \times 2 \times 3$, which is **12**.

E1 (a) (i) Write 64 as a product of prime factors.

(ii) Write 168 as a product of prime factors.

(b) Use your prime factorisations to find the HCF of 64 and 168.

E2 Use prime factorisation to find the HCF of these.

(a) 72 and 180   (b) 90 and 525   (c) 165 and 154   (d) 104 and 234

Example

Find the LCM (lowest common multiple) of 84 and 105.

• Write each number as a product of primes and look for common factors.

$$84 = 2 \times 2 \times \underline{3} \times \underline{7}$$
$$105 = \underline{3} \times 5 \times \underline{7}$$

• Look for common factors (underlined) and write the product of the common factors.

$$3 \times 7$$

• Multiply this product by all of the remaining (non-common) factors.

$$3 \times 7 \times 2 \times 2 \times 5$$

So the lowest number which is a multiple of 84 **and** a multiple of 105 is

$$3 \times 7 \times 2 \times 2 \times 5, \text{ which is } \textbf{420}.$$

E3 (a) Find the prime factorisations of 18 and 42.

(b) Use your prime factorisations to find the LCM of 18 and 42.

E4 Use prime factorisation to find the LCM of these.

(a) 12 and 20　　(b) 14 and 15　　(c) 45 and 165　　(d) 42 and 350

E5 Di wants to make a patchwork quilt 204 cm by 374 cm.
She is going to use red and yellow square patches.
The width of each patch is to be a whole number
of centimetres.

What is the largest size she can use for the patches?

374 cm

204 cm

*E6 Ten friends swim at the local pool on 1 January and make a New Year's resolution.

The first person is going to swim every day, the second person
every second day, the third every third day and so on.

How many days later do ten people again swim on the same day?

*E7 The HCF of two numbers is 20. The LCM of the same two numbers is 420.
Both the numbers are over 50. What are the numbers?

Test yourself

T1 (a) Find all the factors of 90.

(b) Write down the prime numbers between 10 and 30.

(c) Write down all the powers of 3 between 20 and 100.

(d) What is the highest common factor of 7 and 19?

(e) What is the lowest common multiple of 2 and 7?

T2 Evaluate these.　　　　(a) 3^7　　　(b) 13^2　　　(c) 10^1

T3 Solve these equations.　　(a) $x^5 = 1$　　(b) $2^x = 128$　　(c) $5^x = 5$

T4 Write the answers to these using indices.

(a) $2^5 \times 2^9$　　　(b) 3×3^8　　　(c) $5^2 \times 5^3 \times 5^2$

T5 Simplify $2^5 \times 3^2 \times 2 \times 3^7$.

T6 Find the prime factorisation of 234 and write it using index notation.

T7 Use prime factorisation to find

(a) the LCM of 12 and 15　　　　(b) the HCF of 84 and 126.

T8 A green light flashes every 15 seconds. A red light flashes every 55 seconds.
The lights are switched on and both flash together.
How many seconds do you have to wait until both flash together again?

13 Negative numbers

You should know how to substitute in expressions such as $x^2 + 1$, $3(x + 4)$, $\frac{x}{3} - 1$, the rules about the order of calculating with $+, -, \times, \div$ and brackets, and how to solve equations.

This work will help you calculate with positive and negative numbers and substitute into a variety of expressions.

A Calculating with positive and negative numbers
level 6

Examples

• To add a negative, subtract the corresponding positive.	$6 + {}^-9 = 6 - 9$ $= {}^-3$ ${}^-7 + {}^-1 = {}^-7 - 1$ $= {}^-8$
• To subtract a negative, add the corresponding positive.	$6 - {}^-9 = 6 + 9$ $= 15$ ${}^-7 - {}^-1 = {}^-7 + 1$ $= {}^-6$
• Multiplying or dividing two negatives gives a positive.	${}^-8 \times {}^-2 = 16$ ${}^-14 \div {}^-7 = 2$
• Multiplying or dividing a negative and a positive gives a negative.	$5 \times {}^-3 = {}^-15$ ${}^-12 \div 4 = {}^-3$

A1 (a) Copy and complete the addition below using three different numbers from the loop.

$$\boxed{} + \boxed{} = \boxed{}$$

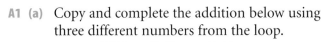

(b) Make as many different additions like this as you can.

(c) Copy and complete the subtraction here using three different numbers from the loop.

$$\boxed{} - \boxed{} = \boxed{}$$

(d) Make eight different subtractions like this.

A2 Copy and complete each multiplication table.

(a)

×		⁻2
⁻5		
4	12	

(b)

×		
⁻1	⁻5	
6		⁻18

(c)

×		⁻7
	8	28
6		

A3 This is a 'division triangle'.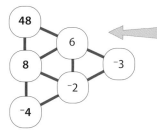

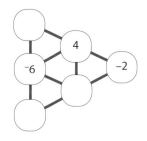
To find each number, divide the left-hand pair of numbers:
top number ÷ bottom number
(48 ÷ 8 = 6)

Copy and complete each division triangle.

(a)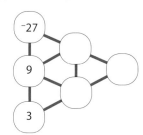

(b)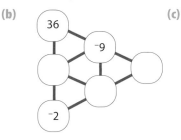

(c)

A4 Copy and complete each magic square, so that each row, column and diagonal adds to give the same total.

(a)

		0
	1	
2	⁻3	

(b)

⁻4	1	0
⁻2	⁻3	

(c)

	5	
	⁻3	
3	⁻11	

A5 Find the next two numbers in each sequence.

(a) 11, 9, 7, 5, 3, …

(b) ⁻11, ⁻8, ⁻5, ⁻2, …

(c) 5, 3.5, 2, 0.5, …

(d) 1, ⁻2, 4, ⁻8, 16, …

A6 Work these out.

(a) $10 + (^-3 \times 2)$

(b) $^-3 \times (^-2 + ^-5)$

(c) $2 \times (1 - 9)$

(d) $(^-3)^2 - 4$

(e) $6 - ^-4 \times ^-2$

(f) $7 - (1 - 5)$

(g) $\dfrac{^-12}{3} + 1$

(h) $^-5 + \dfrac{^-16}{^-4}$

(i) $\dfrac{^-8 - 2}{5}$

(j) $\dfrac{^-10 - ^-8}{^-2}$

(k) $\dfrac{20}{^-5} - ^-3$

(l) $^-2 - \dfrac{^-15}{5}$

*A7 Find the missing number in each of these calculations.

(a) $^-5 \times 3 \times \blacksquare = 30$

(b) $6 + 2 \times \blacksquare = 4$

(c) $(\blacksquare - 5) \times 3 = ^-9$

(d) $4 - ^-2 \times \blacksquare = 14$

(e) $\blacksquare - ^-3 \times ^-2 = ^-4$

(f) $10 + \blacksquare \times ^-5 = 0$

(g) $\dfrac{10 - \blacksquare}{^-4} = ^-3$

(h) $\dfrac{\blacksquare}{^-3} - 9 = ^-1$

(i) $^-1 - \dfrac{10}{\blacksquare} = 4$

B Substitution

Examples

Find the value of
$4x - 7$ when $x = 1$.

$$4x - 7 = 4 \times 1 - 7$$
$$= 4 - 7$$
$$= {}^-3$$

Find the value of
$\dfrac{6 - a}{9}$ when $a = {}^-3$.

$$\frac{6 - a}{9} = \frac{6 - {}^-3}{9}$$
$$= \frac{9}{9}$$
$$= 1$$

Find the value of
$^-5(n - 7)$ when $n = 2$.

$$^-5(n - 7) = {}^-5 \times (2 - 7)$$
$$= {}^-5 \times {}^-5$$
$$= 25$$

B1 What is the value of each expression when $x = 4$?

(a) $2x - 9$ 　　(b) $19 - 6x$ 　　(c) $10 - x^2$ 　　(d) $\dfrac{x}{^-2} + 8$

B2 Find the value of each expression when $y = {}^-3$.

(a) $2y + 1$ 　　(b) $y^2 + 5$ 　　(c) $8 - y$ 　　(d) $\dfrac{y}{^-3}$

B3 What is the value of each expression when $p = {}^-6$?

(a) $3p - 2$ 　　(b) $2(p + 5)$ 　　(c) $1 - 2p$ 　　(d) $p^2 - 9$

(e) $\dfrac{p}{3} - 1$ 　　(f) $(p + 3)^2$ 　　(g) $5 - \dfrac{p^2}{4}$ 　　(h) p^3

Examples

Find the value of
$4(x^2 - 7)$ when $x = 2$.

$$4(x^2 - 7) = 4 \times (2^2 - 7)$$
$$= 4 \times (4 - 7)$$
$$= 4 \times {}^-3$$
$$= {}^-12$$

Find the value of
$\dfrac{6 - 3h}{^-2}$ when $h = {}^-4$.

$$\frac{6 - 3h}{^-2} = \frac{6 - 3 \times {}^-4}{^-2}$$
$$= \frac{6 - {}^-12}{^-2}$$
$$= \frac{18}{^-2}$$
$$= {}^-9$$

Find the value of
$4a^2 - 38$ when $a = {}^-3$.

$$4a^2 - 38 = 4 \times ({}^-3)^2 - 38$$
$$= 4 \times 9 - 38$$
$$= 36 - 38$$
$$= {}^-2$$

B4 What is the value of each expression when $h = 5$?

(a) $5(2h - 11)$ 　　(b) $\dfrac{10 - 6h}{5}$ 　　(c) $3(10 - h^2)$ 　　(d) $\dfrac{4h}{^-2} + 3$

B5 What is the value of each expression when $k = {}^-4$?

(a) $2k^2 + 1$ (b) $3(2k + 5)$ (c) $5(2 - 3k)$ (d) $\frac{1}{2}k^2 - 1$

(e) $\dfrac{8 - k^2}{{}^-4}$ (f) $\dfrac{k^2}{8} - 10$ (g) $\dfrac{(k - 2)^2}{9}$ (h) $5 - \dfrac{k^2}{2}$

B6

$\dfrac{3n - 17}{2}$	$5 - n^2$	$3n^2 - 11$	$\dfrac{4n + 3}{{}^-5}$	$2(n - 5)$	$2(n^2 - 7)$

(a) When $n = 3$, three expressions above have a value of $^-4$.
Find these expressions.

(b) When $n = {}^-2$, three expressions above have the same value.
Find these expressions.

B7 Sixteen expressions are arranged in a square grid
giving four horizontal, four vertical and
two diagonal sets of expressions.

For example, a set of expressions is coloured
yellow on the grid.

(a) What is the value of each expression on
a yellow square when $n = 8$?

What do you notice?

(b) When $n = 2$, find a set of expressions (in a row,
column or diagonal) that each have a value of 1.

$\dfrac{n - 3}{2}$	$2n$	$n^2 - 3$	$n - 1$
$\dfrac{2n^2}{{}^-6}$	$4(12 - n)$	$\dfrac{6 - n}{4}$	$3n + 11$
$4n + 9$	$\dfrac{n^2}{4}$	$\dfrac{5 - n}{7}$	$2n + 5$
$\dfrac{4n - 3}{5}$	$n + 8$	$3n^2$	$\dfrac{n^2}{2} - 25$

(c) When $n = {}^-1$, which set of expressions each have a value of $^-2$?

(d) Find sets where each expression has the same value when

(i) $n = {}^-2$ (ii) $n = {}^-3$ (iii) $n = {}^-6$

B8 (a) Find the value of the expression $4n - 3$ when

(i) $n = 1$ (ii) $n = 0$ (iii) $n = {}^-2$

(b) Find the value of the expression $3n - 18$ when

(i) $n = 1$ (ii) $n = 0$ (iii) $n = {}^-2$

(c) There is one value of n for which both expressions have the same value.

(i) By putting $4n - 3$ equal to $3n - 18$ and solving the equation,
find this value of n.

(ii) Check that the value is correct by substituting it in both expressions.

C Equations with negative solutions

C1 (a) Solve the equation $2n + 10 = 4$.

(b) Check that your answer fits the original equation.

C2 Solve each of these equations. Check each of your answers.

(a) $3k + 5 = 2$ (b) $4n - 1 = {}^-7$ (c) $6p + 3 = {}^-12$

C3 Solve the equation $4m + 21 = 3m + 16$. Check your answer works.

C4 Solve and check each of these.

(a) $3k + 14 = 2k + 10$ (b) $5g + 3 = 4g + 1$ (c) $6n + 7 = 4n + 1$

(d) $7b + 2 = 3b - 10$ (e) $2t + 5 = 5t + 8$ (f) $2x - 6 = 6x + 2$

C5 Solve and check each of these.

(a) $12 + n = 8 - n$ (b) $4t + 28 = 10 - 2t$ (c) $12 - 3b = 8 - 4b$

C6 Solve and check each of these.

(a) $4(m + 5) = 12$ (b) $3(2d - 3) = {}^-12$ (c) $5(1 - 3h) = 8$

C7 Solve and check each of these.

(a) $2q + 4 = 3(q + 2)$ (b) $4(r + 10) = 3(10 - 2r)$ (c) $8(t + 3) = 2t$

(d) $6v + 5 = 7(2 + v)$ (e) $5(1 - w) = 3(2 - w)$ (f) $6(5 - 3x) = 5(4x + 25)$

Test yourself

T1 Evaluate these.

(a) ${}^-3 - 6$ (b) ${}^-3 \times {}^-4$ (c) $4 + {}^-8$

(d) ${}^-3 \times (2 - 9)$ (e) $\dfrac{{}^-7 + {}^-8}{-5}$ (f) $7 - \dfrac{{}^-8}{4}$

T2 What is the value of each expression when $n = {}^-8$?

(a) $2n - 10$ (b) $5(n + 1)$ (c) $\dfrac{3n}{4} + 12$ (d) $\dfrac{n^2 + 1}{5}$

(e) ${}^-3(n - 7)$ (f) $2n^2 - 100$ (g) $\dfrac{20 - 2n}{-9}$ (h) $3 - \dfrac{n}{4}$

T3 Solve each of these equations and check that your answers work.

(a) $3x + 8 = 2$ (b) $2m + 3 = {}^-7$ (c) $5w + 11 = 2w + 5$

(d) $7n + 3 = 4n - 6$ (e) $3d + 25 = 5 - d$ (f) $5(2y - 4) = 2(9y + 2)$

14 Drawing and using linear graphs

You will draw straight-line graphs and use them to solve problems.

A Drawing straight-line graphs

A **linear** equation connecting x and y is one whose graph is a straight line. Linear equations are those such as $y = 2x + 1$ and $3y - \frac{1}{2}x = 10$ that connect a number of ys with a number of xs.

Only two points are needed to plot a straight line, but finding the coordinates of three points gives a useful check and often a more accurately drawn line.

In the example below, three points are found for $y = 2x - 1$ using the x-values $^-2$, 0 and 2. Then these three points are used to plot the graph.

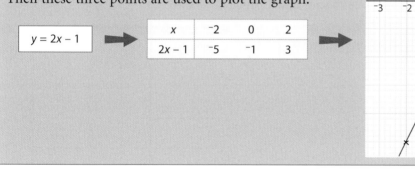

x	$^-2$	0	2
$2x - 1$	$^-5$	$^-1$	3

$y = 2x - 1$

A1 Which of these are linear equations?

A $2y + 3x = 1$ **B** $y = 3x^2 - 1$ **C** $x + y = 1$ **D** $y = x^2 - 1$ **E** $y = 2x - 1$ **F** $y = x^2 + 5$

A2 (a) Copy and complete this table for $y = 2x + 3$.

x	$^-2$	0	2
$2x + 3$			

(b) On graph paper, draw axes with x from $^-3$ to 3 and y from $^-4$ to 10. Draw and label the graph of $y = 2x + 3$.

A3 (a) Copy and complete this table for $y = 6 - 2x$.

x	0	2	4
$6 - 2x$			

(b) On graph paper, draw axes with x from $^-1$ to 5 and y from $^-4$ to 8. Draw and label the graph of $y = 6 - 2x$.

A4 (a) Copy and complete this table of values for $y = \frac{1}{2}x - 2$.

x	-2	0	2
$\frac{1}{2}x - 2$	-3		

(b) On graph paper, draw axes with x from $^-2$ to 5 and y from $^-4$ to 4.
Draw and label the graph of $y = \frac{1}{2}x - 2$.

(c) Copy and complete this table of values for $y = 2 - x$.

x	-2	0	2
$2 - x$	4		

(d) On your diagram from part (b), draw and label the graph of $y = 2 - x$.

(e) What are the coordinates of the point where the two graphs meet, correct to 1 d.p?

A5 (a) Copy and complete this table of values for $y = 3$.

x	-3	-2	-1	0	1	2	3
y	3	3	3				

(b) Draw and label the graph of $y = 3$. Choose your own values on the axes.

A6 The diagram shows the graphs of four equations,
$x = 3$, $x = ^-1$, $y = 3$ and $y = ^-1$.

Which line goes with which equation?

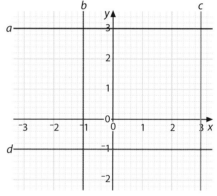

A7

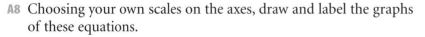

The diagram shows four straight lines.
Write down the equation of each line.

A8 Choosing your own scales on the axes, draw and label the graphs of these equations.

(a) $y = 4$ (b) $y = ^-4$ (c) $x = 4$ (d) $x = ^-4$

Drawing the graph of an equation such as $2x + 3y = 12$

- Try to spot any 'easy' values of x and y that fit.
  For example, when x is 3, you need to find y so that $6 + 3y = 12$. This gives $y = 2$.
- Find the value of y when $x = 0$. Solving the equation $3y = 12$ gives $y = 4$.
- Find the value of x when $y = 0$. Solving the equation $2x = 12$ gives $x = 6$.
- You can summarise your results in a table.

x	0	3	6
y	4	2	0

- Plot your points and draw the line $2x + 3y = 12$.

A9 The graph of $x + 2y = 8$ is a straight line.

   (a) What is the value of y when $x = 2$?

   (b) Work out the value of y when x is 0.

   (c) What is the value of x when $y = 0$?

   (d) Copy and complete this table for $x + 2y = 8$.

x	0	2	
y			0

   (e) On graph paper, draw axes with x from $^-2$ to 10 and suitable values of y.
Draw the graph of $x + 2y = 8$.

   (f) From your graph, what is the value of y when $x = ^-0.8$?

A10 (a) Copy and complete this table for $3x + y = 6$.

x	0	1	
y			0

   (b) On graph paper, draw axes with x from $^-1$ to 3 and suitable values of y.
On your axes draw the graph of $3x + y = 6$.

A11 (a) Copy and complete this table for $3x + 2y = 12$.

x	0	2	
y			0

   (b) Draw axes with x from $^-1$ to 5 and suitable values of y.
On your axes draw the graph of $3x + 2y = 12$.

   (c) From your graph, what is the value of y when $x = 2.5$?
(Give your answer to one decimal place.)

A12

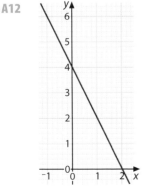

Look at the straight-line graph on the left.

   (a) Check that when $x = 0$, $y = 4$.

   (b) Copy and complete this table of values for the line.

x	y
0	4
1	
2	

   (c) Which of the equations below is the equation of the straight line?

     P $y = x + 1$ **Q** $y = 2x - 1$ **R** $x + y = 4$

     S $2x + y = 4$ **T** $x + y = 2$ **U** $x + 2y = 4$

A13 Draw axes with both x and y labelled from $^-10$ to 10.
Draw the graph of each of these.

(a) $y = 2x - 3$ (b) $y = 6 - x$ (c) $x = 9$

(d) $y = \frac{1}{4}x + 2$ (e) $y = {}^-3$ (f) $2x + y = 10$

A14 (a) On a suitable set of axes, draw the graphs of $y = \frac{1}{3}x + 1$ and $y = 6 - 3x$.

(b) Give the coordinates of the point where the graphs cross.

B Using graphs to solve problems   level 6

B1 You can put an advertisement into the *Evening News*.
The paper charges £25 to typeset the advert,
and then £4 for each centimetre of depth.

(a) What would the total cost be for this advert?

(b) How much would an advert 20 cm deep cost?

(c) Copy and complete this table for adverts.

(d) On graph paper, draw axes with d going across
from 0 to 20 and with c going up from 0 to 110.
Plot the points from your table and join them.

Depth (d)	5	10	20
Cost in £ (c)			

(e) Sue spends £75 on an advert. What is the depth of her advert in cm?

B2 Mendip Mushrooms supply mushroom compost to gardeners.
They charge £35 delivery and then £6 per tonne of compost.

(a) How much would 4 tonnes of compost cost delivered to your door?

(b) How much would 1 tonne cost?

(c) Copy and complete this table for deliveries
of Mendip Mushrooms compost.

Weight (w)	1	4	6
Cost in £ (c)			

(d) Draw axes with w going across from 0 to 8 and c going up from 0 to 90.
Plot the points from your table and join them.

(e) Dave asks for £55 worth of compost to be delivered.
How much will he get, to the nearest $\frac{1}{10}$th of a tonne?

(f) Find a formula that connects w (the weight delivered in tonnes)
and c (the cost in £).

B3 Fuming Fertilisers also supply compost.
The formula they use for working out the cost of a delivery is $c = 10 + 10w$.
c is the cost in £; w is the weight in tonnes.

(a) Copy and complete this table for Fuming Fertilisers' prices.

Weight (w)	1	4	7
Cost in £ (c)			

(b) On the axes you used for B2, draw the graph of $c = 10 + 10w$.

(c) What do Fuming Fertilisers charge for a delivery of 5.5 tonnes of compost?

(d) Use the graph to say which company is cheaper for 10 tonnes of compost. Explain your answer carefully.

B4 Reliable Repairs repair electrical equipment.
The formula they use for working out the cost of a repair is $c = 18 + 0.2t$.
c is the cost of the repair in £, and t is the time taken in minutes to do the repair.

(a) Draw a graph that shows the costs for all repairs that take an hour or less.

Bright Sparks also repair electrical equipment.
The formula they use is $c = 0.7t$.

(b) On the axes you used for Reliable Repairs, draw a graph for Bright Sparks.

(c) Ellie has a video that needs to be repaired.
She has been told that it will take between 30 and 50 minutes to repair.
Where would you advise her to take her video, Reliable Repairs or
Bright Sparks? Explain your decision.

Test yourself

T1 (a) Copy and complete this table for $y = 2x - 2$.

x	-1	0	3
$2x - 2$			

(b) On graph paper, draw axes with x from -3 to 3 and y from -4 to 4.
Draw the graph of $y = 2x - 2$.

T2

(a) Write down the equation of line a.

(b) What is the equation of line b?

T3 (a) On a suitable set of axes, draw the graphs of $y = \frac{1}{2}x - 2$ and $2y + 3x = 6$.

(b) Estimate the coordinates of the point where the graphs cross.

15 Using a calculator

You should know

● what brackets mean in a calculation

● how to round to a number of decimal places or significant figures

This work will help you

● use a calculator for complex calculations

● work with squares, square roots and negative numbers

A Brackets and order of operations
level 5

| Four add two, multiplied by three | Four, add two multiplied by three |

The position of the comma alters the calculation.
Brackets make the calculations clear.

$(4 + 2) \times 3$ $4 + (2 \times 3)$

Scientific calculators do not need the brackets in the second calculation.
They automatically multiply or divide before they add or subtract.

$4 + 2 \times 3 = 4 + 6 = 10$

A1 For each of the calculations below
   (i)   predict what the result will be without using a calculator
   (ii)   then check with a calculator

  (a) $7 + 5 \times 4$ (b) $5 \times (6 - 2)$ (c) $20 - (6 - 2)$ (d) $20 + 12 \times 4$

  (e) $5 \times 6 + 3$ (f) $5 \times 3 + 7 \times 4$ (g) $5 \times (3 + 7) \times 4$ (h) $4 + 2 \times 8 + 3$

A2 Do these on a calculator.
Round each answer to two decimal places.

  (a) $(4.82 + 2.94) \times 6.5$ (b) $4.82 + 2.94 \times 6.5$

  (c) $3.74 \times 2.81 - 1.66$ (d) $12.65 - 2.91 \times 0.36$

  (e) $8.64 + 2.37 \times 1.08 - 2.67$ (f) $0.85 \times (3.47 + 1.26) - 2.55$

  (g) $4.22 \times 3.14 + 0.88 \times 2.57$

A3 Do these on a calculator.
Round each answer to three significant figures.

  (a) $2.62 + 3.91 \times 4.5$ (b) $(1.82 + 4.94) \times 2.5$

  (c) $40.4 \times (17.31 - 8.86)$ (d) $665 - 16.1 \times 13.2$

  (e) $7.14 - 1.47 \times 1.13 + 4.61$ (f) $0.65 \times (3.52 - 1.46) + 3.58$

  (g) $8.12 \times 0.64 - 0.92 \times 3.82$

B Division

In written calculations, a bar is often used for division.

Written	On calculator	
$6 + \dfrac{24}{3}$	$6 + 24 \div 3$	Brackets are not needed here. The calculator automatically does $24 \div 3$ first.
$\dfrac{6 + 24}{3}$	$(6 + 24) \div 3$	The division bar does a similar job to brackets.
$\dfrac{24}{7 + 3}$	$24 \div (7 + 3)$	
$\dfrac{6 + 24}{7 + 3}$	$(6 + 24) \div (7 + 3)$	

B1 Do these on your calculator.
All the answers should be whole numbers.

(a) $\dfrac{8.71 - 3.01}{1.9}$

(b) $\dfrac{130.9}{18.7} + 5$

(c) $(6.5 + 5.5) \times 1.5$

(d) $4.95 + 2.5 \times 2.02$

(e) $2.8 + \dfrac{2.88}{2.4}$

(f) $\dfrac{109.8}{4.4 + 1.7}$

(g) $\dfrac{17.38 + 2.22}{6.13 - 1.23}$

(h) $\dfrac{22.4}{0.76 + 0.64}$

(i) $\dfrac{14.08 - 6.93}{0.88 + 0.55}$

B2 Match each written calculation to one you would do on a calculator.

Written

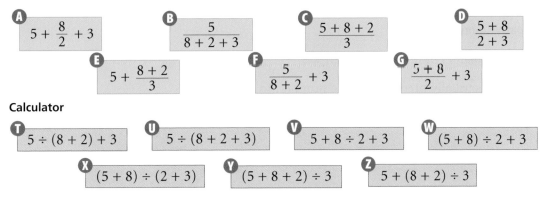

A $5 + \dfrac{8}{2} + 3$

B $\dfrac{5}{8 + 2 + 3}$

C $\dfrac{5 + 8 + 2}{3}$

D $\dfrac{5 + 8}{2 + 3}$

E $5 + \dfrac{8 + 2}{3}$

F $\dfrac{5}{8 + 2} + 3$

G $\dfrac{5 + 8}{2} + 3$

Calculator

T $5 \div (8 + 2) + 3$

U $5 \div (8 + 2 + 3)$

V $5 + 8 \div 2 + 3$

W $(5 + 8) \div 2 + 3$

X $(5 + 8) \div (2 + 3)$

Y $(5 + 8 + 2) \div 3$

Z $5 + (8 + 2) \div 3$

B3 Calculate each of these, giving the result to two decimal places.

(a) $\dfrac{4.75 - 1.08}{2.03}$

(b) $0.68 + \dfrac{2.95}{1.07}$

(c) $\dfrac{4.86}{2.57 - 1.08}$

(d) $\dfrac{4.18 - 1.92}{7.15 - 3.28}$

(e) $\dfrac{115.4}{8.76 - 2.54}$

(f) $\dfrac{9.08 + 7.12}{6.48 - 3.25}$

C1 Amber had to calculate $\dfrac{21.39 + 37.78}{4.85}$. She got the answer 29.18, which is wrong.

She should have checked her answer by making a rough estimate:

21.39 is roughly 20, 37.78 is roughly 40 and 4.85 is roughly 5.

(a) Use these numbers to get a rough estimate of the answer to the calculation.

(b) Do the actual calculation on your calculator.

C2 Pat wants to get a rough estimate for $\dfrac{0.49 \times 216}{3.88}$.

(a) Write down a calculation Pat could do to get a rough estimate.

(b) Work out the rough estimate without using a calculator.

(c) Use a calculator to work out $\dfrac{0.49 \times 216}{3.88}$ and compare the result with your estimate.

C3 For each calculation below

(i) work out a rough estimate   (ii) calculate the result, to three significant figures

(a) $\dfrac{57.2}{9.13 - 2.78}$

(b) $4.13 \times (38.5 - 18.8)$

(c) $\dfrac{41.4}{0.97 \times 7.89}$

(d) $\dfrac{207.4 \times 0.48}{28.4 - 9.7}$

(e) $\dfrac{77.31 + 38.84}{5.86 \times 9.75}$

(f) $\dfrac{286 - 18.7}{47.9 + 18.8}$

D Other keys

Negative numbers

Most calculators have a 'change sign' key $\boxed{+/-}$ for entering negative numbers.

This key is usually pressed after the number: to enter ⁻5 press $\boxed{5}$ $\boxed{+/-}$.

Squaring

The squaring key is often labelled $\boxed{x^2}$. To do 4^2, press $\boxed{4}$ $\boxed{x^2}$.

Square root

On some calculators, the square root key is pressed before the number.

On others it is pressed after. So $\sqrt{9}$ may be $\boxed{\sqrt{}}$ $\boxed{9}$ or $\boxed{9}$ $\boxed{\sqrt{}}$.

D1 Do each of these first without a calculator.
Then use a calculator to check your answer.

(a) $7 + {}^-2$ (b) ${}^-5 - {}^-5$ (c) ${}^-3 \times {}^-4$ (d) ${}^-10 \div 2$ (e) ${}^-1 + {}^-2.5$

D2 (a) Without a calculator, work out $(^-3)^2$.
Then use a calculator to check your answer.

(b) Use a calculator for these.

    (i) $(^-4.3)^2$ **(ii)** $3.2^2 - 2.7^2$ **(iii)** $(7.19 - 4.42)^2$ **(iv)** $7.19 - 4.42^2$ **(v)** $(3.2 - 6.7)^2$

D3 Use a calculator to work these out.
Give each answer correct to two decimal places.

    (a) $\sqrt{19}$ **(b)** $6 \times \sqrt{19}$ **(c)** $\sqrt{6 \times 19}$ **(d)** $\dfrac{\sqrt{19}}{6}$ **(e)** $\sqrt{\dfrac{19}{6}}$

D4 Use a calculator for each of these.
Give each answer correct to two decimal places.
Estimate each answer roughly first.

    (a) $16.7 - \sqrt{8.91}$ **(b)** $(2.83 - 1.64)^2$ **(c)** $4.67 + \left(\dfrac{2.56}{3.2}\right)^2$

    (d) $\dfrac{4.94 - 1.8^2}{2.5}$ **(e)** $3.28 + \dfrac{\sqrt{7.29}}{1.03}$ **(f)** $\dfrac{4.86}{2.57 - \sqrt{1.69}}$

    (g) $\sqrt{4.4^2 + 1.9^2}$ **(h)** $\dfrac{13.4}{\sqrt{5.76} - 1.54}$ **(i)** $\sqrt{\dfrac{9.8 + 7.2}{6.8 - 3.5}}$

Test yourself

T1 Calculate the value of $\dfrac{21.7 \times 32.1}{16.20 - 2.19}$.

Give your answer correct to three significant figures.   *Edexcel*

T2 (a) Estimate the value of

$$S = \frac{738 \times 19}{593 + 392}$$

Do not use your calculator.
Show all your approximations and working.

(b) Now use your calculator to work out the value of *S*.

    (i) Write down all the figures in your calculator display.

    (ii) Write your answer correct to three significant figures.   *OCR*

T3 Use your calculator to work out the value of $\dfrac{\sqrt{12.3^2 + 7.9}}{1.8 \times 0.17}$.

Give your answer correct to one decimal place.   *Edexcel*

T4 (a) Calculate the value of $\dfrac{5.3^2 + \sqrt{8.7}}{1.8 \times 7.2}$.

Give your answer correct to two decimal places.

(b) Write down a calculation you can do in your head to check your answer to (a).
Write down the answer to this calculation.

16 Changing the subject

You should know

- how to solve equations like $3a + 2 = 17$ or $4a - 2 = 10$
- that an expression like $\frac{b-6}{10}$ means 'take 6 off b and divide the result by 10'

This work will help you change the subject of a formula with letters and numbers in it, for example $a = 4d + 5$ and $h = 2k - 3$.

A Forming and using formulas
level 5

Stella is a garden designer who plants ornamental vegetable beds.
To keep away pests, she plants rows of artichokes, with marigolds by them in this pattern.

This table shows the number of marigolds for rows of artichokes of various lengths.

Number artichokes (a)	1	2	3	4	5
Number of marigolds (m)	6	8	10	12	14

A rule for finding the number of marigolds needed is

number of marigolds = number of artichokes × 2 + 4

If a stands for the number of artichokes and m stands for the number of marigolds we can write this rule as a **formula** using letters:

$m = a \times 2 + 4$ or even shorter as $m = 2a + 4$.

A1 Use the formula to complete these shopping lists. Each is for one row of artichokes.

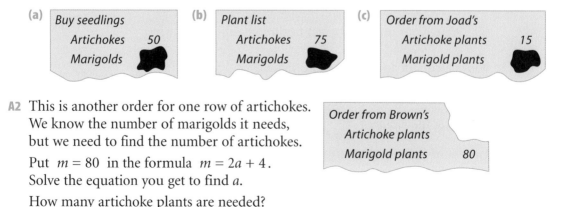

(a)
> Buy seedlings
> Artichokes   50
> Marigolds

(b)
> Plant list
> Artichokes   75
> Marigolds

(c)
> Order from Joad's
> Artichoke plants   15
> Marigold plants

A2 This is another order for one row of artichokes.
We know the number of marigolds it needs,
but we need to find the number of artichokes.

Put $m = 80$ in the formula $m = 2a + 4$.
Solve the equation you get to find a.

How many artichoke plants are needed?

> Order from Brown's
> Artichoke plants
> Marigold plants   80

A3

Stella also plants rows of broccoli.
She puts ornamental cabbages above and below each row of broccoli
and at the ends in the pattern shown above.

(a) Copy and complete this table for her broccoli and cabbage rows.

Number of broccoli plants (b)	1	2	3	4	5	10	100
Number of cabbage plants (c)					22		

(b) Given that b stands for the number of broccoli plants and
c stands for the number of cabbage plants, write a formula connecting b and c.

(c) Use your formula to say how many cabbage plants she needs in a row that has
   (i) 15 broccoli plants   (ii) 25 broccoli plants

This is an order for one row of broccoli plants.
We need to find the number of
broccoli plants to order.

> Order from Brown's
> Broccoli plants
> Cabbage plants   90

(d) Put $c = 90$ in your formula.
   Solve the equation you get to find b.

(e) How many broccoli plants does Stella need?

A4 Stella grows Spanish onions
and garlic in patterns like this.

Suppose s stands for the
number of Spanish onions
in a row and g stands for
the number of garlic bulbs.

Spanish onion

Garlic

(a) Explain why the formula connecting s and g is $g = 6s + 4$.

(b) How many garlic bulbs does Stella need if she plants
   50 Spanish onions in one row?

(c) For one row of onions, Stella plants 100 garlic bulbs.
   How many Spanish onions are in the row?

For Stella's onion and garlic rows, the formula $g = 6s + 4$
connects the letters g and s.

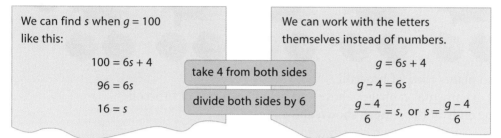

We can find s when $g = 100$
like this:

$$100 = 6s + 4$$
$$96 = 6s$$
$$16 = s$$

take 4 from both sides

divide both sides by 6

We can work with the letters
themselves instead of numbers.

$$g = 6s + 4$$
$$g - 4 = 6s$$
$$\frac{g-4}{6} = s, \text{ or } s = \frac{g-4}{6}$$

Each time, we do the same thing to both sides of the formula.
We call this 'rearranging the formula to make s the subject' or
'making s the subject of the formula'.

Now we can find the value of s easily for different values of g.

We can check the rearrangement by using values of g and s.
For example, when $s = 10$ in the original formula, $g = 6 \times 10 + 4 = 64$.
Now check this in the rearranged formula.
When $g = 64$, $s = \dfrac{64-4}{6} = \dfrac{60}{6} = 10$ which checks.

B1 For Stella's onion and garlic pattern, a formula is $s = \dfrac{g-4}{6}$.
s stands for the number of Spanish onions in a row
and g stands for the number of garlic bulbs.

(a) If $g = 160$, what is s?

(b) When $g = 400$, what is s?

(c) There are 82 garlic bulbs in one row.
How many onions are there in this row?

B2 Stella plants red and white onions in rows like this.

Suppose r stands for the number of red onions
and w stands for the number of white onions.

(a) Explain why $w = 3r + 2$ in this pattern.

(b) What is the value of w when $r = 20$?

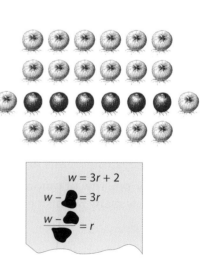

(c) Copy and complete this working
to make r the subject of the formula.

(d) What is the value of r when $w = 50$?

(e) How many red onions are there in a row
that has 68 white onions in it?
Check your answer works in the formula for w.

$$w = 3r + 2$$
$$w - ⬛ = 3r$$
$$\frac{w - ⬛}{⬛} = r$$

B3 For this pattern of red and white onions, $w = 2r + 4$.

   (a) Rearrange the formula $w = 2r + 4$
to make r the subject.

   (b) Work out r when $w = 88$.

   (c) How many red onions are there in a row with 128 white?

B4 **(a)** In the formula $f = 3g + 2$, find f when $g = 10$.

   (b) Make g the subject of the formula $f = 3g + 2$.

   (c) Check your rearrangement is correct by substituting
the value of f from (a) into your new formula.

B5 **(a)** Rearrange the formula $s = 5t + 1$ to make t the subject.

   (b) Find a pair of values of s and t that fit the original formula $s = 5t + 1$.
Use this pair of values to check that your rearrangement is correct.

B6 Make the bold letter the subject of each of these formulas.
For each one, check your rearrangement by using a pair of values
that fit the original formula.

   (a) $b = 8\boldsymbol{w} + 7$ **(b)** $u = 5\boldsymbol{v} + 2$ **(c)** $g = 6\boldsymbol{d}$ **(d)** $y = 12 + 3\boldsymbol{x}$

   (e) $t = 3\boldsymbol{b} + 5$ **(f)** $f = 8 + 3\boldsymbol{d}$ **(g)** $h = \boldsymbol{k} + 5$ **(h)** $w = 7\boldsymbol{d} + 1$

B7 **(a)** Copy and complete this working to make x
the subject of the formula $y = 5x - 6$.

   (b) Use your new formula to find x when $y = 129$.

   (c) Substitute $y = 129$ and the value of x you found
in (b) into the original formula to check
that your rearrangement is correct.

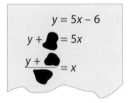

$y = 5x - 6$

$y + \blacksquare = 5x$

$\dfrac{y + \blacklozenge}{\blacksquare} = x$

B8 Which of the following are correct rearrangements of $a = 2b - 10$?

  A $b = \dfrac{a - 10}{2}$ **B** $b = \dfrac{a}{2} + 5$ **C** $b = \dfrac{a + 10}{2}$ **D** $b = \dfrac{a + 2}{10}$ **E** $b = \dfrac{a - 2}{10}$ **F** $b = \dfrac{10 + a}{2}$

B9 Make the bold letter the subject of each of these formulas.

   (a) $a = 8\boldsymbol{w} - 6$ **(b)** $b = 4\boldsymbol{h} - 1$ **(c)** $h = 2\boldsymbol{f} - 2$ **(d)** $y = \boldsymbol{x} - 15$

   (e) $z = 2\boldsymbol{r} - 15$ **(f)** $k = 2\boldsymbol{d} - 3$ **(g)** $b = \boldsymbol{g} - 5$ **(h)** $l = 2\boldsymbol{m} - 1$

B10 Here are eight formulas. Find four matching pairs of equivalent formulas.

A
$$y = 12x - 4$$

B
$$x = \frac{y - 12}{4}$$

C
$$y = 4x - 12$$

D
$$x = \frac{y - 4}{12}$$

E
$$y = 4x + 12$$

F
$$x = \frac{y + 4}{12}$$

G
$$y = 12x + 4$$

H
$$x = \frac{y + 12}{4}$$

B11 Rearrange each of these formulas to make the bold letter the subject.

(a) $a = 30 + 3\boldsymbol{b}$ (b) $s = 2\boldsymbol{t} - 40$ (c) $t = 12\boldsymbol{g} - 60$ (d) $f = 3\boldsymbol{b} + 12$

(e) $y = 12 + 8\boldsymbol{x}$ (f) $r = 5\boldsymbol{s} - 20$ (g) $a = 3\boldsymbol{b}$ (h) $v = 7\boldsymbol{u} - 10$

(i) $y = 35 + \boldsymbol{x}$ (j) $8 + 4\boldsymbol{j} = d$ (k) $k = 8\boldsymbol{j} - 45$ (l) $7\boldsymbol{z} - 1 = w$

Test yourself

T1 Make the bold letter the subject of each of these formulas.

(a) $a = 6\boldsymbol{r} + 8$ (b) $b = 4\boldsymbol{s} + 6$ (c) $c = 12 + 5\boldsymbol{t}$ (d) $d = 8 + 4\boldsymbol{u}$

T2 (a) Copy and complete this working to make m the subject of the formula $n = 3m - 2$.

(b) Find a pair of values of n and m that fit the formula $n = 3m - 2$.

(c) Use this pair of values to check your rearrangement.

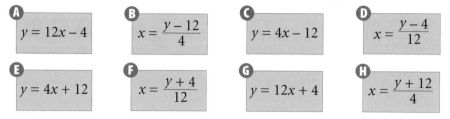

$n = 3m - 2$

$n + \blacksquare = 3m$

$\dfrac{n + \bullet}{\blacksquare} = m$

T3 Which of these rearrangements of $y = 2x - 3$ are correct?

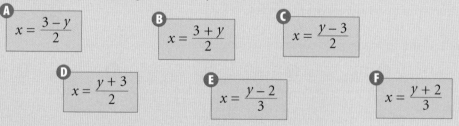

A
$$x = \frac{3 - y}{2}$$

B
$$x = \frac{3 + y}{2}$$

C
$$x = \frac{y - 3}{2}$$

D
$$x = \frac{y + 3}{2}$$

E
$$x = \frac{y - 2}{3}$$

F
$$x = \frac{y + 2}{3}$$

T4 Rearrange each of these formulas to make the bold letter the subject.

(a) $e = 4\boldsymbol{v} - 12$ (b) $f = 2\boldsymbol{w} - 15$ (c) $g = \boldsymbol{x} - 12$ (d) $h = 5\boldsymbol{y} - 10$

T5 Make the bold letter the subject of each formula.

(a) $n = 8 + 5\boldsymbol{t}$ (b) $s = 4\boldsymbol{t} - 7$ (c) $y = 2\boldsymbol{x} + 12$ (d) $m = 3\boldsymbol{u} - 5$

(e) $j = 5\boldsymbol{v} + 12$ (f) $f = 15 + 5\boldsymbol{w}$ (g) $k = 3\boldsymbol{x}$ (h) $8\boldsymbol{y} + 4 = b$

17 Grid totals

You will

● form and solve simple linear equations

● use algebra to derive and prove some simple general statements

A Expressions from patterns on a number grid   level 6

A1 This grid of numbers has ten columns.

An L-shape outlines some numbers.

1	2	3	4	5	6	7	8	9	10
11	12	13	14	15	16	17	18	19	20
21	22	23	24	25	26	27	28	29	30
31	32	33	34	35	36	37	38	39	40

(a) What is the total of the numbers in the L-shape above?

(b) Find totals for the L-shape in different positions on the grid.

(c) Suppose the grid is continued downwards.

    (i) Copy and complete this L-shape for the grid above.

    (ii) What is its total?

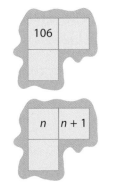

(d) (i) Copy and complete this L-shape for the grid above.

    (ii) Find an expression for the total.

(e) What numbers are in the L-shape that has a total of 614 on this grid?

(f) Explain why you can't have an L-shape with a total of 154 on this grid.

A2 This grid of numbers has ten columns.

A T-shape outlines some numbers.

(a) What is the total of the numbers in this T-shape?

(b) Find totals for the T-shape in different positions on the grid.

1	2	3	4	5	6	7	8	9	10
11	12	1.	14	15	16	17	18	19	20
21	22	23		25	26	27	28	29	30
31	32	33	34	35	36	37	38		
4			44	45	46				

(c) Suppose the grid is continued downwards.

(i) Copy and complete this T-shape for the grid above.

(ii) What is its total?

103

(d) (i) Copy and complete this T-shape for the grid above.

(ii) Find an expression for the total.

n

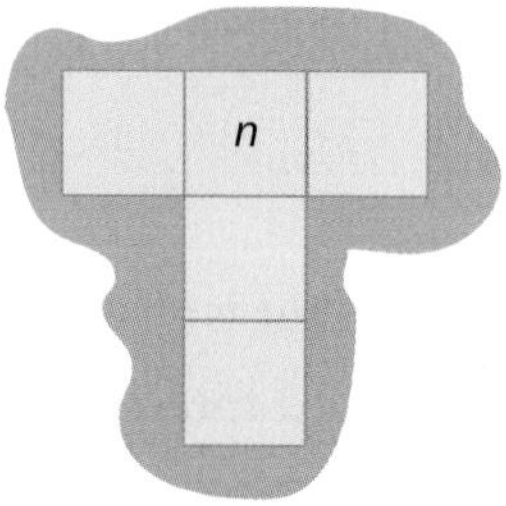

(e) Draw the T-shape that has a total of 1020 on this grid.

(f) Explain why you can't have a T-shape with a total of 231 on this grid.

A3 Another grid of numbers has six columns.

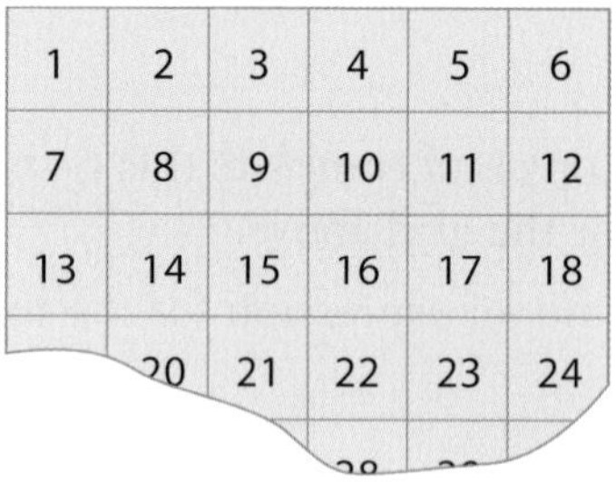

1	2	3	4	5	6
7	8	9	10	11	12
13	14	15	16	17	18
	20	21	22	23	24
		28			

(a) (i) Copy and complete this T-shape for the six-column grid.

(ii) Find an expression for the total.

n

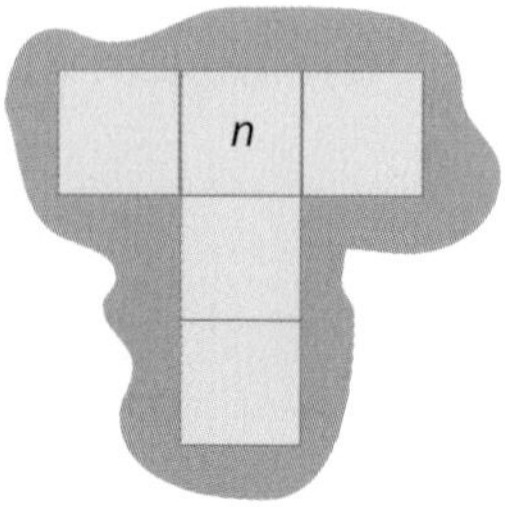

(b) Investigate T-shape totals for grids with different numbers of columns.

A4 A grid of numbers
    has twelve columns.

1	2	3	4	5	6	7	8	9	10	11	12
13	14	15	16	17	18	19	20	21	22	23	24
25	26	27	28	29	30	31	32	33	34	35	36

(a) What is the total of the numbers in the shaded shape.

(b) Find totals for this shape in three more different positions on the grid.

(c) Copy and complete this shape for this grid.

n

(d) Explain why you cannot find a position on this grid for
     this shape that gives a total of 84.

(e) Show that any total for this shape on this grid must be a multiple of 4.

T1 Part of a number grid with seven columns is shown below.

1	2	3	4	5	6	7
8	9	10	11	12	13	14
15	16	17	18	19	20	
	23	24	25	26		
	21					

(a) What is the total of the numbers in the shaded square above?

(b) Find totals for a square this size in two more different positions on the grid.

(c) Copy and complete this square for the grid above.

(d) Draw the square that has a total of 200 on this grid.

(e) Explain why you cannot find a position on this grid for
     a square this size that gives a total of 62.

(f) Show that you cannot find an odd total for any square of this size on this grid.

(g) Can you find a position on this grid for the square that gives a total of 100?
     Explain your answer carefully.

Review 2

1   **P** $\boxed{2n + 1}$ **Q** $\boxed{2(3n - 5)}$ **R** $\boxed{\dfrac{n + 5}{2}}$ **S** $\boxed{13 - 2n}$ **T** $\boxed{(n - 3)^2}$

    (a)   Find the value of each expression above when

       (i) $n = 3$ (ii) $n = 2$ (iii) $n = {}^{-}3$

    (b)   Which expression has the smallest value when $n = {}^{-}1$?

2   Which is larger, 2^6 or 3^4?

3   Work out   (a) ${}^{-}2 \times ({}^{-}6 + 1)$ (b) $5 - \dfrac{{}^{-}16}{8}$ (c) $\dfrac{{}^{-}3 - 9}{{}^{-}4}$

4   Multiply out the brackets in $7(3p - 5)$.

5   Write down all the prime numbers between 30 and 40.

6   Jane and Ayse have n sweets each. They each give away 2 sweets.
    Which expressions give the number of sweets they now have altogether?

    $\boxed{2n - 2}$ $\boxed{n - 2}$ $\boxed{2n - 4}$ $\boxed{2(n - 2)}$ $\boxed{2(n - 1)}$

7   Simplify these expressions.

    (a) $6 + 3p - 1 - 5p$ (b) $\dfrac{10b}{5} + 1$ (c) $\dfrac{12 - 18k}{6}$

8   Write down the number missing from the statement $7^6 \times 7^{\blacksquare} = 7^{10}$.

9   Solve these equations.

    (a) $3x + 5 = 5x - 7$ (b) $5x - 18 = 3 - 2x$ (c) $5x + 9 = 3x + 1$

    (d) $5n + 11 = 3(3n - 5)$ (e) $6(2n + 1) = 9(3 - n)$ (f) $n - 6 = 9(n + 2)$

10   (a)   Find the prime factorisation of 300 and write it using index notation.

     (b)   Find the prime factorisation of 198 and write it using index notation.

     (c)   Find the highest common factor of 198 and 300.

11   (a)   Find an expression for the perimeter of this rectangle.

     (b)   What is the perimeter when $n = 10$?

     (c)   What value of n gives a perimeter of 95?

     (d)   What value of n gives a square?

12   Find the missing length in this triangle.

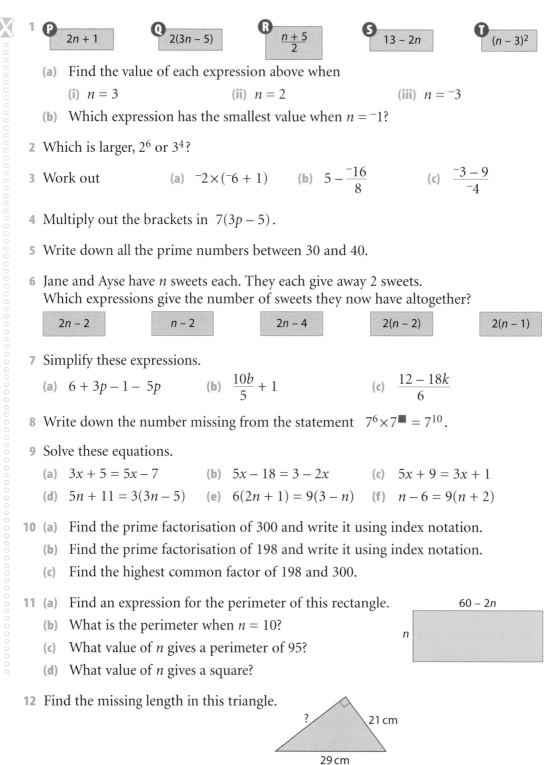

13 (a) Write a formula for the perimeter of this rectangle.
$P = \ldots$

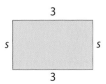

(b) Rearrange the formula to make s the subject.

(c) Use your rearranged formula to find the length s when the perimeter is 15 units.

14 Find the missing length.

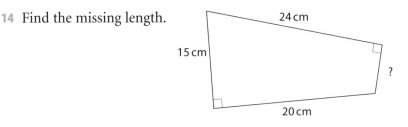

15 (a) On a suitable set of axes, draw and label the graphs with these equations.

(i) $x = 2$ (ii) $y = 3x + 2$ (iii) $y = \frac{1}{4}x - 1$ (iv) $4y - x = 8$

(b) Name the quadrilateral that is enclosed by these four lines.

16 (a) Use rough estimates to decide on these.

(i) Which calculation gives the greatest result?

(ii) Which gives the smallest result?

(b) Now use your calculator to work out the answers, correct to three significant figures.

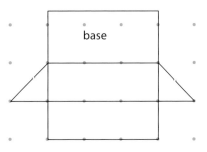

17 Rearrange the formula $v = 7h - 9$ to make h the subject.

18 The net is drawn on square cm dotty paper. It folds up to make the solid below.

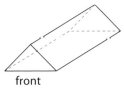

(a) Calculate the area of the base of the solid, correct to the nearest $0.1 \, cm^2$.

(b) How many planes of symmetry has the solid?

(c) Draw an accurate side view of the solid.

19 Work these out on a calculator, giving your answers to two decimal places.

(a) $(5.71 + 3.82) \times 6.7$ (b) $4.45 - 1.82 \times 1.42$ (c) $\dfrac{6.31}{8.22 - 7.46}$

(d) $\sqrt{7.6 \times (4.2 + 8.1)}$ (e) $(4.2 - 8.9)^2$ (f) $\dfrac{4.3^2 + 0.62}{4.3 + 0.62^2}$

20 The diagonals of a rhombus measure 6.5 cm and 10.2 cm. What is the perimeter of the rhombus?

18 Ratio

You will revise using ratios given in the form $a:b$ and $a:b:c$.

This work will help you divide a quantity in a given ratio.

A Writing a ratio in its simplest form

Here are some recipes for fruit drinks, using cordial and sugar syrup.

* In some of the recipes the ratio **cordial : syrup** is **2 : 3**.
  Which are they?

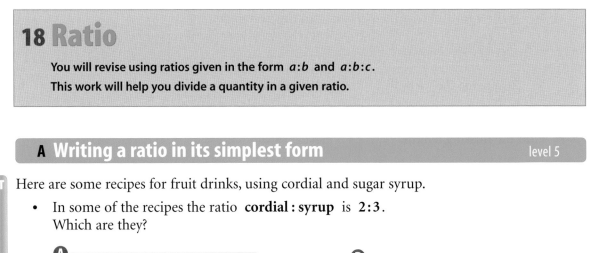

A 400 ml cordial needs 600 ml syrup.

B To every 2 glasses of cordial add 3 glasses of syrup.

C 5 teaspoons of cordial should be mixed with 8 teaspoons of syrup.

D Mix cordial to syrup in the ratio 4 : 6.

E To 1 litre of cordial add 12 litres of syrup.

F For every 20 ml of cordial you will need 30 ml of syrup.

G Cordial to syrup should be 10 parts to 15 parts.

H Mix 8 parts of cordial with 12 parts of syrup.

A1 Match up these ratios in pairs.

1 : 4   6 : 10   150 : 200   20 : 80   3 : 4   25 : 75   3 : 5   2 : 6

A2 A recipe requires 250 g flour and 100 g sugar.

(a) Write the ratio of flour to sugar in its simplest form.

(b) Write the ratio of sugar to flour in its simplest form.

A3 Write each of these ratios in its simplest form.

(a) 4 : 16   (b) 5 : 15   (c) 6 : 8   (d) 20 : 25   (e) 12 : 6

(f) 45 : 50   (g) 18 : 12   (h) 40 : 25   (i) 21 : 14   (j) 21 : 15

(k) 48 : 16   (l) 30 : 35   (m) 12 : 32   (n) 100 : 40   (o) 18 : 42

A4 Simplify these ratios as far as possible.

   (a) 200 g : 500 g   (b) 10 m : 25 m   (c) 8 cm : 20 cm

A5 A plank of wood is 10 centimetres wide and 5 metres long.
Dean says the ratio of width to length is 2 : 1.

   (a) Why is his answer wrong?   (b) Write down the correct ratio.

A6 Simplify these ratios as far as possible.

   (a) 20 cm : 1 m   (b) 300 g : 1 kg   (c) 40 cm : 2 m   (d) 8 mm : 3 cm

   (e) 3 kg : 250 g   (f) 5 km : 500 m   (g) 2 m : 10 cm   (h) 6 cm : 5 mm

---

Ratios of the form $a:b:c$

A recipe for blackberry and apple jam needs 8 kg blackberries, 2 kg apples and 6 kg sugar.

The ratio **blackberries : apples : sugar** is **8 : 2 : 6**.

This can be simplified (by dividing by 2) as **4 : 1 : 3**.

A7 A recipe for orange and grapefruit marmalade needs 15 kg oranges,
5 kg grapefruit and 10 kg sugar.
Write the ratio oranges : grapefruit : sugar in its simplest form.

A8 A salad recipe needs 1 kg potatoes, 200 g cucumber and 250 g tomatoes.
Write the ratio potatoes : cucumber : tomatoes in its simplest form.

A9 Joan mixes 2 litres of white paint with 500 ml of blue and 200 ml of yellow.
Write the ratio white : blue : yellow in its simplest form.

A10 Steve is making cakes.
He mixes 1.5 kg sultanas with 250 g cherries and 100 g candied peel.
Write the ratio sultanas : cherries : candied peel in its simplest form.

A11 Write each of these ratios in its simplest form.

   (a) 3 : 12 : 18   (b) 10 : 15 : 25   (c) 40 : 60 : 100   (d) 48 : 36 : 24

A12 The length of this cuboid is 18 cm.
Its width is 9 cm and its height 6 cm.

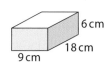

   (a) Write the ratio length : width : height in its simplest form.

   (b) Which of the following cuboids have the same ratio
of length : width : height as the one above?

     A length 3 m, width 1.5 m, height 1 m

     B length 90 cm, width 45 cm, height 20 cm

     C length 1.2 m, width 60 cm, height 40 cm

B Finding a value from a given ratio

Example

The alloy cupro-nickel is made from 2 parts of nickel to 5 parts of copper.
If 80 kg of nickel is used, how much copper will be needed?

Method 1

nickel : copper

=   2 : 5

(Multiply both numbers by
40, to make 2 become 80.)

=   80 : **200**

So **200 kg** copper is needed.

Method 2

Nickel is 2 parts.

2 parts is 80 kg.

So 1 part is 40 kg.

Copper is 5 parts = 5×40 kg

            = **200 kg**

Method 3

2 kg nickel needs 5 kg copper.

So 1 kg nickel needs 2.5 kg copper.

So 80 kg nickel needs 80×2.5

            = **200 kg** copper.

B1 Rose pink paint is made by mixing
red and white in the ratio $1:3$.
Copy and complete this mixing table.

Red (1 part)	White (3 parts)
2 litres	
	9 litres
0.5 litre	
	12 litres

B2 Panther pink is made by mixing
red and white in the ratio $2:3$.
Copy and complete this mixing table.

Red (2 parts)	White (3 parts)
6 litres	
	15 litres
8 litres	
	1.5 litres

B3 Tracy knew that she had to mix 2 parts of yellow paint with 5 parts of blue
to get the shade of green she liked.

(a) If she had 1 litre of yellow paint, how much blue paint would she need?

(b) If she had 250 ml of blue paint, how much yellow paint would she need?

B4 On a school trip, the ratio of adults to children is one to eight.

(a) If 5 adults are going on the trip, how many children can go?

(b) If 200 children want to go on the trip, how many adults will be needed?

B5 The ratio of sailing dinghies to motor cruisers moored in a harbour is $4:1$.
If there are 24 dinghies in the harbour, how many motor cruisers are there?

B6 In a herd, the ratio of male to female animals is $5:8$.
There are 40 males. How many females are there?

B7 A tea blender mixes Indian and African teas in the ratio $3:5$.

  (a) How much African tea does she mix with 15 kg Indian tea?

  (b) How much Indian tea does she mix with 20 kg African tea?

B8 Copy and complete the quantities in this table.

Ratio	Quantities
1:5	15 kg : ... kg
2:3	50 g : ... g
5:4	20 m : ... m
3:8	... g : 320 g

B9 Bob is 7 years old and his sister Hayley is 11 years old.
Their Nan gives them some money in the ratio of their ages.

  (a) If Bob gets £2.10, how much does Hayley get?

  (b) If Hayley gets £5.50, how much does Bob get?

B10 In a new housing development, the ratio of starter homes to family homes
is 3 to 5.

  (a) If 48 starter homes are built, how many family homes will there be?

  (b) If 25 family homes are built, how many starter homes will there be?

B11 When choosing tiles for a bathroom floor, Pat wants
2 patterned tiles for every 15 plain tiles.
If he buys 120 plain tiles, how many patterned tiles will he need?

B12 Karen makes purple paint by mixing red and blue in the ratio $2:3$.
How much blue paint does she mix with 5 litres of red?

B13 Sophie mixes orange juice and pineapple juice in the ratio $4:5$.
How much pineapple juice does she mix with 10 litres of orange juice?

B14 To make 'Pago fizz' you mix pineapple juice, mango juice
and fizzy water in the ratio $5:2:3$.

  (a) You have 120 ml of pineapple juice.
  How much mango juice and how much fizzy water do you need?

  (b) You have 150 ml of fizzy water.
  How much pineapple juice and how much mango juice do you need?

B15 The animals on a farm consist of sheep, cows and pigs in the ratio $9:5:2$.
There are 162 sheep.
How many cows and how many pigs are there?

B16 On another farm the sheep, cows and pigs are in the ratio $3:8:1$.
There are 112 cows.
How many animals are there altogether?

Example

Ali and Ben share a pizza which weighs 450 g.
The ratio of Ali's piece to Ben's piece is 2:3.
How much does each person get?

Ali gets 2 parts and Ben 3.
That's 5 parts altogether.

Each part is 450 g ÷ 5 = 90 g

So   Ali gets 2 × 90 g   = 180 g
and   Ben gets 3 × 90 g   = 270 g

Check: the two shares add up to 450 g.

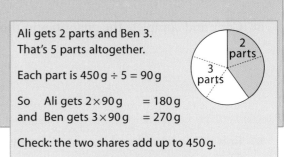

C1   Colin and Dilip share £200 in the ratio 1:3.
How much does each of them get?

C2   Emma and Farnaz share £160 in the ratio 3:5.
How much does each of them get?

C3   Sharon makes a drink by mixing pineapple juice and mango juice in the ratio 3:2.
She wants to make 1 litre of the drink.

(a)   How much pineapple juice will she need?

(b)   How much mango juice will she need?

C4   An alloy using 9 parts of silver to 1 part of copper is often used for jewellery.
A chain of mass 50 g is made out of this alloy.

(a)   What mass of silver does it contain?   (b)   What mass of copper does it contain?

C5   (a)   Divide £12 in the ratio 1:3.   (b)   Share £35 in the ratio 2:5.

(c)   Divide 60 kg in the ratio 3:7.   (d)   Divide £4.50 in the ratio 7:2.

C6   Paula has a collection of stamps.
She has twice as many foreign stamps as British stamps.

(a)   What is the ratio of foreign to British stamps in her collection?

(b)   If she has 480 stamps altogether, how many of them are foreign?

C7   Some material is woven from cotton and polyester mixed in the ratio 7 to 3.
How many grams of cotton are there in 2 kg of the material?

C8   Paul, Steph and Ronnie share £24 in the ratio 1:2:3.
How much does each get?

C9   2 litres of aquamarine paint is mixed using blue, yellow and white paint
in the ratio 1:3:4.
How much of each colour is needed?

C10 A biscuit tin contains chocolate, cream and plain biscuits in the ratio $2:2:3$.
If there are 35 biscuits altogether, how many of each kind are there?

C11 A silver coloured alloy is made using copper, nickel and zinc in the ratio $2:2:1$.
How much of each metal is needed to make a candlestick weighing $350\,\text{g}$?

D Converting between ratios, fractions and percentages   level 6

Example

A packet contains round balloons and long balloons in the ratio $3:1$.
What fraction of all the balloons are round?

Drawing a picture helps.

There are 3 round balloons for every 1 long balloon.

Out of every 4 balloons, 3 are round. So $\frac{3}{4}$ of all the balloons are round.

D1 A bag of chocolates contains milk and dark chocolates in the ratio 4 milk to 1 dark.
What fraction of all the chocolates are dark chocolates?

D2 The ratio of male fish to female fish in a tank is $1:7$.
What fraction of the fish are   (a) male   (b) female

D3 The ratio of girls to boys in a choir is $3:2$.

(a) What fraction of the choir are girls?

(b) What percentage are girls?

D4 In a primary school class, $\frac{1}{2}$ the children are boys.
Is the ratio of boys to girls $1:2$, $2:1$, $1:1$, or none of these?

D5 In a pet shop, $\frac{1}{3}$ of the kittens are male.
What is the ratio of male to female kittens?

M   F   F

D6 In the pet shop, $\frac{1}{4}$ of the rabbits are male.
What is the ratio of male to female rabbits?

D7 In the pet shop, $\frac{1}{6}$ of the guinea pigs are male.
What is the ratio of male to female guinea pigs?

D8 In the pet shop, $\frac{3}{5}$ of the puppies are male.
What is the ratio of male to female puppies?

M   M   M   F   F

D9 Put these statements into pairs so that the statements in each pair say the same thing.

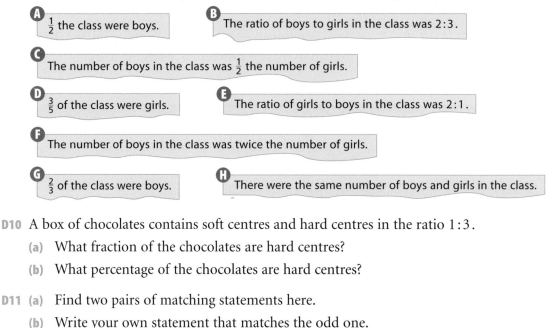

A $\frac{1}{2}$ the class were boys.

B The ratio of boys to girls in the class was 2:3.

C The number of boys in the class was $\frac{1}{2}$ the number of girls.

D $\frac{3}{5}$ of the class were girls.

E The ratio of girls to boys in the class was 2:1.

F The number of boys in the class was twice the number of girls.

G $\frac{2}{3}$ of the class were boys.

H There were the same number of boys and girls in the class.

D10 A box of chocolates contains soft centres and hard centres in the ratio 1:3.

   (a) What fraction of the chocolates are hard centres?

   (b) What percentage of the chocolates are hard centres?

D11 **(a)** Find two pairs of matching statements here.

    (b) Write your own statement that matches the odd one.

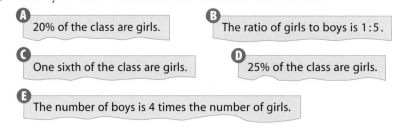

A 20% of the class are girls.

B The ratio of girls to boys is 1:5.

C One sixth of the class are girls.

D 25% of the class are girls.

E The number of boys is 4 times the number of girls.

D12 An alloy is made from copper and nickel.
If 20% of the alloy is nickel, what is the ratio of copper to nickel?

E Writing in the form $k:1$ and $1:k$ level 6

It is often convenient to use ratios where one of the parts is 1,
even if the other part is then not a whole number.

Example

A school with 1560 pupils has 100 teachers.
The ratio pupils:teachers is 1560:100.

If we divide both numbers by 100, we get **15.6:1** (15.6 pupils for every teacher).

This ratio could be compared with other schools.

E1 To make orange paint, red and yellow are mixed in the ratio $3:2$.
How much red is needed to mix with 1 litre of yellow?

E2 Write each of the following ratios in the form $k:1$.

(a) $7:2$ (b) $10:4$ (c) $250:200$ (d) $33:10$ (e) $2:5$

E3 By dividing both parts by 2, write the ratio $2:11$ in the form $1:k$.

E4 Write each of the following ratios in the form $1:k$.

(a) $2:5$ (b) $10:35$ (c) $4:18$ (d) $10:7$ (e) $4:3$

E5 Fat makes up 5% of the ingredients of some biscuits.
Write the ratio of fat to the other ingredients in the form $1:k$.

E6 One Saturday afternoon at a cinema there are 7 children for every 2 adults.
Write the ratio children:adults in the form $k:1$.

E7 Sterling-silver contains silver and copper in the ratio $23:2$.

(a) Write this ratio in the form $k:1$.

(b) How much silver needs to be mixed with 50 g of copper?

Test yourself

T1 Rashid has 35 sweets.
He shares them in the ratio $4:3$ with his sister.
Rashid keeps the larger share.
How many sweets does Rashid keep?   Edexcel

T2 There were 1200 fans at the game between City and United.

(a) The ratio of City fans to United fans was $3:2$.
How many fans of each team were there?

150 of the fans attending were women and children.

(b) What fraction of the fans were women and children?
Give your answer in its simplest form.   OCR

T3 Wayne shares £360 between his children, Sharon and Liam, in the ratio of their ages.
Sharon is 13 years old and Liam is 7 years old.

(a) Work out how much each child receives.

(b) What percentage of the £360 does Sharon receive?   Edexcel

T4 Anna, Beth and Cheryl share the total cost of a holiday in the ratio $6:5:4$.
Anna pays £294.

(a) Work out the total cost of the holiday.

(b) Work out how much Cheryl pays.   Edexcel

19 Substitution

You should know how to work out expressions such as $\frac{h-6}{10}$, $35 - 2h$, $4h^2 - 40$, $\frac{h^2}{10}$ and $200 - h^2$ when you know the value of h.

This work will help you

- substitute into expressions involving cubes
- substitute into more complex expressions, and those involving units
- substitute into expressions involving several letters

A Substitution review

A1 Work out the value of each of these expressions when $h = 4$.

(a) $2h^2$
(b) $100 - h^2$
(c) $\frac{100}{5h}$
(d) $\frac{64}{h^2}$
(e) $\frac{1 - h^2}{5}$

A2 Use a calculator to work out the value of these expressions.

(a) $8a^2$ when $a = 2.5$
(b) $7.2 - 2b^2$ when $b = 1.1$
(c) $4.5c - 2.7$ when $c = 1.5$

(d) $\frac{9}{2d - 3}$ when $d = 2.4$
(e) $1.5(2.2e + 1)$ when $e = 2$
(f) $\frac{f^2}{5} - 3f$ when $f = 4.5$

A3 The circumference of a circle is given by the formula $C = 2\pi r$.
C stands for the circumference and r for the radius.

Work out the circumference, in centimetres, of each of these circles.
Give your answers to one decimal place.

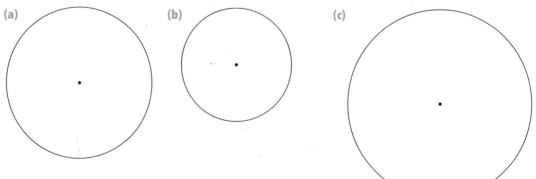

(a)   (b)   (c)

A4 The area of a circle is given by the formula $A = \pi r^2$.
Work out the areas of the circles in A3. Give each answer to the nearest $0.1\,\text{cm}^2$.

A5 (a) Which of the expressions in the boxes has the highest value when $x = 5$?

(b) Which expression has the lowest value when $x = 5$?

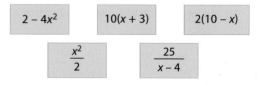

$2 - 4x^2$ $10(x + 3)$ $2(10 - x)$

$\frac{x^2}{2}$ $\frac{25}{x - 4}$

A6 Which numbers in this list fit each equation below?
More than one number may fit an equation.

$$-5 \quad -1 \quad 1 \quad 3.5 \quad 4 \quad 5$$

(a) $5x - 20 = 0$ (b) $2x^2 - 50 = 0$ (c) $4(2x - 5) = 8$ (d) $\dfrac{1}{x^2} = 1$

B   Expressions with more than one letter

When you have several letters in an expression, you treat them just like numbers.

Evaluate $a - bc$ when $a = 5, b = 2, c = 8$.

$$a - bc \quad \longleftarrow \quad bc \text{ means } b \times c$$
$$= 5 - 2 \times 8$$
$$= 5 - 16 = -11$$

Evaluate $a(b - c)^2$ when $a = 5, b = 2, c = 8$.

$$a(b - c)^2 \quad \longleftarrow \quad a(b - c)^2 \text{ means } a \times (b - c)^2$$
$$= 5 \times (2 - 8)^2$$
$$= 5 \times (-6)^2 = 5 \times 36 = 180$$

B1 Calculate the values of each of the following expressions
when $p = 2, q = 3, r = 6$.

(a) $r(p + q)$ (b) $rp + q$ (c) $\dfrac{r}{pq}$ (d) $\dfrac{q + r}{p}$ (e) $5r^2$

Check that you can make your calculator agree with you.

B2 Calculate the values of each of the following expressions
when $f = 2, g = -6, h = 4$.

(a) $f + gh$ (b) $\dfrac{f}{g - h}$ (c) $(f + g)^2$ (d) $10g^2$ (e) $f^2 + h^2$

Check that you can make your calculator agree with you.

B3 Evaluate each of the expressions in B2 when $f = 7.9, g = 5.7, h = 3.8$.
Give your answers correct to one decimal place.

B4 Given that $u = 2.1, v = 3.1$ and $w = 5.9$, evaluate each of these expressions,
giving answers correct to two decimal places.

(a) $\dfrac{u}{v + w}$ (b) $w - \dfrac{u}{v}$ (c) $u + vw$ (d) $\dfrac{u + v}{v + w}$ (e) uv^2

B5 Evaluate each of these expressions when $a = -4.5, b = 0.5$ and $c = -2.5$.
Round to 2 d.p. if necessary.

(a) $\dfrac{a^2}{b^2 + c^2}$ (b) $(c - 2b)^2$ (c) $3b^2$ (d) $(3b)^2$ (e) $ab + bc + ca$

B6 Evaluate each of the following expressions when $w = \frac{1}{2}, x = \frac{1}{3}$ and $y = \frac{3}{4}$.

(a) $2w$ (b) $2w - y$ (c) $w + x$ (d) $w + x + y$ (e) $w + x - y$

B7 Given that $a = 2$ and $b = 3$, calculate the values of these.

(a) $a^2 b$ (b) ab^2 (c) $(ab)^2$

If any of your answers are the same, you have made a mistake.
In that case, find it!

C Units in formulas

When using a formula for a real problem, you must be careful about the units.

To find the area of this triangle we must work entirely in either centimetres or millimetres.

The area of a triangle is given by $A = \frac{1}{2}bh$ or $\frac{bh}{2}$

where b is the base and h is the height.

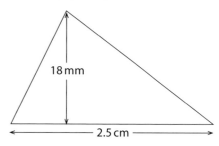

Working in centimetres, $A = \dfrac{bh}{2} = \dfrac{2.5 \times 1.8}{2}$

$$= \frac{4.5}{2} = 2.25$$

So the area is $2.25\,\text{cm}^2$.

When using formulas

- be clear what each letter stands for
- think carefully about the units of any quantities
- give answers complete with any units

C1 The area of a triangle is given by the formula $A = \dfrac{bh}{2}$.

Work out the areas of triangles where

(a) $b = 25\,\text{cm}$, $h = 10\,\text{cm}$

(b) $b = 1.2\,\text{m}$, $h = 90\,\text{cm}$

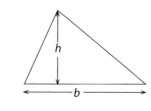

C2 The area, A square units, of a trapezium is given by the formula $A = \frac{1}{2}(a + b)h$.
(a, b and h are shown on the diagram.)

Use the formula to calculate the areas of trapeziums for which

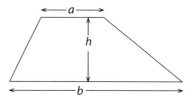

(a) $a = 60\,\text{cm}$, $b = 80\,\text{cm}$, $h = 40\,\text{cm}$

(b) $a = 50\,\text{cm}$, $b = 1.8\,\text{m}$, $h = 80\,\text{cm}$

C3 The power, W, used by an electrical appliance is measured in watts.
The current, A, the appliance needs in amps is given by the formula $A = \dfrac{W}{230}$.

(a) Work out the current needed by these.

   (i) A 250 watt television   (ii) A 90 watt computer

   (iii) A 60 watt light bulb   (iv) A 5 kilowatt cooker | 1 kilowatt = 1000 watts |

   (Give your answers to one significant figure.)

(b) A shower needs a current of 30 amps.
How many kilowatts does it use?

C4 Calculate the area of each of these trapeziums.
Make sure you include units in your answers.

(a)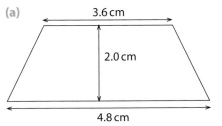

(b)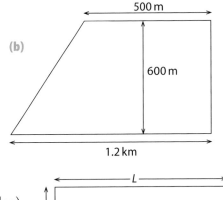

C5 A rectangle has length L and width W.
Its perimeter P (the total distance round the edge)
can be found using the formula $P = 2(L + W)$.

Use this formula to find the perimeters of
the following rectangles.

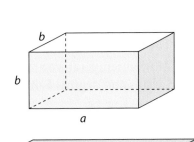

(a) A field 120 m long and 200 m across

(b) A poster 40 cm wide and 65 cm high

(c) A postage stamp measuring 18 mm across and 2.5 cm from top to bottom

(d) A doormat measuring 1.2 m by 75 cm

C6 This cuboid has square ends.
Its volume V is given by the formula $V = ab^2$.

Calculate the volume of each of these cuboids
with square ends.

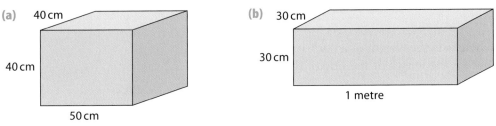

(a) 40 cm
40 cm
50 cm

(b) 30 cm
30 cm
1 metre

C7 A cuboid with square ends, as in C6, has a surface area A,
given by the formula $A = 4ab + 2b^2$.

Calculate the surface area of these.

(a) A cuboid that is 10 cm long, with ends 4 cm by 4 cm

(b) A cuboid that is 1.2 metres long, with ends 75 centimetres square

D1 To convert temperatures between Celsius and Fahrenheit you can use one of these formulas.

$$C = \frac{5(F-32)}{9} \qquad\qquad F = \frac{9C}{5} + 32$$

C stands for the temperature in °C, F stands for the temperature in °F.

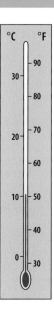

(a) The freezing point of water is 0 °C. What is it in Fahrenheit?

(b) The boiling point of water is 100 °C. What is it in Fahrenheit?

(c) A comfortable room temperature is about 72 °F. What is it in Celsius?

(d) The temperature in a domestic fridge should be about 36 °F. What is this in Celsius?

(e) The melting point of iron is about 2800 °F. What is this in Celsius?

(f) The temperature at the centre of the Sun may be about 27 000 000 °F. What is it in Celsius?

(g) In 1895 a temperature of ⁻17 °F was recorded in Scotland. What is this in Celsius?

(h) In 1983 a temperature of ⁻128 °F was recorded in Antarctica. What is this in Celsius?

(i) The freezing point of mercury is ⁻38.86 °C. What is it in Fahrenheit?

(j) At what temperature are the measurements in degrees Celsius and degrees Fahrenheit exactly the same?

D2 Building bricks are supplied in cube-shaped packs on a pallet. The weight of a pack can be worked out using the formula

$$w = 2000l^3$$

where w is the weight of a pack in kilograms and l is the length of the side of the pack in metres.

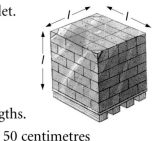

Work out the weights of packs of bricks with these side lengths.

(a) 1.0 metres (b) 1.5 metres (c) 50 centimetres

D3 ProPlanters make large cubical lead planters. The weight of a planter, filled with earth, is given by the formula $w = 0.6S^2 + 2.2S^3$.

w is the weight of the full planter in tonnes and S is the length of the side of the planter in metres.

(a) Work out the weight of a full planter with a side of 1.1 metres.

(b) Work out the weight of a full planter that has a side of 1 m 50 cm.

(c) Four gardeners can lift about 300 kg between them. Could they lift a full 50 cm planter?

D4 The weight in kilograms that can be supported at the middle of an oak beam is given by the formula

$$w = \frac{60bd^2}{l}$$

where w stands for the weight in kilograms, and b, d and l for the breadth, depth and length of the beam in centimetres.

Calculate the load that can be supported by an oak beam 4 m long, 20 cm broad and 30 cm deep.

D5 A child drops a stone from the top of a cliff which is 80 m above the level of the sea.

As it falls, the height of the stone above the sea can be calculated using the formula $h = 80 - 5t^2$.

t is the time in seconds since the stone was dropped.
h is the height of the stone in metres above sea level.

(a) Copy and complete this working to find the value of h when $t = 3$.

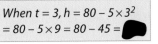

When $t = 3, h = 80 - 5 \times 3^2$
$= 80 - 5 \times 9 = 80 - 45 = $ ⬤

(b) Calculate the values of h when t is 0, 1, 2, and 4. Make a table of the results, like this.

t	0	1	2	3	4
h					

(c) Describe where the stone is when $t = 0$.

(d) Does the stone fall at the same speed all the time, or does it speed up, or does it slow down?

(e) After how many seconds does the stone hit the sea?

D6 Copy this number grid puzzle on to squared paper. To solve the puzzle, first work out the value of each of the expressions below.

Then fit the values you worked out into the grid puzzle.

To help you, the value of one of the expressions has been fitted into the grid.

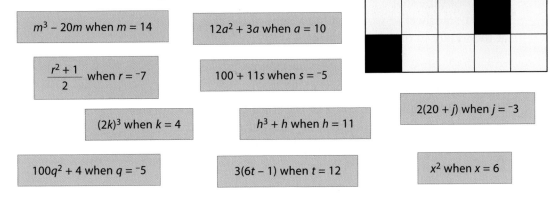

$m^3 - 20m$ when $m = 14$

$12a^2 + 3a$ when $a = 10$

$\dfrac{r^2 + 1}{2}$ when $r = ^-7$

$100 + 11s$ when $s = ^-5$

$(2k)^3$ when $k = 4$

$h^3 + h$ when $h = 11$

$2(20 + j)$ when $j = ^-3$

$100q^2 + 4$ when $q = ^-5$

$3(6t - 1)$ when $t = 12$

x^2 when $x = 6$

E Using formulas in a spreadsheet

 A spreadsheet is ideal when you have a lot of calculations to do using a formula. For example, this spreadsheet is set up to work out the areas of trapeziums.

Trapezium spreadsheet

	A	B	C	D	E
1	Length of first parallel side (a)	Length of second parallel side (b)	Height (h)	Area	
2					
3	8	12	4	=0.5*(A3+B3)*C3	

The area of a trapezium is usually written as $\frac{1}{2}(a + b)h$.
Notice that we have to put in the formula in a way that the spreadsheet understands.

E1 Set up a spreadsheet as above. Use it to work out the areas of trapeziums where

   (a) $a = 6, b = 5, h = 10$ (b) $a = 7.6, b = 12.2, h = 9.8$

E2 This trapezium has an area of $100\,cm^2$. Use your spreadsheet to find the value of x to one decimal place.

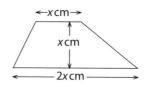

E3 Another trapezium has one parallel side 3 cm longer than the other. The height of the trapezium is the same as the shorter side and its area is $50\,cm^2$. Use your spreadsheet to work out the height of the trapezium to one decimal place.

E4 The area of a semicircle is given by the expression $\frac{1}{2}\pi r^2$. Set up a spreadsheet to work out the areas of semicircles. (You may be able to enter π as PI(); if not use 3.14159.)

Work out the areas of semicircles with these radii.

   (a) 6.5 cm   (b) 8.8 cm   (c) 0.2 km   (d) 100 m

E5 This shape is made from a square and a semicircle. The area of the shape is $200\,cm^2$. Use a spreadsheet to work out the length of the side of the square to one decimal place.

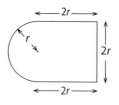

E6 This running track is made up of a square and two semicircles. The distance round the outside of the track must be 400 metres. Use a spreadsheet to work out what the radius of the semicircles must be to the nearest centimetre.

Test yourself

T1 Calculate the values of each of the following expressions
when $a = 2$, $b = 4$, $c = {}^-1$.

(a) $a(b + c)$ (b) $ab - c$ (c) $\dfrac{ab}{c}$ (d) $\dfrac{b - 2c}{a}$ (e) ab^2

T2 Work out the value of the following expressions
when $p = \frac{1}{3}$, $q = \frac{1}{4}$ and $r = \frac{7}{8}$.

(a) $p + q$ (b) $3q$ (c) $3q - p$ (d) $p + q + r$ (e) $r - 2q$

T3 The area A of a trapezium can be written as $A = \frac{1}{2}(a + b)h$.
Work out the areas of each of these.

(a) 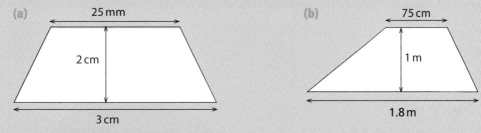 (b)

25 mm   2 cm   3 cm   75 cm   1 m   1.8 m

T4 The length of this metal rod is exactly 1 metre at $0\,°C$.

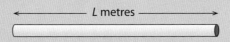

L metres

When the temperature is $T\,°C$, its length, L metres,
is given by the formula $L = 1 + \dfrac{T}{30\,000}$.

Find the length of the rod at these temperatures.

(a) $150\,°C$ (b) $600\,°C$ (c) $^-90\,°C$ (d) $^-200\,°C$

T5 Quattro ponds are made up of a square and four semicircles.
The radius of each semicircle is r.

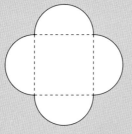

The area of a pond can be written as $2\pi r^2 + 4r^2$.
Work out the area of a Quattro pond when

(a) $r = 1$ (b) $r = 10$ (c) $r = 0.75$

20 Scaling and ratio

You will revise how to recognise and make scaled copies of shapes.

This work will help you

- work with decimal scale factors
- work with ratios within shapes

You will need some A2 paper, tabloid newspaper pages and a metre rule.

A Scaling drawings

A graphic artist has designed a logo for a company.

He is asked to make a copy double the size.
But he isn't happy with his drawing.

What is wrong with it?

Copy

Original

Here is part of another copy of the original logo.
This one is correctly scaled.
How high is the complete copy?

A1 Which of these are scaled copies of the original shape?
Give the scale factor for those that are.

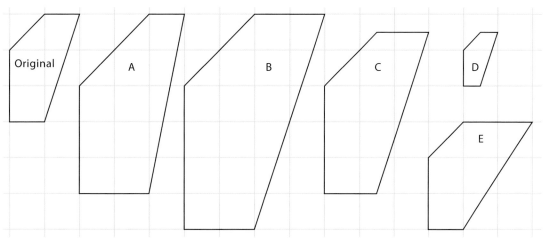

A2 **(a)** Copy the original shape above on to squared paper.
Draw a scaled copy of it using a scale factor of 3.

(b) Draw another scaled copy using a scale factor of 2.5.

A3 The larger picture here is a scaled copy of
the original on the left.

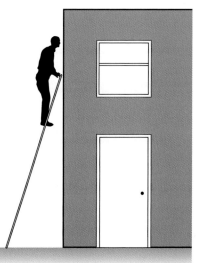

(a) Copy and complete this table of measurements and work out each multiplier.

Measurement	Original length	—⟨× ?⟩➤	Length in copy
Height of building			
Length of ladder			
Height of door			
Width of door			

(b) What is the scale factor of the enlargement?

(c) Measure the angle between the ladder and the ground in the original
and the copy. What do you find?

A4 A picture shows a house, a car and a hedge.
This table compares measurements in the original picture and a scaled copy.
Copy the table and fill in the missing values.

	Original length	Scale factor	Copy length
Width of picture	10 cm		25 cm
Height of picture	6 cm		
Height of house	3 cm		
Length of car			5 cm
Length of hedge			20 cm

You can use a scale factor that is a decimal.

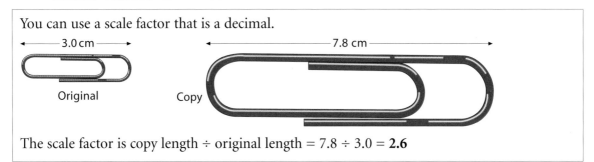

Original   Copy

The scale factor is copy length ÷ original length = 7.8 ÷ 3.0 = **2.6**

A5 Find the scale factor for each of these copies of the original paperclip.

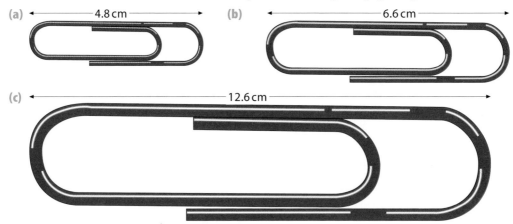

(a) 4.8 cm   (b) 6.6 cm

(c) 12.6 cm

A6 Copy and complete this table for a picture that has been enlarged.

	Original length	Scale factor	Copy length
Width of picture	15.0 cm		54.0 cm
Height of picture	10.0 cm		
Length of bike	13.5 cm		
Height of saddle			27.0 cm
Diameter of wheel			16.2 cm

A7 Bella has a rectangular photo 125 mm by 80 mm.
The photo is enlarged. The longer side of the copy is 350 mm long.
Calculate the length of the shorter side of the copy.

B Scaling down

This pencil is life size.

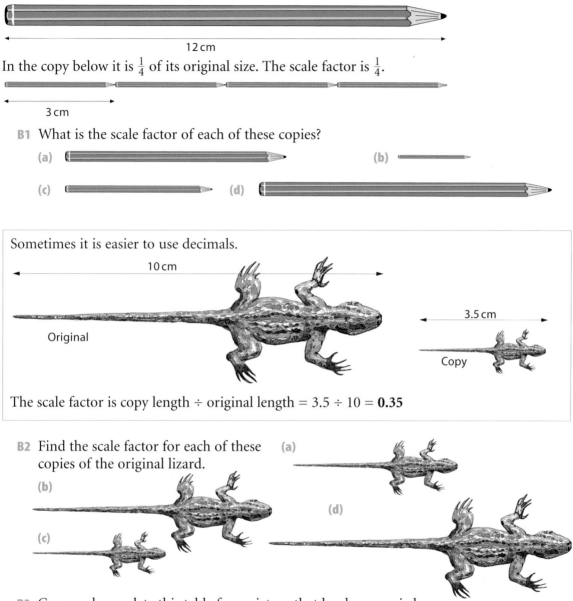

12 cm

In the copy below it is $\frac{1}{4}$ of its original size. The scale factor is $\frac{1}{4}$.

3 cm

B1 What is the scale factor of each of these copies?

(a)

(b)

(c)

(d)

Sometimes it is easier to use decimals.

10 cm

Original

3.5 cm

Copy

The scale factor is copy length ÷ original length = 3.5 ÷ 10 = **0.35**

B2 Find the scale factor for each of these copies of the original lizard.

(a)

(b)

(c)

(d)

B3 Copy and complete this table for a picture that has been copied.

	Original length	Scale factor	Copy length
Width of picture	8 cm		4.8 cm
Height of picture	5 cm		
Height of tree	3 cm		
Length of pond			4.5 cm
Length of fence			5.4 cm

C **Proportion within a shape**

Paper sizes

You need some A2 paper, tabloid newspaper pages and a metre rule.

You will have often used A4 paper. This is a standard metric size.
However, newspapers do not use this system.

- Measure the lengths of the sides of the A2 sheet.
- Fold the sheet in half (to A3) by halving the longer side.
  Measure the sides of the new sheet.
- Repeat this three more times, always halving the longer side.
- Record your results in a table and calculate the ratio $\dfrac{\text{long side}}{\text{short side}}$ each time.

	Metric sizes					Newspaper sizes			
	A2	A3	A4	A5	A6	Tabloid	$\frac{1}{2}$ tabloid	$\frac{1}{4}$ tabloid	$\frac{1}{8}$ tabloid
long side									
short side									
$\dfrac{\text{long side}}{\text{short side}}$									

- Measure a tabloid newspaper page, then repeatedly fold and measure
  it as with the A2 sheet. Record your results in the table.
- What rule applies to the A sizes?
  Does the same rule apply to the newspaper sizes?
- What advantage does the A system have over the newspaper sizes?

A ratio is used to compare two quantities.

For example, if the height of a window is 3 times its width,
we can write

$$\text{height} = 3 \times \text{width}$$

$$\text{or} \quad \frac{\text{height}}{\text{width}} = 3$$

We say 'the ratio of height to width is 3 (or 3 : 1)'.

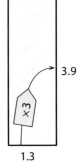

For this window, the height is 0.4 times the width,

$$\text{so the ratio} \quad \frac{\text{height}}{\text{width}} = 0.4$$

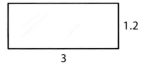

C1 All the pictures below are scaled copies of this original.

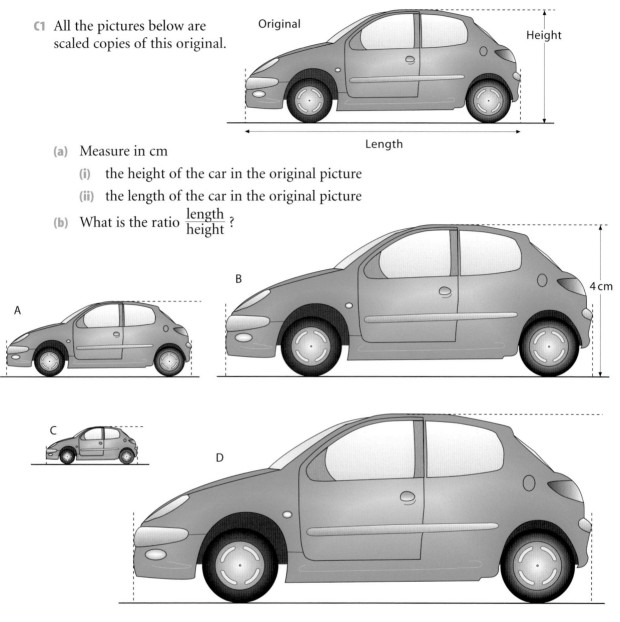

Original

Height

Length

(a) Measure in cm

    (i) the height of the car in the original picture

    (ii) the length of the car in the original picture

(b) What is the ratio $\dfrac{\text{length}}{\text{height}}$?

B

4 cm

A

C

D

(c) Copy and complete this table for the scaled copies.

Copy	A	B	C	D
Length of car				
Height of car				
Ratio $\dfrac{\text{length}}{\text{height}}$				

(d) What do you notice about the ratio each time?

(e) A car is now drawn 7 cm high. How long should it be?

(f) How high would a car 20 cm long be if it were a scaled copy?

C2 For each of these cards find the ratio $\frac{\text{longer side}}{\text{shorter side}}$.
Use this to make pairs that are copies from the same original.

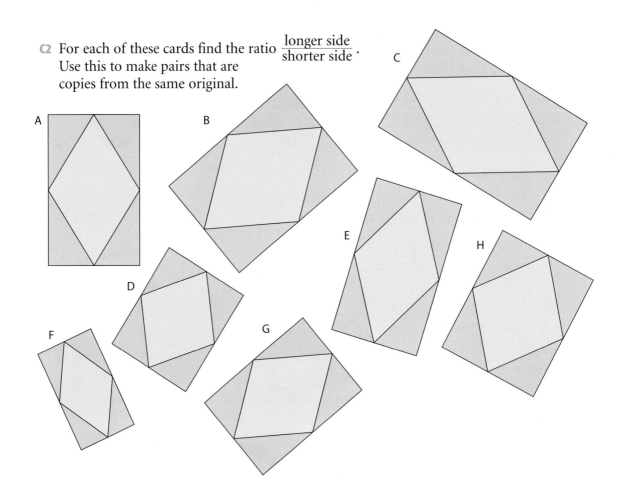

A   B   C   D   E   F   G   H

Test yourself

T1 What scale factor has been used to copy

   (a) shape A to shape B

   (b) shape C to shape B

   (c) shape A to shape C

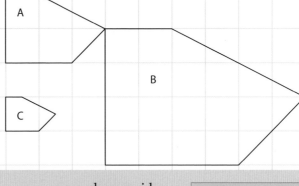

A   B   C

T2 (a) Measure this rectangle and find the ratio $\frac{\text{longer side}}{\text{shorter side}}$.

   (b) If the rectangle is scaled so its shorter side is 44 mm long, how long will its longer side be?

   (c) If it is scaled so its longer side is 15 metres long, how long will its shorter side be?

21 Understanding inequalities

This work will help you

- understand, use and combine inequalities
- convert statements in words to inequalities in symbols

A Single inequalities

- $2 < 3$ means '2 **is less than** 3' so the statement is true.
- $5 > 10$ means '5 **is greater than** 10' so the statement is false.
- $^-2 \leq 4$ means '$^-2$ **is less than or equal to** 4' so the statement is true.
- $3 \geq 3$ means '3 **is greater than or equal to** 3' so the statement is true.

$x \geq {}^-3$ represents the set of numbers that are greater than or equal to $^-3$.
It can be shown on a diagram like this.

The circle is filled in to show that
the number $^-3$ is included.

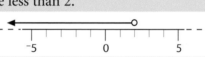

$x < 2$ represents the set of numbers that are less than 2.
It can be shown on a diagram like this.

The circle is empty to show that
the number 2 is not included.

A1 Decide whether each of the following is true or false.

(a) $2 > 1$ 　　(b) $\frac{1}{3} < \frac{1}{4}$ 　　(c) $\sqrt{26} \geq 5$ 　　(d) $11^2 \leq 121$

(e) $7 \leq 7$ 　　(f) $0 \leq {}^-1$ 　　(g) $\frac{1}{3} > 0.33$ 　　(h) $0.1^2 > 0.1$

A2 (a) For the set of values $x \leq 1$, which of the
numbers in the bubble are values of x?

(b) Which are values of n for the set $n > 3$?

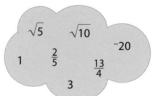

A3 Write an inequality for each of the following diagrams.

(a)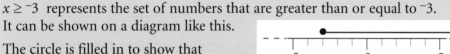

(b)

(c)

(d)

A4 For each of these, sketch a number line and draw the inequality on it.

(a) $x < 4$ (b) $n \geq {}^{-}1$ (c) $p < 5\frac{1}{2}$ (d) $y \geq {}^{-}4$

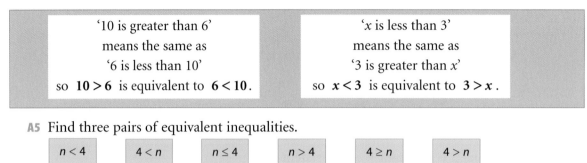

'10 is greater than 6'	'x is less than 3'
means the same as	means the same as
'6 is less than 10'	'3 is greater than x'
so $10 > 6$ is equivalent to $6 < 10$.	so $x < 3$ is equivalent to $3 > x$.

A5 Find three pairs of equivalent inequalities.

$n < 4$ $4 < n$ $n \leq 4$ $n > 4$ $4 \geq n$ $4 > n$

A6 Sketch a number line and draw the inequality $2 \leq x$ on it.

*A7 Given that $x > 3$, decide whether each of the following is

- **always** true   or   **sometimes** true   or   **never** true

(a) $x > 4$ (b) $x > 2$ (c) $x > {}^{-}1$ (d) $x < 1$

(e) $x + 5 > 8$ (f) $x - 1 < 4$ (g) $2x > 3$ (h) $\dfrac{x}{2} < 1$

B Combined inequalities

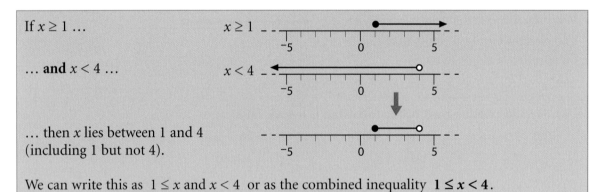

If $x \geq 1$ ...

... **and** $x < 4$ ...

... then x lies between 1 and 4 (including 1 but not 4).

We can write this as $1 \leq x$ and $x < 4$ or as the combined inequality $1 \leq x < 4$.

B1 Match each diagram A to C with its appropriate inequality.

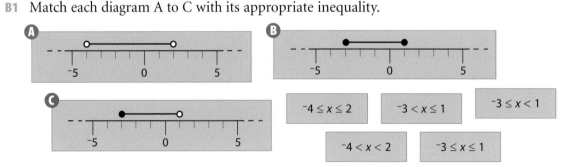

$^{-}4 \leq x \leq 2$ $^{-}3 < x \leq 1$ $^{-}3 \leq x < 1$

$^{-}4 < x < 2$ $^{-}3 \leq x \leq 1$

B2 For each of these, sketch a number line to represent the inequality.

(a) $2 \leq x \leq 4$ (b) $^-3 < x \leq 1$ (c) $0 \leq n < 6$ (d) $1 \leq n < 10$

B3 (a) Which of the numbers in the bubble are in the set of values of x given by $0 < x \leq 5$?

(b) Which are in the set of values of n given by $^-3 \leq n \leq 2$?

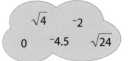

B4 Write inequalities for each of the following diagrams.

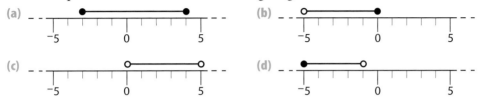

(a)

(b)

(c)

(d)

B5 We say that the values of x that make an inequality true **satisfy** the inequality.

Which of these values of x satisfy $^-2 < x < 3$?

0   1   -1.5   -2.5   3   -2

B6 Write down four whole numbers that satisfy the inequality $0 \leq x \leq 3$.

B7 List five different values of n that satisfy $^-1 \leq n < 2$.

B8 Find two prime numbers p so that $20 < p < 30$.

B9 m is a multiple of 3.
Find three values of m so that $10 \leq m \leq 20$.

B10 Calculate the value of a^2 when $a = 3$.
Does this value of a satisfy the inequality $a^2 > 8$?

B11 Calculate the value of x^2 when $x = {}^-5$.
Does this value of x satisfy the inequality $x^2 \leq 20$?

B12 Which of the numbers n, below, satisfy $n^2 < 100$?

    20   10.5   9 $^-$7 $^-$11   10   0

B13 **Integers** are positive and negative whole numbers, including zero.
Find all the integers, n, so that $n^2 < 20$.
(There are nine of these integers altogether.)

B14 Find two integers x so that $10 < x^2 < 17$.

B15 List three whole numbers n that satisfy $4 \leq 2n \leq 12$.

B16 List three different integers p so that $9 \leq 2p \leq 23$.

*B17 List all the values of n, where n is an integer, such that $4 \leq n + 5 < 7$.

'There are fewer than 10 bananas' leads to the inequality $b < 10$ where b stands for 'the **number** of bananas': the letter b is not just shorthand for the word 'bananas'.

Match each of the statements A to D with the appropriate inequality from the set below.

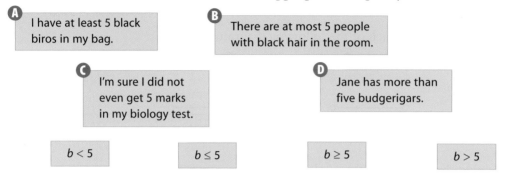

A I have at least 5 black biros in my bag.

B There are at most 5 people with black hair in the room.

C I'm sure I did not even get 5 marks in my biology test.

D Jane has more than five budgerigars.

$b < 5$ $b \leq 5$ $b \geq 5$ $b > 5$

C1 Write each of these as a mathematical statement.
For each one, use t to stand for the temperature in °C.

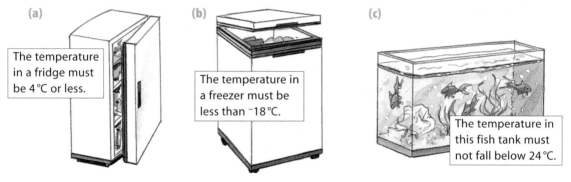

(a) The temperature in a fridge must be 4°C or less.

(b) The temperature in a freezer must be less than ⁻18°C.

(c) The temperature in this fish tank must not fall below 24°C.

C2 Translate this statement into mathematics.
Use w to stand for the weight of hand baggage in kg.

IMPORTANT NOTICE
Hand baggage must not weigh more than 7 kilos.

C3 Write each of the following statements using mathematical symbols.

(a) There are at least 20 pupils in my class.

(Use n for the number of pupils.)

(b) **New Stadium holds at most 35000!**

"Scandal" says Jo Bloggs, Mayor of Bigsville, speaking at this year's bingo binge bash.

The Mayor was also quoted as saying 'Never before in my life have I seen such a huge gathering of people at such an unimportant occasion. If only the general public would put more effort into the exciting opportunities to support their local communities.' Whereas members of the public participating in the bingo binge bash had a fantastic time with the support being overwhelming. Many came to see and experience the atmosphere of the new stadium, which by all accounts, was electric. Fiona Wilkinson is the PR assistant to the m... financial departm... many more occas... welcome to all ag... looking forward...

A local supporter of the annual bingo bash at the new ... has been bigger ... than ever before ... tracting far more ... ople in total than ... evious... ear

(Use s for the number of people the stadium holds.)

C4 Make up a sentence for each of these. Say what the letters stand for.

(a) $n \leq 35$ (b) $p > 100$ (c) $m < 20$

T1 State whether each of the following is true or false.

(a) $9 \geq 10$ (b) $9 \leq 9$ (c) $(^{-}3)^2 < 2$ (d) $0.29 \leq 0.3$ (e) $^{-}2 > ^{-}6$

T2 Write down an inequality for each of these diagrams.

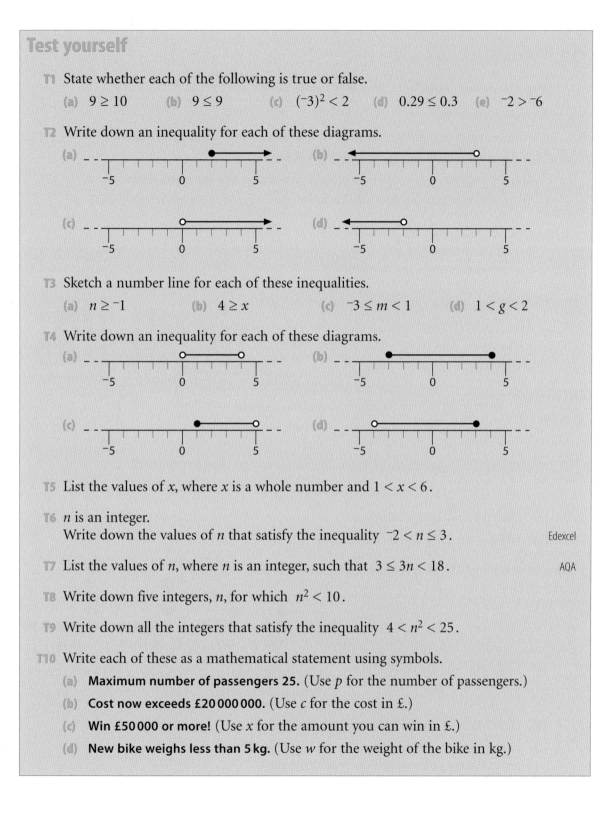

T3 Sketch a number line for each of these inequalities.

(a) $n \geq ^{-}1$ (b) $4 \geq x$ (c) $^{-}3 \leq m < 1$ (d) $1 < g < 2$

T4 Write down an inequality for each of these diagrams.

T5 List the values of x, where x is a whole number and $1 < x < 6$.

T6 n is an integer.
Write down the values of n that satisfy the inequality $^{-}2 < n \leq 3$.   Edexcel

T7 List the values of n, where n is an integer, such that $3 \leq 3n < 18$.   AQA

T8 Write down five integers, n, for which $n^2 < 10$.

T9 Write down all the integers that satisfy the inequality $4 < n^2 < 25$.

T10 Write each of these as a mathematical statement using symbols.

(a) **Maximum number of passengers 25.** (Use p for the number of passengers.)

(b) **Cost now exceeds £20 000 000.** (Use c for the cost in £.)

(c) **Win £50 000 or more!** (Use x for the amount you can win in £.)

(d) **New bike weighs less than 5 kg.** (Use w for the weight of the bike in kg.)

22 Sequences

You should know how to find the value of simple expressions such as $10 - 2n$, $n^2 + 3$.

This work will help you

- form sequences of numbers such as odd, even, square and triangle numbers
- find and use rules to continue a variety of sequences
- find and use rules for the nth term of linear and simple non-linear sequences
- find a sequence from a context, find a rule for the nth term and explain how you did so

A Sequences from shapes
level 5

These designs are made by arranging counters in squares.

design 1   design 2   design 3   design 4   design 5

The number of counters in each design is shown in this table.

Design number	1	2	3	4	5
Number of counters	1	4	9	16	25

The numbers in the sequence 1, 4, 9, 16, 25, ... are called **square numbers**.

A1 (a) Find the 6th square number.

(b) What is the 20th square number?

A2 These designs are made by arranging counters in L-shapes.

design 1   design 2   design 3   design 4   design 5

(a) Copy and complete this table for these designs.

Design number	1	2	3	4	5
Number of counters	1				

(b) How many counters are in the 6th design?

(c) How many counters are needed to make the 15th design? Explain how you worked out your answer.

(d) Which design uses 99 counters?

(e) Is it possible to make one of these designs with 40 counters? Explain your answer.

A3 These designs are made by arranging counters in triangles.

 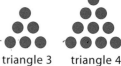

triangle 1   triangle 2   triangle 3   triangle 4

(a) Draw the next two designs.

(b) Copy and complete this table.

Design number	1	2	3	4	5	6
Number of counters			6			

(c) The numbers of counters are called **triangle numbers**.
So, for example, the third triangle number is 6.

List the first ten triangle numbers.

A4 These lattice designs are all models of salt crystals.
They are cube-shaped.

(a) Work out the number of ions in
crystal 3 without counting them all.

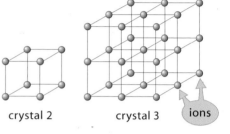

crystal 1   crystal 2   crystal 3   ions

(b) Copy and complete this table.

Crystal number	1	2	3
Number of ions		8	

(c) Without drawing, work out how many ions will be in crystal 4.

(d) The numbers of ions are called **cubic numbers** or cubes.
So, for example, the second cubic number is 8.

What is the 10th cubic number?

B Continuing linear sequences

In a sequence of numbers, there is often a rule to go from one term to the next.
These are some examples.

Sequence	Rule
8, 16, 24, 32, 40, …	Add 8 to the previous term
8, 16, 32, 64, 128, …	Multiply the previous term by 2
4, 5, 7, 10, 14, …	Add 1, then add 2, then add 3 and so on
4, 5, 9, 14, 23, …	Add the previous two terms together

Sequences where the rule is to **add or subtract the same amount** each time are **linear**.

B1 A sequence of numbers begins   5, 9, 13, ...
The rule to continue this sequence is 'add 4 to the previous term'.

(a)   What is the next term?   (b)   What is the 8th term?

(c)   Is the sequence linear?

B2 A sequence of numbers begins   5, 9, 17, ...
The rule to continue this sequence is 'multiply the previous term by 2 and subtract 1'.

(a)   What is the next term?   (b)   What is the 6th term?

(c)   Is the sequence linear?

B3 (a)   Write down the next two numbers in this sequence   4, 7, 10, 13, 16, ...

(b)   Write down a rule to find the next two numbers.

B4 Write down the next two terms in the sequence   0, 2, 6, 14, ...

B5 A sequence of numbers begins   3, 4, 6, 9, 13, 18, ...

(a)   Describe a rule to go from one term to the next.

(b)   Using your rule, what is the 7th term of this sequence?

(c)   Is the sequence linear?

B6 For each of the following sequences

- describe a rule to go from one term to the next
- find the 8th term

(a)   1, 8, 15, 22, 29, ...   (b)   35, 30, 25, 20, 15, ...   (c)   1.5, 3, 6, 12, 24, ...

(d)   800, 400, 200, 100, ...   (e) $\frac{1}{9}, \frac{1}{3}$, 1, 3, 9, ...   (f)   1, 4, 13, 40, 121, ...

B7 The first four terms of a sequence are   1, 4, 7, 10, ...
Explain how you can work out the 30th term of this sequence.

B8 Copy each sequence and fill in the missing numbers.

(a)   5, 7, 9, __ , 13, __ , 17, 19, ...   (b)   1, 3, 7, 13, 21, 31, __ , 57, __ , ...

(c)   __ , 0.5, 1, 2, 4, 8, __ , 32, ...   (d)   1, 1, 2, 3, 5, 8, 13, __ , 34, 55, __ , ...

(e)   1, 5, 13, 29, __ , 125, __ , ...

B9 Each sequence below is linear.
Copy each sequence and fill in the missing numbers.

(a)   4, 6, __ , __ , __ , 14, ...   (b)   25, __ , 19, __ , 13, 10, ...

(c)   1, __ , 11, __ , 21, __ , ...   (d)   __ , 10, __ , __ , 19, __ , ...

*B10 Find the missing expression in each linear sequence below.

(a) x, $x + 4$, _____ , $x + 12$, ...   (b) a, $a + b$, $a + 2b$, _____ , ...

(c) $n - 5$, $n - 3$, $n - 1$, _____ , ...   (d) x, $x - y$, _____ , $x - 3y$, ...

We can work out any term of a sequence if we have an expression for its *n*th term.

Example

The *n*th term of a sequence is $2n + 5$. Find the first six terms.

The 1st term is $2 \times 1 + 5 = \mathbf{7}$
The 2nd term is $2 \times 2 + 5 = \mathbf{9}$
The 3rd term is $2 \times 3 + 5 = \mathbf{11}$ … and so on.

We can show our results in a table.

Term numbers (*n*)	1	2	3	4	5	6	…
Terms of the sequence ($2n + 5$)	7	9	11	13	15	17	…

C1 Linear sequences can be found on this grid.
Two are shown on the diagram.

44	34	24	14	4	3	6	9	12
40	30	5	20	10	11	5	8	1
44	37	30	23	16	9	2	7	3
4	11	23	21	22	12	1	6	9
1	7	26	20	28	9	8	5	0
3	31	10	15	34	30	12	4	8
36	6	11	13	40	0	1	3	2

(a) Find seven more linear sequences that have four terms or more.

Write down each sequence as an **increasing** sequence and find its next term.

(b) The expressions below give the *n*th terms of these sequences.
Match each expression to its sequence.

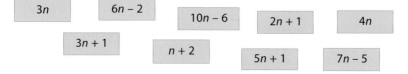

$3n$ $6n - 2$ $10n - 6$ $2n + 1$ $4n$

$3n + 1$ $n + 2$ $5n + 1$ $7n - 5$

C2 An expression for the *n*th term of a sequence is $4n - 3$.
Work out the fourth and fifth terms of the sequence.

C3 The *n*th term of a sequence is $2n + 3$.

(a) Write down the first six terms of the sequence.

(b) Calculate the 100th term.

C4 The *n*th terms of six different sequences are:

A $7n - 2$ **B** $10 - n$ **C** $\frac{1}{2}n - 3$ **D** $n^2 + 1$ **E** $\frac{60}{n}$ **F** 2^n

(a) Calculate the first five terms of each sequence.

(b) Calculate the 20th term of each sequence.

(c) Which of these sequences are linear?

Find the *n*th term of the linear sequence   3, 7, 11, 15, 19, …

Term numbers (*n*)	1	2	3	4	5	…
Terms of the sequence	3	7	11	15	19	…

+4　+4　+4　+4

The differences are all 4 so the expression begins 4*n*.

Term numbers (*n*)	1	2	3	4	5	…
4*n*	4	8	12	16	20	
Terms of the sequence	3	7	11	15	19	…

– 1

To get from 4 to 3 you can subtract 1. This works for all terms.

So an expression for the *n*th term of the linear sequence   3, 7, 11, 15, 19, …   is $4n - 1$.

D1　For each of the following sequences

- find an expression for the *n*th term
- use your expression to work out the 50th term

(a)　4, 7, 10, 13, 16, …　　(b)　1, 10, 19, 28, 37, …　　(c)　2, 7, 12, 17, 22, …

(d)　4, 9, 14, 19, 24, …　　(e)　3, 5, 7, 9, 11, …

D2　This diagram shows house numbers on North Street.

2　4　6　8　10

(a)　What is the number of the 15th house?

(b)　Find an expression for the number of the *n*th house on North Street.

This diagram shows house numbers on South Street.

1　3　5　7　9

(c)　What is the number of the 10th house?

(d)　Find an expression for the number of the *n*th house on South Street.

(e)　What are the house numbers of the 50th house in each street?

D3 (a) Copy and complete this table for the linear sequence 40, 38, 36, 34, 32, …

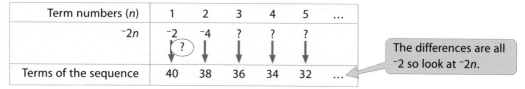

Term numbers (n)	1	2	3	4	5	…
−2n	−2	−4	?	?	?	
Terms of the sequence	40	38	36	34	32	…

The differences are all −2 so look at −2n.

(b) What is an expression for the *n*th term of the sequence?

(c) Calculate the 20th term in the sequence.

D4 For each of the following sequences, find an expression for the *n*th term.

(a) 30, 28, 26, 24, 22, …   **(b)** 40, 37, 34, 31, 28, …

(c) 33, 28, 23, 18, 13, …   **(d)** 60, 54, 48, 42, 36, …

E The *n*th term of other sequences

Each of the expressions below gives the *n*th term of a sequence.

- Investigate these sequences.
  What do you notice about the differences each time?

A n^2 **B** $n^2 + 4$ **C** $n^2 - 2$ **D** $2n^2$ **E** $2n^2 + 3$ **F** $5n^2$

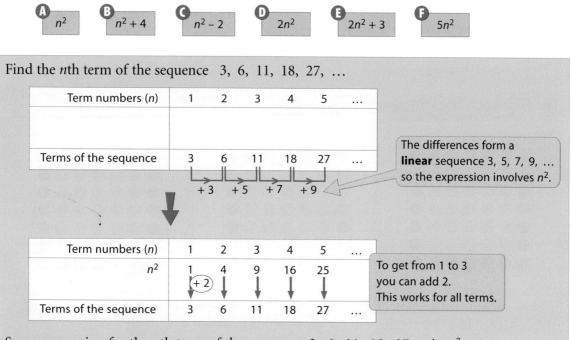

Find the *n*th term of the sequence 3, 6, 11, 18, 27, …

Term numbers (n)	1	2	3	4	5	…
Terms of the sequence	3	6	11	18	27	…

+3   +5   +7   +9

The differences form a **linear** sequence 3, 5, 7, 9, … so the expression involves n^2.

Term numbers (n)	1	2	3	4	5	…
n^2	1	4	9	16	25	
Terms of the sequence	3	6	11	18	27	…

(+2)

To get from 1 to 3 you can add 2. This works for all terms.

So an expression for the *n*th term of the sequence 3, 6, 11, 18, 27 … is $n^2 + 2$.

E1 A sequence of numbers begins 2, 5, 10, 17, 26, 37, …

(a) What is the next term in the sequence?

(b) Explain how you can tell that the sequence is not linear.

(c) What is an expression for the *n*th term of this sequence?

E2 **(a)** A sequence of numbers begins   4, 7, 12, 19, 28, ...
What is an expression for the nth term of this sequence?

   (b) Calculate the 15th term.

E3 **(a)** A sequence of numbers begins   3, 12, 27, 48, 75, ...
What is an expression for the nth term of this sequence?

   (b) Calculate the 10th term.

E4 **(a)** A sequence of numbers begins   2, 8, 18, 32, 50, 72, ...
What is an expression for the nth term of this sequence?

   (b) What is the nth term of the sequence   3, 9, 19, 33, 51, 73, ...?

E5 For each of the following sequences, find an expression for the nth term.

   (a) 0, 3, 8, 15, 24, ...   **(b)** 11, 14, 19, 26, 35, ...

   (c) 4, 16, 36, 64, ...   **(d)** 5, 17, 37, 65, ...

F Ways of seeing

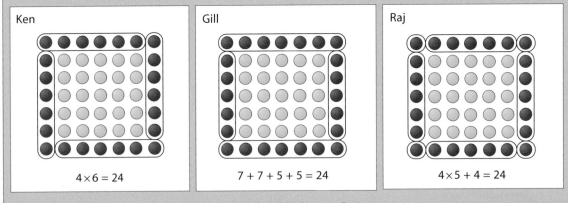

Some disco light units are designed as shown.
They use red and yellow lights.

design 1

design 2

design 3

The diagrams below show how some students counted the red lights in design 5.

Ken	Gill	Raj
$4 \times 6 = 24$	$7 + 7 + 5 + 5 = 24$	$4 \times 5 + 4 = 24$

They each found a rule for the number of red lights in design n.

$r = (n + 2) + (n + 2) + n + n$ $r = 4n + 4$ $r = 4(n + 1)$

- Who do you think found each rule?
- Show that all three rules are equivalent.
- What is the rule for the number of yellow lights?

F1 Here is another design for square light units.

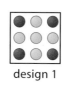
design 1

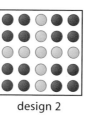
design 2

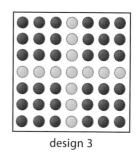
design 3

(a) Draw a diagram to show design 4.

(b) For design 4, what is the number of yellow lights?

(c) How many yellow lights would you need for design 10?

(d) Find a rule for the number of yellow lights in design n. Explain how you found your rule.

(e) How many yellow lights would you need for design 50?

(f) Find a rule for the number of red lights in design n.

F2 Here are some rectangular units.

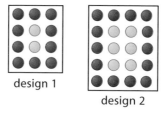
design 1
design 2

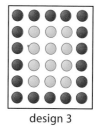
design 3

(a) For design 3, what is the number of red lights?

(b) How many red lights would you need for design 8?

(c) Find a rule for the number of red lights in design n. Explain how you found your rule.

(d) How many red lights would you need for design 100?

(e) Find a rule for the number of yellow lights in design n.

F3 Here are some triangular units.

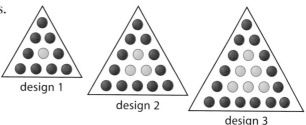
design 1
design 2
design 3

(a) Find a rule for the number of red lights in design n. Explain how you found your rule.

(b) How many red lights would you need for design 100?

G Ways of seeing further

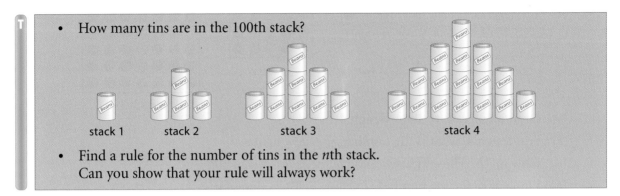

- How many tins are in the 100th stack?

stack 1   stack 2   stack 3   stack 4

- Find a rule for the number of tins in the *n*th stack.
  Can you show that your rule will always work?

*G1 For each set of patterns below
  - draw pattern 5
  - find a rule for the number of black tiles in the *n*th pattern
  - find a rule for the number of white tiles in the *n*th pattern

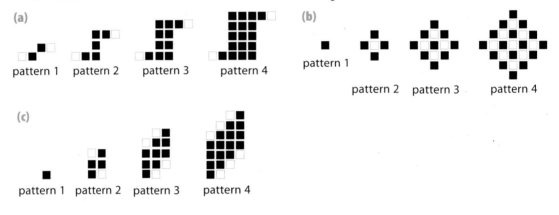

(a)

pattern 1   pattern 2   pattern 3   pattern 4

(b)

pattern 1   pattern 2   pattern 3   pattern 4

(c)

pattern 1   pattern 2   pattern 3   pattern 4

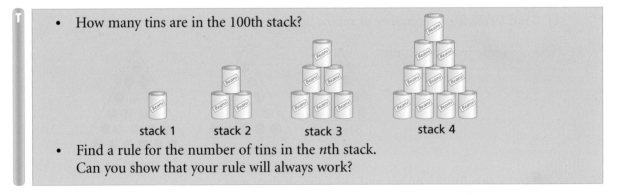

- How many tins are in the 100th stack?

stack 1   stack 2   stack 3   stack 4

- Find a rule for the number of tins in the *n*th stack.
  Can you show that your rule will always work?

*G2 The diagrams below show how to draw a 'mystic rose'.

This is a 7-point mystic rose.

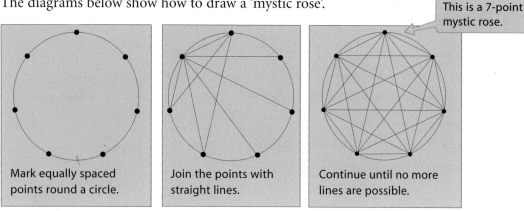

Mark equally spaced points round a circle.

Join the points with straight lines.

Continue until no more lines are possible.

(a) Draw three different mystic roses.
How many straight lines are in each of your designs?

(b) How many lines would be in a 20-point mystic rose?

(c) Find a rule for the number of lines in a n-point mystic rose.

Test yourself

T1 Write down the next two terms in the sequence 10, 11, 13, 16, 20, ...

T2 (a) Find the eighth term of the sequence whose nth term is $4n - 1$.

(b) Find the nth term of the sequence whose first four terms are

  2 8 14 20

OCR

T3 Each of these patterns uses black tiles.

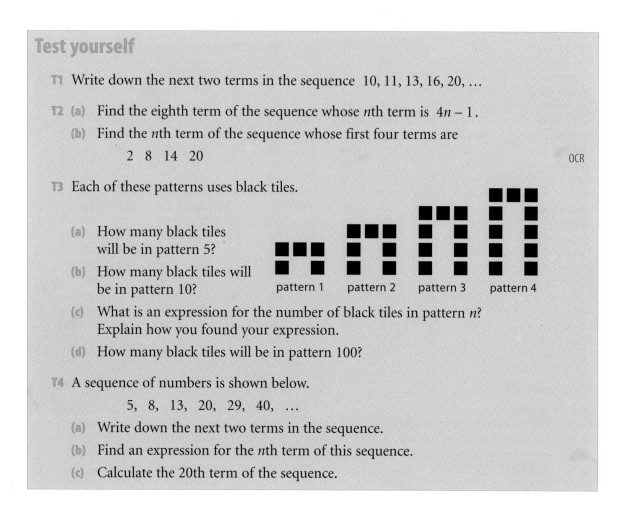

(a) How many black tiles will be in pattern 5?

(b) How many black tiles will be in pattern 10?

pattern 1   pattern 2   pattern 3   pattern 4

(c) What is an expression for the number of black tiles in pattern n?
Explain how you found your expression.

(d) How many black tiles will be in pattern 100?

T4 A sequence of numbers is shown below.

  5, 8, 13, 20, 29, 40, ...

(a) Write down the next two terms in the sequence.

(b) Find an expression for the nth term of this sequence.

(c) Calculate the 20th term of the sequence.

23 Paired data

You will revise how to

- draw a scatter diagram using pairs of data
- recognise the different types of correlation

This work will help you

- draw a line of best fit on a scatter diagram
- use a line of best fit to estimate results

A Scatter diagrams and correlation level 6

Car database

Make	Price	m.p.g.	Engine	Power	Speed	Boot	Tank	Length	Width	Height	Weight
Porsche Turbo	98 000	18	3600	408	181	123	77	425	177	129	1500
Aston Martin DB7	83 000	19	3250	335	159	174	89	465	183	124	1700
Honda Legend	34 000	23	3500	202	134	450	68	498	181	143	1650
Saab 9000	32 000	32	3000	225	149	623	66	476	178	142	1440
Citroen XM	28 000	40	2500	130	124	456	80	470	180	140	1570
Peugeot 406	24 500	25	3000	191	141	430	70	473	177	141	1540
Toyota MR2	21 500	34	2000	168	137	187	55	418	170	123	1280
Ford Scorpio	20 000	32	2000	114	120	465	70	483	188	139	1480
Mercedes C180	20 000	33	1800	122	120	430	62	449	172	141	1340
Renault Espace	19 500	27	2000	115	106	510	78	443	179	169	730
Volvo V40	16 000	33	2000	140	130	369	60	448	172	139	1270
Rover 618	15 000	42	1800	113	121	397	65	465	172	138	1260
Audi A3	14 400	37	1600	99	117	350	55	415	174	142	1090
Ford Mondeo	13 800	39	1600	89	112	470	62	456	175	137	1220
Vauxhall Tigra	12 600	41	1400	89	118	215	46	392	181	134	1050
Peugeot 306	11 100	42	1400	75	102	340	60	399	169	138	1010
Ford Escort	10 800	40	1300	59	95	380	55	414	188	135	980
Toyota Starlet	10 300	44	1300	73	102	214	45	374	164	140	840
Daewoo Nexia	8800	40	1500	75	101	390	50	426	166	139	1000
Ford Fiesta	8400	44	1300	59	96	250	42	383	163	132	950
Renault Clio	8200	46	1100	60	100	265	43	370	162	139	850
Citroen Saxo	7400	46	1100	60	101	280	40	372	160	137	800
Nissan Micra	7300	47	1000	59	93	206	38	370	178	142	835
Suzuki Swift	6800	51	1000	52	90	250	36	373	160	135	780

Key to columns

Price	New list price in pounds
Engine	Engine capacity in cubic centimetres (c.c.)
Speed	Maximum speed of car in miles per hour in test conditions
Tank	Amount of fuel in a full tank in litres
Width	Width of car in centimetres
Weight	Weight of car in kilograms

m.p.g.	Average fuel economy in miles per gallon
Power	Power of engine in brake horse power (b.h.p.)
Boot	Capacity of the boot in litres
Length	Total length of car in centimetres
Height	Height of car in centimetres

T Opposite is a database about a selection of different models of cars.
This is a scatter diagram showing the engine size and top speed of these cars.

- Describe the relationship between the engine size and top speed of these cars.

- Are there any cars that have a low top speed for the size of their engine?

- Are there any cars that have a high top speed for the size of their engine?

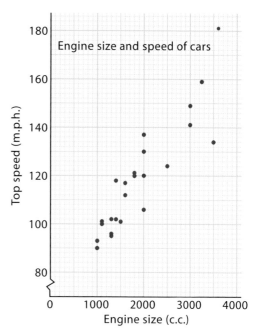

A1 (a) Draw a scatter diagram with engine size on the horizontal scale and power on the vertical scale.

(b) Is there any correlation between the power and the engine size? If so, what type of correlation is this?

A2 (a) Draw a scatter diagram with engine size on the horizontal scale and fuel economy (m.p.g.) on the vertical scale.

(b) Describe any correlation between the fuel economy and the engine size.

(c) Why do you think these two variables are related in this way?

A3 (a) Draw a scatter diagram with height on the horizontal axis and fuel economy on the vertical axis. Use a jagged line on the horizontal scale to show the scale does not start at zero.

(b) Describe the relationship between the heights of the cars and their fuel economy.

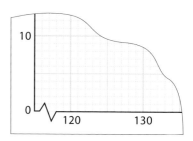

A4 (a) Draw a scatter diagram with the length of the car on the horizontal axis and the size of the boot on the vertical scale. Use these scales.

(b) Describe any correlation shown by the scatter diagram.

(c) Does the diagram support a statement in a magazine that longer cars usually have bigger boots?

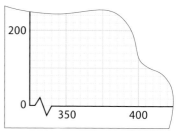

Forensic scientists sometimes have to decide what someone looked like by examining individual bones.

This scatter diagram shows the heights of some males and the length of their femur (thigh bone).

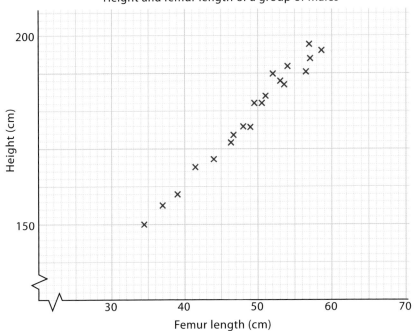

Height and femur length of a group of males

- What correlation is there between femur length and height?

- Roughly how long would you expect a femur to be on a male who is 180 cm tall? How accurate do you think your estimate is?

- Police find a male femur in a pit. It is 42 cm long. How tall would you estimate its owner was? How accurate do you think your estimate is?

- What would you estimate the height of a male to be if his femur is 65 cm long? How accurate do you think this estimate is?

When points on a scatter diagram show strong correlation, it can be useful to draw a straight line through them. This is called a **line of best fit**.

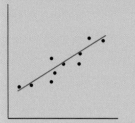 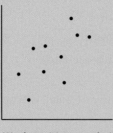  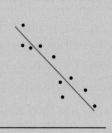

Strong positive correlation – worth drawing a line of best fit

Weak positive correlation – **not** worth drawing a line of best fit

Weak negative correlation – **not** worth drawing a line of best fit

Strong negative correlation – worth drawing a line of best fit

You should draw a line of best fit to look like a 'spine' for the points, with roughly the same number of points on each side.

The line can be used to estimate new values. But extending the line beyond the given points to estimate values is less reliable.

B1 An ice cream seller records the maximum daily temperature and the number of ice creams he sells each day.

His results for a period of ten days are shown in the table.

Maximum temperature, °C	22	26	25	27	25	20	24	26	28	27
Number of ice creams sold	85	102	94	103	92	72	89	100	107	105

(a) Draw a scatter diagram for these results.

(b) Draw a line of best fit.

(c) The weather forecast for the next day gives a maximum temperature of 23 °C. Use your line of best fit to estimate the number of ice creams sold on the next day.

B2 Eight students take two maths tests, one in the morning and one in the afternoon. The table below shows the eight pairs of marks.

Morning test mark	49	74	62	40	27	32	82	78
Afternoon test mark	46	68	60	35	25	26	74	72

(a) Draw a scatter diagram for this data.

(b) Draw a line of best fit.

(c) A ninth student scored 56 in the morning test, but was absent for the afternoon test. Use your line of best fit to estimate a mark for this student in the afternoon test.

B3 This data shows the engine size and the fuel economy of a range of petrol cars.

Engine size (litres)	4.0	3.5	3.0	2.0	1.7	1.6	1.4	1.3	1.2	1.1	1.0
Fuel economy (m.p.g.)	18	25	32	34	35	37	41	44	43	46	49

(a) Show this information on a scatter diagram.
Draw a line of best fit on your scatter diagram.

(b) Describe the correlation between the engine size and fuel economy of these cars.

(c) Use your graph to estimate the fuel economy of a car whose engine capacity is 2.5 litres.

(d) What capacity engine would you estimate would be needed to obtain a fuel economy of more than 50 m.p.g?

(e) A Lamborghini Diablo has a 5.7 litre engine.
What fuel economy would you expect from this car?
How reliable do you think this estimate is?

In an experiment some students add weights to a strong elastic band.
They measure the length of the elastic band with each weight.
These are their results.

Weight (g)	50	100	150	200	250	300	350	400
Length (cm)	15.6	21.8	23.8	28.5	30.8	36.6	39.7	46.1

Since the weights are controlled by the person doing the experiment, correlation does not apply.
A line of best fit can still be drawn for this data and used to estimate results.

B4 (a) Plot the data for weights and lengths on a graph.
Add a line of best fit.

(b) Estimate the length of the elastic band if a weight of 225 g was used.

(c) Estimate the length of the elastic band before any weight was added.

(d) Estimate the length if a weight of 450 g was used.

(e) If your graph was large enough could you reliably estimate the length of the elastic band if a 1 kg weight was used?

 By searching on the web you can find many sets of paired data that are worth investigating for correlation. Where you find correlation you can consider whether it would be useful to draw a line of best fit.

 By putting paired data on a spreadsheet in two adjacent columns with each pair in its own row, you can use the spreadsheet's charting facility to draw a scatter diagram quickly and accurately.

c Interpreting scatter diagrams

This data shows the weight in kilograms and the top speed of the cars in the database.

- What type of correlation is there between the top speed and weight of these cars?

- It has been suggested that lighter cars go faster. Does this graph support this hypothesis?

- Can you suggest an explanation for the correlation here?

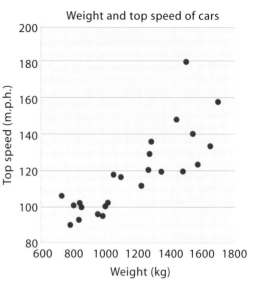

Weight and top speed of cars

C1 (a) Draw a scatter diagram using the data on page 168, with the tank size on the horizontal axis and the top speed on the vertical axis.
The horizontal scale should go from 30 to 100.
The vertical scale should go from 80 to 200.

(b) Describe any correlation shown by the graph.
What might explain it?

C2 This data shows the age and shoulder height of 20 bull elephants from a game reserve in Kenya.

Age (years)	41	9	19	38	3	6	55	10	2	27	1	29	21	15	12	17	5	33	32	10
Height (cm)	293	215	257	287	135	165	317	227	108	272	95	287	260	218	237	238	168	270	290	201

(a) Plot this data on a scatter diagram.

(b) Can you use the graph to estimate the height of a 50-year-old bull elephant?

(c) Describe how age and height are related.
Would it be sensible to draw a line of best fit in this case?
Give your reasons.

A likely story!

In a survey in Sweden a researcher found there was a good positive correlation between the number of storks nesting in a village and the number of babies born in the village.

What might explain this?

T1 The table shows the number of units of electricity used in heating a house on
ten different days and the average temperature for each day.

Average temperature (°C)	6	2	0	6	3	5	10	8	9	12
Units of electricity used	28	38	41	34	31	31	22	25	23	22

(a) Copy and complete the scatter graph to show the information in the table.
The first six points have been plotted for you.

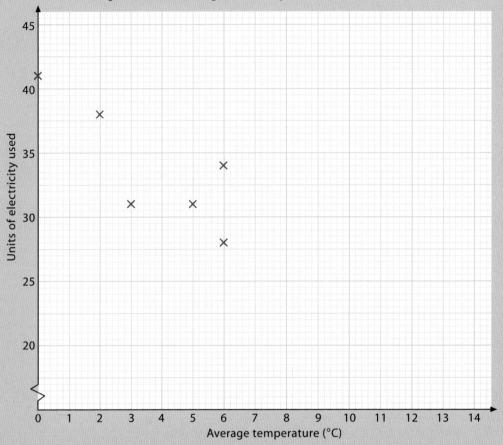

(b) Describe the **correlation** between the number of units of electricity used and
the average daily temperature.

(c) Draw a line of best fit on your scatter graph.

(d) Use your line of best fit to estimate

(i) the average temperature if 35 units of electricity are used

(ii) the units of electricity used if the average temperature is 7°C

Edexcel

24 Working with coordinates

You will revise

- symmetry
- calculating the area of a triangle, parallelogram and circle
- the equation of a straight line
- calculating the length of a line segment using Pythagoras's theorem

This work will help you

- find the mid-point of a line segment
- solve problems involving coordinates

A Shapes on a coordinate grid
level 6

A1 (a) Draw a pair of axes, each numbered from ‾5 to 10.
Plot the points P (‾4, 3), Q (‾2, 7) and R (10, 1). Join P to Q and Q to R.

(b) Plot the point S so that PQRS is a rectangle.
What are the coordinates of S?

(c) Draw the lines of symmetry on the rectangle.
What are the coordinates of the point where the lines of symmetry intersect?

A2 (a) On centimetre squared paper draw a pair of axes, each numbered from ‾6 to 6.
Plot the points A (5, 2), B (‾4, 5) and C (‾5, 2).

(b) Plot the point D so that ABCD is a kite.
What are the coordinates of D?

(c) Work out the area of the kite.

(d) Plot the point E so that ABCE is a rectangle.
What are the coordinates of E?

(e) What is the area of the rectangle?

A3 (a) Plot the points D (5, 1), E (1, 3) and F (8, 5) on a grid.

(b) Plot a fourth point G that makes DEFG a parallelogram.

(c) What symmetry does the shape DEFG have?

A4 (a) Draw a pair of axes, each numbered from ‾4 to 7.
Plot the points K (‾2, ‾1), L (2, 1) and M (6, ‾1).

(b) Plot the point N so that KLMN is a rhombus and write down the coordinates of N.

(c) Draw the lines of symmetry on the rhombus.
Write down the equation of each line.

This number line shows the line segment with end-points 1 and 9.
The **mid-point** of this line segment is 5.

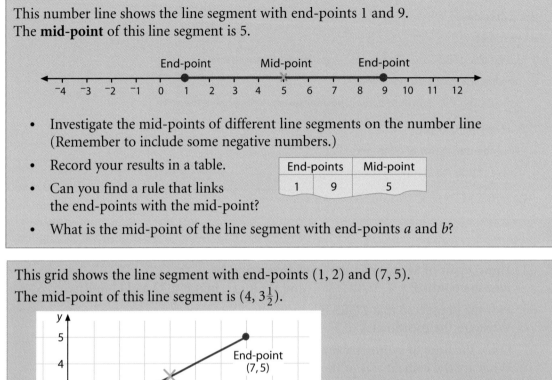

- Investigate the mid-points of different line segments on the number line
  (Remember to include some negative numbers.)

- Record your results in a table.

End-points		Mid-point
1	9	5

- Can you find a rule that links
  the end-points with the mid-point?

- What is the mid-point of the line segment with end-points a and b?

This grid shows the line segment with end-points $(1, 2)$ and $(7, 5)$.
The mid-point of this line segment is $(4, 3\frac{1}{2})$.

- Investigate the mid-points of different line segments on a coordinate grid.

- Can you find a rule that links the end-points with the mid-point?

B1 Which number is half-way between each of these pairs?

   (a) 8 and 12   (b) 3 and 11   (c) 1 and 8   (d) ⁻2 and 6

   (e) $1\frac{1}{2}$ and $7\frac{1}{2}$ (f) ⁻1 and 7   (g) ⁻4 and ⁻2   (h) ⁻9 and ⁻3

B2 8 is the mid-point of a line that has 3 as one of its end-points.
   What is the other end-point?

B3 What is the mid-point of the line segment AB?

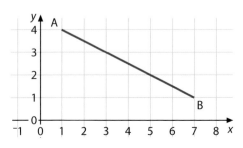

B4 Work out the mid-points of the line segments joining these pairs of points.

(a) $(0, 2)$ and $(6, 8)$ (b) $(1, 5)$ and $(11, 7)$ (c) $(^-2, 5)$ and $(4, 1)$

(d) $(^-3, 6)$ and $(3, 2)$ (e) $(1, 9)$ and $(8, 1)$ (f) $(^-2, 8)$ and $(10, 9)$

B5 $(2, 3)$ is the mid-point of a line segment that has $(5, ^-1)$ as one of its end-points. What is the other end-point?

c Mixed questions

In each question, the coordinates refer to a square centimetre grid.

C1 The line segment AB is one edge of a parallelogram ABCD.
The point A has coordinates $(0, 3)$.
The point B has coordinates $(6, 5)$.
The diagonals of the parallelogram cross at the point $(3, 2)$.

(a) Draw the whole parallelogram.

(b) Write down the coordinates of points C and D.

(c) Calculate the area of the parallelogram.

C2 M is the mid-point of the line segment KL.
The point K has coordinates $(^-2, ^-6)$.
The point L has coordinates $(4, 12)$.

(a) Find the equation of the line through M that is parallel to the y-axis.

(b) Find the equation of the line through M that is parallel to the x-axis.

C3 The line segment XY is the diameter of a circle.
The point X has coordinates $(^-1, 0)$.
The point Y has coordinates $(5, 8)$.

(a) What are the coordinates of the centre of the circle?

(b) Use Pythagoras's theorem to calculate the length of XY.

(c) Calculate the area of the circle, correct to two decimal places.

C4 (a) Plot and join the points A $(5, 9)$, B $(13, 10)$ and C $(1, 2)$.

(b) (i) Calculate the length of AB.

(ii) Calculate the length of AC.

(iii) What is the special name for triangle ABC?

(c) (i) Plot M, the mid-point of BC, and write down its coordinates.

(ii) Explain how you know that $\angle AMB = 90°$.

(d) Write down the coordinates of D so that shape ABDC is a rhombus.

C5 The diagram shows a triangle PQR.
P, Q and R have coordinates (⁻2, 4), (5, 3) and (⁻1, ⁻1.5) respectively.
X is a point on RQ with coordinates (1, 0).

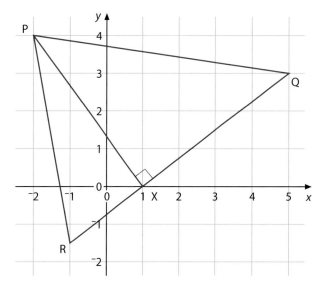

(a) Calculate the length PX.

(b) Calculate the length QR.

(c) Find the area of triangle PQR.

C6 (a) Draw a pair of axes, each numbered from ⁻6 to 8.
Plot and join the points A (1, 2) and B (4, 5).

A and B are vertices of a square ABCD.
Points C and D are on the line $y = x - 5$.

(b) Draw the line and plot the points C and D.
Give the coordinates of points C and D.

(c) Find the area of the square.

(d) Find the area of a circle that passes through A, B, C and D.

C7 ABCD is a parallelogram whose vertices are all above the x-axis.

- A and B are points on the line $y = 2x + 1$.
- The point D has coordinates (2, 1).
- The edge AD is parallel to the x-axis.
- The area of the parallelogram is 8 cm².

Draw the parallelogram in the correct position on a coordinate grid.

T1 A is the point (4, 2), B is the point (4, 0) and C is the point ($^-$1, $^-$3).

ABCD is a kite.

On a suitable set of axes, draw the kite ABCD and write down the coordinates of D.

T2

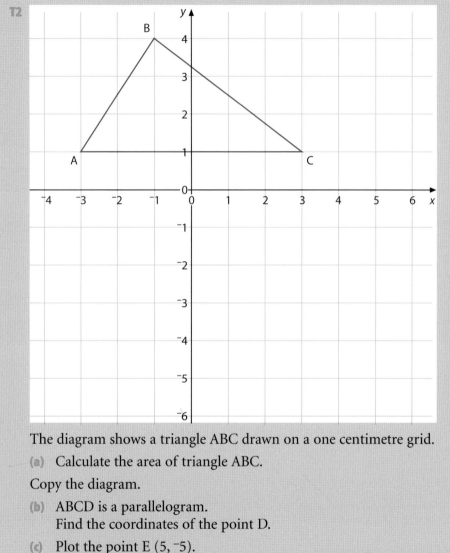

The diagram shows a triangle ABC drawn on a one centimetre grid.

(a) Calculate the area of triangle ABC.

Copy the diagram.

(b) ABCD is a parallelogram.
Find the coordinates of the point D.

(c) Plot the point E (5, $^-$5).
What kind of quadrilateral is ABCE?

OCR

T3 The line segment AB has end-points A ($^-$5, 6) and B (10, $^-$2).

(a) Draw suitable axes and show these points on the grid.

(b) Find the coordinates of the mid-point of AB.

(c) Find the length of the line segment AB.

25 Brackets and equations

You should know how to

- simplify an expression such as $1 - 2x + 6 - 3x$ to give $7 - 5x$
- multiply out brackets such as $2(3x + 4)$ to give $6x + 8$
- simplify divisions such as $\frac{8n - 2}{2}$ to give $4n - 1$
- solve linear equations such as $6 + 3x = 10 - x$

This work will help you

- add and subtract expressions with brackets such as $(5 + 4x) - (3x + 4)$ and $4(3x - 5) - 2(4x - 1)$
- use algebra to prove statements like 'The result for this puzzle will always be 4.'
- solve complex linear equations

A Adding and subtracting expressions in brackets

To **add** an expression in brackets you can remove the brackets and then simplify.

Examples

$100 + (6 + 2)$	$100 + (6 - 2)$	$6 + (2p + 1)$	$(3n + 5) + (n - 6)$
$= 100 + 6 + 2$	$= 100 + 6 - 2$	$= 6 + 2p + 1$	$= 3n + 5 + n - 6$
$= 108$	$= 104$	$= 7 + 2p$	$= 4n - 1$

To **subtract** an expression in brackets you need to be careful with signs.

Examples

$100 - (6 + 2)$	$100 - (6 - 2)$	$6 - (2p + 1)$	$(3n + 5) - (n - 6)$
$= 100 - 6 - 2$	$= 100 - 6 + 2$	$= 6 - 2p - 1$	$= 3n + 5 - n + 6$
$= 92$	$= 96$	$= 5 - 2p$	$= 2n + 11$

- Can you explain why removing the brackets here changes the sign inside them?

A1 Simplify the following expressions.

(a) $6z + (2z - 3)$ (b) $(y + 5) + (2y - 1)$ (c) $(3x + 2) + (x - 6)$

(d) $(10 + w) + (5 - 2w)$ (e) $(2v - 1) + (5v - 3)$ (f) $(6 - u) + (2 - 3u)$

A2 Simplify the following expressions.

(a) $7t - (2t + 9)$ (b) $10 - (s - 1)$ (c) $3r - (5 + 2r)$

(d) $10q - (3 - 2q)$ (e) $(8p + 6) - (5 + 3p)$ (f) $(2n + 1) - (9 - 2n)$

A3 Find four pairs of equivalent expressions.

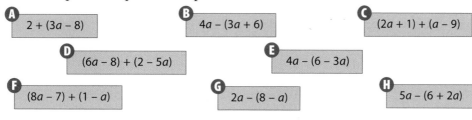

Ⓐ $2 + (3a - 8)$

Ⓑ $4a - (3a + 6)$

Ⓒ $(2a + 1) + (a - 9)$

Ⓓ $(6a - 8) + (2 - 5a)$

Ⓔ $4a - (6 - 3a)$

Ⓕ $(8a - 7) + (1 - a)$

Ⓖ $2a - (8 - a)$

Ⓗ $5a - (6 + 2a)$

A4 Simplify the following expressions.

(a) $(m + 3) + (5m - 9)$ (b) $10k - (3k - 8)$ (c) $(6j + 9) - (4j + 5)$

(d) $(7h - 3) + (5 - 2h)$ (e) $(7g - 3) - (5 - 2g)$ (f) $(f + 2) - (5 - f)$

(g) $(9 - 3e) - (7 + 8e)$ (h) $(5d - 6) - (3d - 5)$ (i) $(5c - 6) + (3c - 5)$

(j) $(10 - 5b) + (2 - 3b)$ (k) $(10 - 5a) - (2 - 3a)$ (l) $(6x + 3) - (7x + 1)$

A5 Solve the puzzle on sheet HT–2.

*A6 (a) Try some numbers for this puzzle and describe what happens.

(b) Copy and complete the algebra box to explain how the puzzle works.

Puzzle

Think of a number

• Add 5

• Subtract **from** 30

• Add the number you first thought of

What is the result?

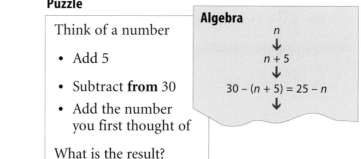

Algebra

n
↓
$n + 5$
↓
$30 - (n + 5) = 25 - n$
↓

*A7 For each puzzle below,

(i) try some numbers and describe what happens

(ii) use algebra to explain how the puzzle works

(a)
Think of a number

• Multiply by 3

• Add 9

• Subtract from 12

• Divide by 3

• Add the number you first thought of

What is the result?

(b)
Think of a number

• Subtract from 20

• Multiply by 2

• Subtract from 100

• Divide by 2

• Subtract 30

What is the result?

(c)
Think of a number

• Subtract 1

• Multiply by 4

• Subtract from 40

• Divide by 4

• Add the number you first thought of

What is the result?

It is often a good idea to multiply out any brackets and simplify divisions before sorting out any signs.

Examples

$(3n + 5) - 2(n + 6)$

$= (3n + 5) - (2n + 12)$

$= 3n + 5 - 2n - 12$

$= n - 7$

$2(5n - 4) - 3(2n - 6)$

$= (10n - 8) - (6n - 18)$

$= 10n - 8 - 6n + 18$

$= 4n + 10$

$\dfrac{3n + 6}{3} + 2(n + 5)$

$= \dfrac{3n}{3} + \dfrac{6}{3} + (2n + 10)$

$= n + 2 + 2n + 10$

$= 3n + 12$

B1 Simplify the following expressions.

(a) $6n + 7(n + 1)$ (b) $(3n + 5) + 2(2n - 1)$ (c) $2(n + 3) + 6(2n - 3)$

(d) $9(n - 3) + 5(3 - n)$ (e) $2(2n + 1) + 4(3 - n)$ (f) $3(n - 2) + 6(n + 1)$

B2 Simplify the following expressions.

(a) $\dfrac{9n + 3}{3} + 5(n + 2)$ (b) $\dfrac{10n + 8}{2} + 3(5n - 2)$ (c) $\dfrac{6n + 9}{3} + 2(5 - n)$

B3 Simplify the following expressions.

(a) $12 - 2(x + 3)$ (b) $(7x + 5) - 3(x + 1)$ (c) $5(3x + 3) - 4(2x - 3)$

(d) $7(x - 3) - 3(3 + x)$ (e) $10x - 3(2x - 5)$ (f) $4(2x + 3) - 6(2 - x)$

B4 Simplify the following expressions.

(a) $\dfrac{20x + 8}{4} - 3(2 + x)$ (b) $\dfrac{14x + 21}{7} - 3(6 - 2x)$ (c) $\dfrac{10x - 14}{2} - 2(5 - x)$

B5 Simplify the following expressions.

(a) $5p + 2(5 - 4p)$ (b) $(10p - 3) - 6(p + 2)$ (c) $2(5p + 3) - 9(p - 2)$

(d) $\frac{1}{4}(8p - 20) + 2(6 - p)$ (e) $\dfrac{45p + 40}{5} - 2(3 + 2p)$ (f) $\dfrac{12p + 36}{6} - 3(2 - 3p)$

*B6 Copy and complete each statement.

(a) $2(3x + 1) + \blacksquare(x - \blacksquare) = 11x - 13$

(b) $\blacksquare - 3(2 - p) = 13p - 6$

(c) $2(3m - \blacksquare) - \blacksquare(2m - 5) = 13$

(d) $\dfrac{8h - 12}{\blacksquare} - 3(\blacksquare - h) = 5h - 6$

C Simplifying to solve an equation

Example

$$10x - 2(x + 5) = 3(15 - x) \quad \text{[multiply out brackets]}$$
$$10x - (2x + 10) = 45 - 3x \quad \text{[deal with the subtracted bracket]}$$
$$10x - 2x - 10 = 45 - 3x \quad \text{[simplify]}$$
$$8x - 10 = 45 - 3x \quad \text{[+ 3x]}$$
$$11x - 10 = 45 \quad \text{[+ 10]}$$
$$11x = 55 \quad \text{[÷ 11]}$$
$$x = 5$$

C1 (a) Simplify the expression $5n + 3(n - 5)$.

    (b) Use the result of part (a) to solve the equation $5n + 3(n - 5) = 1$.

C2 (a) Simplify the expression $10 - (5 - c)$.

    (b) Use the result of part (a) to solve the equation $10 - (5 - c) = 20$.

C3 (a) Simplify the expression $12 - 3(1 + e)$.

    (b) Use the result of part (a) to solve the equation $12 - 3(1 + e) = 21$.

C4 Solve these equations.

    (a) $17 + 5(c - 4) = 47$ (b) $16 - 2(d + 3) = 7$ (c) $6f - 3(2 - f) = 12$

    (d) $5 - (g - 6) = 1$ (e) $h + 3(h - 1) = 3$ (f) $25 - 5(3k + 4) = 20$

    (g) $3m - 5(2 - m) = 10$ (h) $2(3 - 2n) + 5(n + 1) = 8$ (i) $3(p + 1) - 2(1 - 4p) = 34$

C5 Solve these equations.

    (a) $12 - (3 + q) = q - 1$ (b) $5r + 2(6 + r) = 3r + 8$

    (c) $10s - 3(2s - 1) = 6(s - 1)$ (d) $6(t - 2) - 5(1 - 3t) = 2(t + 1)$

Test yourself

T1 Simplify these expressions.

    (a) $10 - (4 + 5x)$ (b) $2(n + 3) + 5(n - 6)$ (c) $4(3m - 2) + 3(2m - 1)$

    (d) $\dfrac{4n + 16}{4} - 3n$ (e) $10k - 3(1 - 2k)$ (f) $5(3x - 4) - 7(2x - 5)$

T2 Solve these equations.

    (a) $6m + 2(m - 3) = 58$ (b) $2(c + 6) + 3(c - 1) = 4$

    (c) $n - 3(2 - n) = 4$ (d) $3(2k - 5) + 5(3k + 1) = 179$

T3 Solve these equations.

    (a) $5s + 2(8 - s) = 17(s - 4)$ (b) $2(x + 1) - 3(x - 5) = 5(x + 7)$

26 Roots

You will revise

● squares and square roots

● cubes and cube roots

● positive indices

A Squares and cubes

level 6

- 6 squared (or the square of 6) $= 6^2 = 6 \times 6 = 36$ so 36 is a **square** number.
- 2 cubed (or the cube of 2) $= 2^3 = 2 \times 2 \times 2 = 8$ so 8 is a **cube** (or cubic) number.

A1 Which of the following numbers are square numbers?

8, 4, 121, 80, 49, 13, 1

A2 (a) Find a square number between 160 and 170.

(b) Is there a square number between 170 and 180?

A3 Which of the following numbers are cube numbers?

9, 16, 27, 1, 30, 64, 1000

A4 Find a cube number between 100 and 200.

A5 Evaluate these.

(a) 3 squared   (b) The cube of 4   (c) 5^2 (d) 3^3

A6 Find two square numbers that add to make 29.

A7 Evaluate these.

(a) 11^2 (b) 1^3 (c) 15^2 (d) 10^3

A8 Hannah makes patchwork quilts.
She has 150 identical square pieces.

She wants to use these pieces to make
the largest **square** quilt she can.

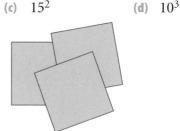

(a) How many pieces will she use?

(b) If each piece is 20 cm by 20 cm, how long will each edge of the quilt be?

A9 125 sugar cubes fit exactly into a cube-shaped box.
How many sugar cubes touch the bottom of the box?

A10 (a) Copy and complete this 'number spiral' using numbers from 1 to 100.

(b) Circle all the square numbers. What do you notice? Can you explain this?

	5	4	3	
	6	1	2	
	7	8	9	10

B Square and cube roots

B1 Evaluate these.

(a) $(^-5)^2$ (b) 5^2 (c) $(^-10)^2$ (d) 2^3 (e) $(^-2)^3$

---

3 squared is $3^2 = 3 \times 3 = 9$ so the **positive square root** of 9 is 3.

$(^-3)$ squared is $(^-3)^2 = ^-3 \times ^-3 = 9$ so the **negative square root** of 9 is $^-3$.

B2 (a) Write down the positive square root of 100.

(b) Write down the negative square root of 100.

B3 What is the negative square root of 36?

B4 Find two numbers that fit each statement.

(a) $\blacksquare^2 = 49$ (b) $\blacksquare^2 = 4$ (c) $\blacksquare^2 = 1$ (d) $\blacksquare^2 = 81$

B5 What are the square roots of 121?

---

6 cubed is $6^3 = 6 \times 6 \times 6 = 216$ so the **cube root** of 216 is 6.

$(^-2)$ cubed is $(^-2)^3 = ^-2 \times ^-2 \times ^-2 = ^-8$ so the **cube root** of $^-8$ is $^-2$.

B6 Find the cube root of these.

(a) 8   (b) 27   (c) 1   (d) 64   (e) $^-27$

B7 (a) A cube has a volume of $125 \, \text{cm}^3$. What is the length of one edge?

(b) What is the cube root of 125?

$125 \, \text{cm}^3$

?

B8 Solve these equations.

(a) $n^2 = 16$ (b) $m^2 + 6 = 150$ (c) $\dfrac{x^3}{2} = 108$

(d) $2n^2 = 32$ (e) $5k^3 = 40$ (f) $4n^3 = 4$

*B9 Explain why a number cannot have more than **one** cube root.

Part of the graph of $y = x^2$ is shown below.

Part of the graph of $y = x^3$ is shown below.

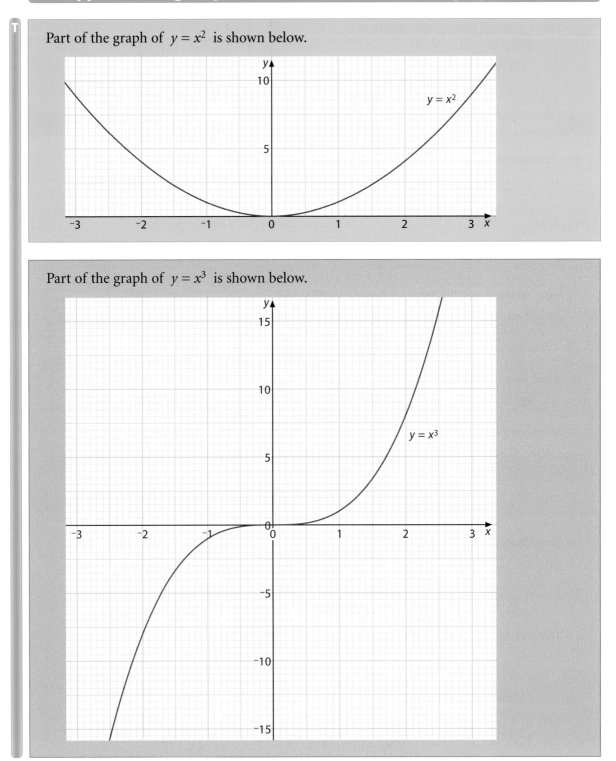

C1 (a) Use the first graph to estimate these.

(i) The square of 2.5   (ii) The square of $^-1.4$ (iii) $(^-2.8)^2$

(b) Check your results to (a) with a calculator.

C2 (a) Use the graph to estimate these.

(i) The positive square root of 3   (ii) The negative square root of 7

(b) Check your results to (a) by using the square root key on a calculator.

C3 (a) Use the graph to estimate the positive square root of 10.

(b) Use a calculator to find the positive square root of 10 correct to 2 d.p.

(c) What is the negative square root of 10 correct to 2 d.p.?

C4 (a) Use the second graph to estimate these.

(i) The cube of 1.5   (ii) $(^-1.8)^3$ (iii) $(2.3)^3$

(b) Check your results to (a) with a calculator.

C5 Use the graph to estimate the cube root of these.

(a) 10   (b) $^-10$ (c) 5   (d) $^-5$ (e) 7.5

D Cube roots on a calculator

The cube root of 20 can be written as $\sqrt[3]{20}$.

Your calculator may have a $\sqrt[3]{}$ key which is the cube root key.

D1 Evaluate these.   (a) $\sqrt[3]{2197}$ (b) $\sqrt[3]{-2744}$ (c) $\sqrt[3]{3.375}$

D2 Check your answers to C5 by using the cube root key on a calculator.

D3 Use the appropriate graph to estimate the solution to $x^3 = 3$, correct to 1 d.p. Use your calculator to find the solution correct to 3 d.p.

D4 Evaluate these, correct to 2 d.p.

(a) $\sqrt[3]{30}$ (b) $\sqrt[3]{14 + 28}$ (c) $\sqrt[3]{\dfrac{25}{3}}$ (d) $\sqrt[3]{\dfrac{20}{\pi}}$

(e) $\sqrt[3]{12.5} + \sqrt{8.62}$ (f) $\sqrt[3]{85.2} + \left(\dfrac{12.6}{18.2}\right)^2$ (g) $\sqrt[3]{\dfrac{6.25^2}{1.81}}$ (h) $\sqrt[3]{\dfrac{4.2 + 3.7}{7.5 - 5.4}}$

D5 (a) Estimate the answer to $\sqrt[3]{9.6^2 + 5.2^2}$. Write down the calculation that you do.

(b) Use your calculator to find the value of $\sqrt[3]{9.6^2 + 5.2^2}$. Give your answer correct to one decimal place.

D6 A formula to find the radius of a sphere is

$$r = \sqrt[3]{\frac{0.75V}{\pi}}$$

where r is the radius and V is the volume.

  (a) When $V = 800$, what is the value of r correct to 2 d.p?

  (b) A ball uses $1000\,cm^3$ of rubber.
    What is the radius of the ball, correct to the nearest 0.1 cm?

Test yourself

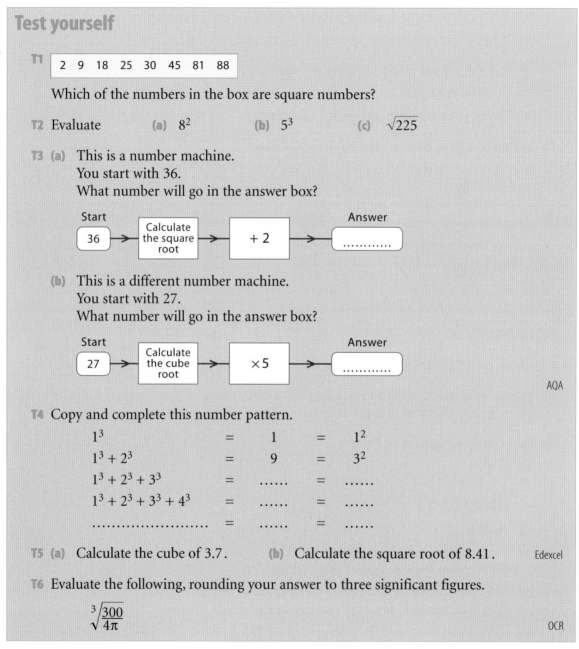

T1

| 2 | 9 | 18 | 25 | 30 | 45 | 81 | 88 |

Which of the numbers in the box are square numbers?

T2 Evaluate   (a) 8^2 (b) 5^3 (c) $\sqrt{225}$

T3 (a) This is a number machine.
    You start with 36.
    What number will go in the answer box?

Start → [Calculate the square root] → [+ 2] → Answer ....

  (b) This is a different number machine.
    You start with 27.
    What number will go in the answer box?

Start → [Calculate the cube root] → [× 5] → Answer ....

AQA

T4 Copy and complete this number pattern.

1^3	$=$	1	$=$	1^2
$1^3 + 2^3$	$=$	9	$=$	3^2
$1^3 + 2^3 + 3^3$	$=$	......	$=$	......
$1^3 + 2^3 + 3^3 + 4^3$	$=$	......	$=$	......
....	$=$	......	$=$	......

T5 (a) Calculate the cube of 3.7.   (b) Calculate the square root of 8.41.   Edexcel

T6 Evaluate the following, rounding your answer to three significant figures.

$$\sqrt[3]{\frac{300}{4\pi}}$$

OCR

Review 3

1 There are 18 girls and 12 boys in a class.
What is the ratio of girls to boys in its simplest form?

2 What is the value of $\dfrac{3n^2}{2}$ when $n = {}^-4$?

3 Work out   (a)   the cube of 6   (b)   the cube root of $^-64$

4 What is the value of $3a - b + c$ when $a = \frac{1}{2}$, $b = \frac{2}{5}$ and $c = \frac{7}{10}$?
Write your answer as a mixed number in its lowest terms.

5 (a)   On a number line, show the set of values of n that satisfy the inequality $1 \le n < 4$.

    (b)   What values in the oval satisfy
the inequality $1 \le n < 4$?

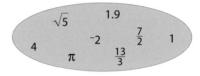

6 Grace is 5 years old, Bob is 8 years old and Hayley is 12 years old.
Their gran gives them £500 to share in the ratio of their ages.

    (a)   How much does Bob receive?

    (b)   What percentage of the money does Hayley receive?

7 Solve these equations.

    (a) $x^2 - 5 = 4$ (b) $3k^3 = 375$ (c) $n^3 + 10 = 2$

8 Write inequalities to describe the following number line diagrams.

9 For each of these sequences,

      (i)   describe a rule to go from one term to the next

      (ii)   find the sixth term

    (a)   2, 9, 16, 23, 30, ...   (b)   0.6, 1.8, 5.4, 16.2, 48.6, ...   (c)   1, 3, 7, 15, 31, ...

10 Simplify the following expressions.

    (a) $4w - (9 + 2w)$ (b) $8b - 7 - (3 + 2b)$ (c) $(5x + 3) - (6x + 1)$

    (d) $6q + 3(4 - 5q)$ (e) $11x - 4(3x - 2)$ (f) $2(6a + 4) - 10(2a - 3)$

11 The nth term of a series is $\dfrac{12}{n + 1}$.
Calculate the first six terms of the series, correct to 2 d.p.

12 Sue's recipe for Dry Martini mixes vermouth and gin in the ratio 1:6.

(a) How much gin would Sue mix with 50 ml of vermouth?

(b) How much vermouth would she mix with 180 ml of gin?

(c) What fraction of Sue's Dry Martini is gin?

13 The table on the right shows the heights and weights of some runners.

(a) Show this information on a scatter diagram.

(b) Describe the correlation between the height and weight of the runners.

(c) Draw the line of best fit on your diagram.

(d) Use your graph to estimate the weight of a runner who is 1.9 m tall.

Height (cm)	Weight (kg)
165	45
164	55
159	49
170	62
168	58
161	47
180	69
174	55
197	77
165	55
177	68
167	58
178	58
162	48
155	40
200	82
180	65
168	50
174	60
186	71

14 This key is drawn to its true size.

(a) What scale factor has been used to produce each of these copies?

(i)   (ii)

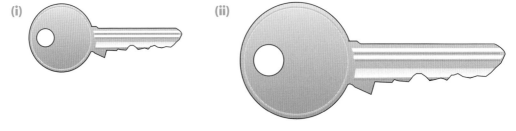

(b) The true width of the key is 25.5 mm.
Another copy is drawn.
On this copy the length is 20 mm.
What is the width on this copy?

15 Calculate the length of the line segment joining ($^-$3, 5) to (7, 1), correct to 1 d.p.

16 For each of these linear sequences,

      (i) find an expression for the nth term

      (ii) use your expression to work out the 100th term

    (a) 5, 8, 11, 14, 17, ...   **(b)** 20, 18, 16, 14, 12, ...   **(c)** $\frac{1}{2}, 1\frac{1}{4}, 2, 2\frac{3}{4}, 3\frac{1}{2}$, ...

17 Write the map scale of 2 cm : 1 km as a ratio in the form 1 : n.

18 The diagram shows a pyramid with a square base.
The volume of this pyramid is given by the formula

$$V = \tfrac{1}{3}b^2h$$

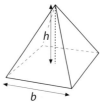

where V is the volume, b is the edge length of
the square base and h is the height.

Find the volume of a square based pyramid where $b = 4.50$ cm and $h = 9.80$ cm.

19 Solve the following equations.

    (a) $5a + 3(7 - a) = 7a - 4$ **(b)** $3(x - 1) - 4(x - 6) = 5(x - 3)$

20 Work out $\sqrt[3]{\dfrac{360}{\pi}}$, giving your answer correct to three significant figures.

21 ABCD is a rhombus and three of its vertices are A (0, 0), B (5, 5) and D ($^-$1, 7).

    (a) What are the coordinates of the centre of the rhombus?

    (b) Find the coordinates of C.

22 Matchsticks are used to make these designs.

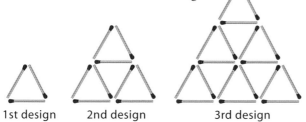

       1st design   2nd design   3rd design

    (a) Draw the 4th design.
        How many matchsticks are needed for it?

    (b) The number of matchsticks in each design gives the sequence 3, 9, 18, ...
        Write down the first six terms of this sequence.
        Is the sequence linear or non-linear?

    (c) Describe a rule to go from one term to the next in the sequence.

    (d) How is the sequence 3, 9, 18, ... related to the sequence of triangle numbers?
        What it is about the designs that makes these sequences related in this way?
        (Use a sketch to help your explanation if you need to)

  *(e) How many matchsticks are in the nth design?

Answers

1 Calculation and estimation

A Decimals and place value (p 8)

A1 (a) 500   (b) $\frac{5}{10}$ or $\frac{1}{2}$ (c) 5 000 000   (d) $\frac{5}{1000}$

A2 (a) 0.18, 0.3, 1.27, 1.9   (b) 0.05, 0.14, 0.25, 0.4
     (c) 0.047, 0.4, 0.407, 0.47   (d) 0.0092, 0.092, 0.902, 0.92

A3 (a) 62.9   (b) 485.1   (c) 1574   (d) 2960
     (e) 21   (f) 40   (g) 5.01   (h) 60.9

A4 (a) 5.61   (b) 0.7231   (c) 0.064   (d) 0.039 87
     (e) 0.307   (f) 0.0013   (g) 0.000 95   (h) 0.024 08

A5 (a) 39.1   (b) 4.25   (c) 869   (d) 0.5263
     (e) 590   (f) 0.03   (g) 0.0156   (h) 21 000

B Multiplying by a decimal (p 9)

B1 (a) 1.2   (b) 0.12   (c) 12   (d) 0.12   (e) 1.2
     (f) 400   (g) 40   (h) 40   (i) 0.4   (j) 400

B2 $0.4 \times 50 = 20$ $50 \times 40 = 2000$ $0.5 \times 400 = 200$

B3 $41 \ (-20, \times 0.5, \times 0.1, + 40)$

B4 N $0.3 \times 0.3 = 0.09$ H $0.02 \times 30 = 0.6$
     F $0.2 \times 0.2 = 0.04$ S $3 \times 0.1 = 0.3$
     I $0.3 \times 0.4 = 0.12$ D $200 \times 0.04 = 8$
     I $0.2 \times 0.4 = 0.08$ E $0.1 \times 8 = 0.8$
     The spelt word is FINISHED.

C Dividing by a decimal (p 10)

C1 (a) 20   (b) 60   (c) 8   (d) 7   (e) 300

C2 (a) 40   (b) 200   (c) 200   (d) 5   (e) 40

C3 (a) 20   (b) 40   (c) 4   (d) 80   (e) 4

C4 $\frac{1.5}{0.3} = 5$ $\frac{15}{30} = 0.5$

C5 $\frac{2.4}{0.8} = 3$ $\frac{24}{0.08} = 300$

C6 $\frac{4}{0.8} = 5$

C7 (a) $\frac{12}{0.4} = 30$ (b) $\frac{4.5}{0.9} = 5$ (c) $\frac{0.5}{0.2} = 2.5$ (d) $\frac{1}{0.05} = 20$

C8 (a) 23.4   (b) 1.4   (c) 0.3   (d) 0.2   (e) 17.2

D Rounding whole numbers (p 11)

D1 (a) 4000   (b) 4400   (c) 4390

D2 (a) 2000   (b) 2400   (c) 2400

D3 (a) 40 790   (b) 40 800   (c) 41 000

D4 (a) 32 100   (b) 48 600

D5 (a) (i) 6 600 000   (ii) 6 590 000
     (b) (i) 8 200 000   (ii) 8 216 000
     (c) All are 7 000 000, to the nearest million. Rounding like this hides the growth in population.

E Rounding decimals (p 11)

E1 (a) 48.3   (b) 8.8   (c) 0.5   (d) 24.0   (e) 70.0

E2 (a) 3.96   (b) 0.09   (c) 0.17   (d) 3.50   (e) 143.64

E3 (a) 3.5   (b) 4.08   (c) 8.057   (d) 0.80   (e) 0.068
     (f) 10.9

E4 (a) 0.76   (b) 13.50   (c) 0.06   (d) 2.80
     (e) 4.45   (f) 0.11   (g) 2.10   (h) 3.00

E5 (a) 0.403   (b) 14.0   (c) 0.350

F Rounding to one significant figure (p 12)

F1 (a) 300   (b) 10 000   (c) 5000   (d) 900
     (e) 300 000   (f) 6000   (g) 400 000   (h) 30 000
     (i) 800 000   (j) 1000

F2 (a) 8   (b) 0.9   (c) 0.7   (d) 0.003   (e) 4
     (f) 20   (g) 0.01   (h) 0.008   (i) 2   (j) 1

F3 $60 \times 30 = 1800$

F4 (a) 1600   (b) 1600   (c) 1200   (d) 1000   (e) 1200
     (f) 9000   (g) 12 000   (h) 20 000   (i) 6400   (j) 40 000

F5 (a) 1.4   (b) 1.5   (c) 0.12   (d) 40   (e) 21
     (f) 0.9   (g) 800   (h) 20   (i) 0.27   (j) 50

F6 (a) £2   (b) £4.50   (c) £60

G Rounding to two or more significant figures (p 13)

G1 (a) 4600   (b) 21 000   (c) 30 000
     (d) 5400   (e) 9600

G2 (a) 43 200   (b) 3330   (c) 28 000
     (d) 601 000   (e) 10 500

G3 (a) 0.053   (b) 2.4   (c) 3.1
     (d) 0.0043   (e) 0.67   (f) 0.000 49
     (g) 52   (h) 0.068   (i) 6.0
     (j) 0.000 97

G4 (a) 0.0237   (b) 8.19   (c) 41.0
     (d) 0.006 41   (e) 0.779   (f) 0.000 156
     (g) 255   (h) 0.0803   (i) 12.1
     (j) 0.006 92

H Sensible accuracy (p 13)

H1 Suggested approximations are 244, $2\frac{1}{2}$, 149 000, 22% or 'over 20%', 11.9 or 12, 186, 35, 144.8 (as is) or 145, 58.3 (as is) or 58, 317 or 'nearly 320', 1284 (as is), 87.6 or 88, 18 500 or 18.5 tonnes, 185 000, 6.8 or 'nearly 7'.

H2 Bickerton 1.73, Naggington 1.67.
Bickerton is doing better (if both are rounded to 1.7, then it appears that the teams are doing equally well).

I Mixed questions (p 14)

I1 (a) 26   (b) 26   (c) 2600   (d) 260   (e) 26 000

I2 (a) 2.38   (b) 238   (c) 2.38   (d) 17   (e) 170
(f) 14   (g) 14   (h) 170

I3 1.8×55, 0.18×550 and 180×0.55
18×0.55, 0.18×55 and 1.8×5.5
18×550 and 180×55
0.18×0.55 and 1.8×0.055

I4 (a) 3 000 000   (b) 2 890 000   (c) 3 000 000

I5 (a) $30 \times 60 = 1800$
(b) 30 is bigger than 28 and 60 is bigger than 59, so 30×60 must be bigger than 28×59.
(c) 1652

I6 (a) $30 \times £7 = £210$ (b) $£200 \times 30 = £6000$

I7 (a) $30 \times 40 = 1200\,\text{m}^2$
(b) It is smaller because 30 is less than 31.2 and 40 is less than 42.3.
(c) $1320\,\text{m}^2$

Test yourself (p 15)

T1 (a) 263   (b) 0.019 05   (c) 45   (d) 0.008 03

T2 (a) 32   (b) 0.32   (c) 0.08   (d) 240
(e) 2.1

T3 (a) 5.166   (b) 5.166   (c) 516.6   (d) 0.5166
(e) 82   (f) 63   (g) 820   (h) 6300

T4 (a) 2100   (b) 2085.2   (c) 2000   (d) 2090

T5 (a) 27   (b) 4.8   (c) 0.15   (d) 1600
(e) 0.5

T6 (a) 45.3   (b) 7500

2 Graphing changes over time

A Fairground graphs (p 16)

A1 (a) P and A, Q and C, R and B
(b) S and B, T and C, U and A

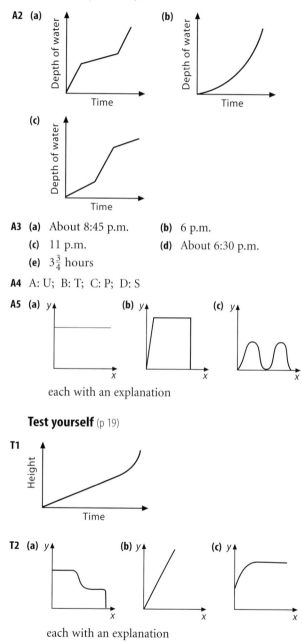

A2 (a)   (b)
(c)

A3 (a) About 8:45 p.m.   (b) 6 p.m.
(c) 11 p.m.   (d) About 6:30 p.m.
(e) $3\frac{3}{4}$ hours

A4 A: U; B: T; C: P; D: S

A5 (a) y   (b) y   (c) y

each with an explanation

Test yourself (p 19)

T1

T2 (a) y   (b) y   (c) y

each with an explanation

3 Unitary method

A Problems (p 20)

A1 (a) 1   (b) 3   (c) 75 g   (d) $1\frac{1}{2}$ tbsp

A2 (a) 20p   (b) £0.90 or 90p   (c) 9

A3 (a) 100 g   (b) 7   (c) 80 g   (d) 75 g

A4 560 kg

A5 20 m

A6 220 g

A7 750 ml

A8 £4.90

A9 240 g

B Cancelling common factors (p 21)

B1 (a) $6 \times 31 = 186$ (b) $25 \times 3 = 75$
    (c) $4 \times 27 = 108$ (d) 4×22 or $8 \times 11 = 88$
    (e) 7×15 or $21 \times 5 = 105$ (f) 5×15 or $25 \times 3 = 75$

B2 (a) $24 \times 2 = 48$ (b) $13 \times 3 = 39$
    (c) $5 \times 13 = 65$ (d) $3 \times 8 = 24$
    (e) $18 \times 1 = 18$ (f) $1 \times \frac{7}{2} = 3\frac{1}{2}$ or 3.5

B3 (a) $5 \times 13 = 65$ (b) $5 \times 7 = 35$
    (c) $11 \times 7 = 77$ (d) $5 \times 4 = 20$
    (e) $\frac{21}{2} \times 1$ or $\frac{7}{2} \times 3 = 10\frac{1}{2}$ or 10.5
    (f) $\frac{9}{2} \times 1$ or $\frac{3}{2} \times 3 = 4\frac{1}{2}$ or 4.5

B4 (a) $\dfrac{12 \times 36}{16}$ (b) $3 \times 9 = 27$

B5 (a) $\dfrac{45 \times 15}{25}$ (b) $9 \times 3 = 27$

B6 16

C Using cancelling (p 23)

C1 (a) $\frac{30}{9} \times 15$ (b) $10 \times 5 = 50$ grams

C2 50 grams

C3 36 grams

C4 250 ml

C5 140 grams

C6 350 grams

C7 175 grams

C8 67.5 grams

D Using a calculator (p 24)

D1 £182.02

D2 160 litres

D3 682 mg

D4 6.6 cm

D5 460 grams

D6 £1.21

D7 £11.25

D8 (a) 5   (b) £13 850

D9 (a) 1250 grams or 1.250 kg
    (b) 173 kg   (c) $8997 \, \text{cm}^3$ or $8996 \, \text{cm}^3$

E Dealing with units of measure (p 25)

E1 43p or £0.43

E2 2.27 kg

E3 6.3 pints

E4 (a) £31.68   (b) 325 km

E5 £3123.64

E6 155 000 won

Test yourself (p 26)

T1 £1.20

T2 (a) 150   (b) 160 grams

T3 (a) 9 slices of bread
      3 eggs
      $1\frac{1}{2}$ pints of milk
      225 g raisins
      15 g margarine
    (b) 5 ounces

T4 7.9 cm

T5 (a) 99 400 forints   (b) £3.65

4 Fractions

A Fractions review (p 27)

A1 (a) $\frac{2}{3} = \frac{10}{15}$ (b) $\frac{5}{6} = \frac{20}{24}$ (c) $\frac{5}{7} = \frac{25}{35}$
   (d) $\frac{4}{9} = \frac{16}{36}$ (e) $\frac{7}{12} = \frac{35}{60}$

A2 (a) $\frac{2}{3}$ (b) $\frac{1}{3}$ (c) $\frac{3}{4}$ (d) $\frac{4}{5}$ (e) $\frac{5}{6}$
   (f) $\frac{3}{4}$ (g) $\frac{3}{5}$ (h) $\frac{2}{3}$ (i) $\frac{2}{5}$ (j) $\frac{3}{4}$

A3 (a) $\frac{5}{4}$ (b) $\frac{5}{3}$ (c) $\frac{16}{5}$ (d) $\frac{13}{8}$ (e) $\frac{21}{10}$

A4 (a) $5\frac{1}{2}$ (b) $2\frac{1}{6}$ (c) $2\frac{6}{7}$ (d) $2\frac{4}{5}$ (e) $2\frac{9}{10}$

A5 (a) $\frac{1}{4}$ (b) $\frac{1}{3}$ (c) $\frac{1}{8}$ (d) $\frac{7}{24}$

A6 (a) $\frac{2}{5}$ (b) $\frac{1}{2}$ (c) $\frac{1}{10}$

A7 (a) $\frac{1}{2}$ (b) $\frac{2}{9}$ (c) $\frac{5}{18}$

A8 Divide by 4 and multiply by 3 (or the other way round).

A9 (a) 4 (b) 8 (c) 12 (d) 8 (e) 32
   (f) 27 (g) 24 (h) 12 (i) 40 (j) 350

B Ordering fractions (p 28)

B1 $\frac{3}{4} = \frac{15}{20}$, so $\frac{17}{20}$ is greater

B2 (a) $\frac{5}{12}$ (b) $\frac{3}{4}$ (c) $\frac{7}{10}$ (d) $\frac{2}{5}$ (e) $\frac{11}{24}$

B3 (a) $\frac{2}{5}$ (b) $\frac{5}{8}$ (c) $\frac{7}{8}$ (d) $\frac{7}{8}$ (e) $\frac{7}{10}$

B4 (a) $\frac{3}{5}$ (b) $\frac{5}{8}$ (c) $\frac{1}{3}$ (d) $\frac{3}{7}$ (e) $\frac{5}{12}$

B5 (a) $\frac{7}{10}, \frac{3}{4}, \frac{4}{5}$ (b) $\frac{7}{10}, \frac{11}{15}, \frac{5}{6}$ (c) $\frac{1}{3}, \frac{3}{8}, \frac{5}{12}$

B6 (a) $\frac{7}{12}$ (b) $\frac{5}{6}$ (c) $\frac{11}{15}$ (d) $\frac{21}{30}$ and $\frac{7}{10}$

C Addition and subtraction (p 29)

C1 (a) $1\frac{2}{5}$ (b) $1\frac{1}{5}$ (c) $\frac{5}{7}$ (d) $\frac{1}{6}$ (e) $1\frac{1}{4}$
   (f) $3\frac{2}{3}$ (g) $\frac{3}{4}$ (h) $1\frac{1}{2}$ (i) $6\frac{1}{5}$ (j) $1\frac{2}{5}$

C2 (a) $\frac{7}{12}$ (b) $\frac{11}{12}$ (c) $\frac{5}{12}$ (d) $\frac{13}{15}$ (e) $\frac{13}{20}$

C3 (a) $\frac{3}{20}$ (b) $\frac{7}{12}$ (c) $\frac{5}{12}$ (d) $\frac{1}{12}$ (e) $\frac{1}{10}$

C4 (a) $\frac{11}{15}$ (b) $\frac{7}{20}$ (c) $\frac{7}{20}$ (d) $\frac{23}{24}$ (e) $\frac{29}{60}$

C5 (a) $1\frac{1}{24}$ (b) $1\frac{7}{12}$ (c) $1\frac{5}{24}$ (d) $2\frac{3}{20}$ (e) $1\frac{2}{5}$
   (f) $3\frac{37}{40}$ (g) $1\frac{3}{20}$ (h) $4\frac{1}{15}$ (i) $2\frac{5}{24}$ (j) $1\frac{11}{14}$

C6 (a) $\frac{1}{5} + \frac{1}{4}$ (b) $\frac{1}{4} + \frac{2}{3}$ or $\frac{1}{6} + \frac{3}{4}$
   (c) $\frac{4}{5} - \frac{1}{3}$ or $\frac{2}{3} - \frac{1}{5}$ (d) $\frac{5}{6} - \frac{1}{6}$
   (e) $\frac{1}{3} + \frac{2}{4} + \frac{1}{4}$ or $\frac{1}{5} + \frac{4}{5} + \frac{1}{4}$ or $\frac{1}{6} + \frac{5}{6} + \frac{1}{4}$ or $\frac{1}{6} + \frac{1}{3} + \frac{3}{4}$
   (f) $\frac{1}{5} + \frac{1}{3} + \frac{5}{6}$ or $\frac{1}{6} + \frac{2}{5} + \frac{4}{5}$

C7 210

C8 $\frac{17}{24}$

D Multiplying a fraction by a whole number (p 30)

D1 (a) 4 (b) 3 (c) 6 (d) 8 (e) 20

D2 $3\frac{3}{4}$ hours

D3 $4\frac{2}{3}$ miles

D4 (a) $3\frac{3}{4}$ (b) $2\frac{2}{3}$ (c) $2\frac{2}{5}$ (d) $1\frac{3}{4}$ (e) $8\frac{1}{2}$

D5 (a) $6\frac{3}{4}$ (b) $6\frac{2}{3}$ (c) $4\frac{4}{5}$ (d) $2\frac{1}{4}$ (e) 4

D6 (a) $\frac{1}{10} \times 5 = \frac{1}{2}$ (b) $\frac{1}{15} \times 5 = \frac{1}{3}$ (c) $\frac{2}{3} \times 6 = 4$

D7 (a) $\frac{2}{3} \times 6 = 4$ or $\frac{2}{4} \times 6 = 3$ or $\frac{3}{6} \times 4 = 2$ or $\frac{4}{6} \times 3 = 2$
   (b) $20 \times \frac{1}{5} = 4$ or $20 \times \frac{1}{4} = 5$ or $10 \times \frac{2}{5} = 4$ or $10 \times \frac{2}{4} = 5$
   (c) $\frac{1}{5}$ of $40 = 8$ or $\frac{1}{8}$ of $40 = 5$ or $\frac{4}{5}$ of $10 = 8$ or $\frac{4}{8}$ of $10 = 5$
   (d) $\frac{3}{4}$ of $20 = 15$ or $\frac{2}{4}$ of $30 = 15$

D8 $5\frac{1}{3}$

D9 (a) $1\frac{3}{4}$ (b) $11\frac{1}{4}$ (c) $6\frac{2}{3}$ (d) $5\frac{3}{5}$

E Dividing a fraction by a whole number (p 31)

E1 (a) $\frac{1}{8}$ (b) $\frac{1}{6}$ (c) $\frac{1}{9}$ (d) $\frac{1}{10}$ (e) $\frac{1}{20}$

E2 (a) $\frac{3}{8}$ (b) $\frac{1}{3}$ (c) $\frac{2}{15}$ (d) $\frac{3}{20}$ (e) $\frac{1}{5}$

E3 (a) $\frac{9}{5} = 1\frac{4}{5}$ (b) $\frac{2}{15}$ (c) $\frac{14}{5} = 2\frac{4}{5}$
   (d) $\frac{3}{16}$ (e) $\frac{24}{5} = 4\frac{4}{5}$

F Fractions of fractions (p 32)

F1 (a) $\frac{2}{3}$ of $\frac{5}{6} = \frac{10}{18} = \frac{5}{9}$ (b) $\frac{5}{8}$ of $\frac{2}{3} = \frac{10}{24} = \frac{5}{12}$
   (c) $\frac{2}{5}$ of $\frac{3}{4} = \frac{6}{20} = \frac{3}{10}$

F2 Diagrams and calculations

F3

$\frac{2}{3}$ of $\frac{4}{5}$ $\frac{4}{5}$ of $\frac{2}{3}$

F4 (a) $\frac{1}{8}$ (b) $\frac{1}{21}$ (c) $\frac{1}{80}$ (d) $\frac{1}{36}$

F5 (a) $\frac{3}{8}$ (b) $\frac{2}{15}$ (c) $\frac{4}{15}$ (d) $\frac{6}{35}$ (e) $\frac{3}{14}$
   (f) $\frac{2}{15}$ (g) $\frac{1}{10}$ (h) $\frac{3}{16}$

G Multiplying fractions together (p 33)

G1 (a) $\frac{1}{10}$ (b) $\frac{1}{24}$ (c) $\frac{2}{15}$ (d) $\frac{8}{15}$ (e) $\frac{9}{20}$

G2 (a) $\frac{1}{2} \times \frac{1}{6} = \frac{1}{12}$ (b) $\frac{1}{3} \times \frac{1}{5} = \frac{1}{15}$ (c) $\frac{2}{3} \times \frac{1}{5} = \frac{2}{15}$
   (d) $\frac{3}{7} \times \frac{5}{8} = \frac{15}{56}$

G3 (a) $\frac{1}{6}$ (b) $\frac{3}{10}$ (c) $\frac{5}{8}$ (d) $\frac{1}{4}$

G4 (a) $\frac{1}{4}$ (b) $\frac{5}{9}$ (c) $\frac{5}{12}$ (d) $\frac{7}{10}$ (e) $\frac{1}{2}$
   (f) $\frac{1}{10}$ (g) $\frac{3}{16}$ (h) $\frac{14}{25}$ (i) $\frac{4}{7}$ (j) 1

G5 (a) $\frac{5}{6}$ (b) $\frac{7}{8}$ (c) $\frac{14}{9} = 1\frac{5}{9}$ (d) $\frac{9}{10}$

G6 (a) $8\frac{5}{9}$ (b) $5\frac{2}{5}$

G7 (a) 2   (b) $\frac{25}{8}$ or $3\frac{1}{8}$ (c) $\frac{35}{9}$ or $3\frac{8}{9}$
   (d) $\frac{25}{6}$ or $4\frac{1}{6}$

H Changing between fractions and decimals (p 34)

H1 (a) $\frac{3}{5}$ (b) $\frac{16}{25}$ (c) $\frac{5}{8}$ (d) $\frac{7}{20}$ (e) $\frac{2}{25}$

    (f) $\frac{33}{40}$ (g) $\frac{7}{200}$ (h) $\frac{18}{25}$ (i) $\frac{1}{250}$ (j) $\frac{19}{125}$

H2 (a) 0.125   (b) 0.625   (c) 0.875

    (d) 0.0625   (e) 0.3125

H3 (a) $0.59, 0.6, \frac{5}{8}, \frac{13}{20}$ (b) $0.7, \frac{37}{50}, 0.77, \frac{4}{5}$

    (c) $\frac{3}{10}, 0.35, 0.4, \frac{9}{20}$ (d) $0.25, 0.3, \frac{7}{20}, \frac{3}{8}$

    (e) $0.4, 0.405, \frac{9}{20}, 0.5$ (f) $\frac{3}{4}, 0.8, 0.85, \frac{7}{8}$

H4 END OF SECTION

I Recurring decimals (p 35)

I1 (a) 0.666 666 6…   (b) 0.111 111 1…

    (c) 0.222 222 2…   (d) 0.444 444 4…

    (e) 0.777 777 7…

I2 (a) 0.142 857 142…   (b) 0.285 714 285…

    (c) 0.428 571 428…   (d) 0.571 428 571…

    (e) 0.714 285 714…   (f) 0.857 142 857…

    An explanation of the pattern

I3 (a) 0.833 333 3…   (b) 0.181 818 1…

    (c) 0.272 727 2…   (d) 0.083 333 3…

    (e) 0.076 923 076…

J Mixed questions (p 35)

J1 (a) $\frac{4}{5}$ (b) $\frac{1}{3}$ (c) $\frac{4}{5}$

J2 $8\frac{3}{4}$ litres

J3 (a) $\frac{27}{4} = 6\frac{3}{4}$ (b) $6\frac{2}{3}$ (c) $6\frac{2}{3}$

    (d) $16\frac{1}{2}$ (e) $\frac{14}{5} = 2\frac{4}{5}$

J4 $\frac{1}{6}$

J5 (a) $\frac{1}{6}$ (b) $\frac{1}{8}$ (c) $\frac{2}{9}$ (d) $\frac{1}{4}$ (e) $\frac{1}{10}$

J6 $\frac{7}{24}$

J7

$+$	$\frac{1}{4}$	$\frac{3}{10}$
$\frac{1}{2}$	$\frac{3}{4}$	$\frac{4}{5}$
$\frac{1}{15}$	$\frac{19}{60}$	$\frac{11}{30}$

J8 (a) $2\frac{1}{12}$ (b) $\frac{4}{5}$ (c) $1\frac{1}{15}$ (d) $\frac{16}{25}$ (e) $3\frac{1}{16}$

J9 250 m

J10

$\times$	$\frac{1}{4}$	$\frac{4}{5}$
$\frac{1}{3}$	$\frac{1}{12}$	$\frac{4}{15}$
$\frac{1}{2}$	$\frac{1}{8}$	$\frac{2}{5}$

Test yourself (p 36)

T1 Jim has more paint.
Jim has $\frac{3}{4} = \frac{9}{12}$ of a tin.
Mary has $\frac{4}{6} = \frac{8}{12}$ of a tin.

T2 $\frac{5}{16}$

T3 $\frac{4}{15}$

T4 (a) $5\frac{1}{6}$ (b) $1\frac{7}{15}$ (c) $2\frac{3}{4}$ (d) $\frac{1}{16}$

T5 (a) $\frac{1}{50}, 0.04, 0.1, \frac{3}{20}$ (b) $\frac{17}{20}, 0.86, \frac{7}{8}, 0.9$

T6 $1\frac{7}{12}$ inches

T7 (a) $\frac{22}{15} = 1\frac{7}{15}$ (b) 2

T8 (a) 0.375   (b) 0.0375

5 Parallel lines and angles

A Angles from parallel lines crossing (p 37)

A1 $a = 130°$, $b = 130°$, $c = 130°$, $d = 130°$, $e = 130°$, $f = 50°$, $g = 50°$, $h = 50°$, $i = 50°$, $j = 50°$

A2 $l = 110°$, $m = 70°$, $n = 70°$, $o = 110°$, $p = 70°$, $q = 110°$, $r = 70°$, $s = 110°$, $t = 110°$, $u = 110°$

A3 (a) f (b) c (c) a and d, e and h

A4 (a) c and d, f and g, h and i
(b) n and p, o and q, t and u

A5 $a = 140°$, $b = 38°$, $c = 50°$, $d = 25°$

A6 (a) r (b) v

A7 (a) a and b, a and c, d and e, f and j
(b) m and n, p and r, q and s, l and u

A8 $a = 78°$, $b = 118°$, $c = 75°$

A9 (a) g (b) b (c) c (d) e

A10 (a) b (b) d (c) e (d) e

A11 $a = 35°$, $b = 88°$, $c = 128°$

A12 r and w, s and v, t and y, u and x

A13 (a) (i) c (ii) d
(b) a and b (c) a and e

A14 p and q, r and s, u and v

A15 $a = 140°$, $b = 95°$, $c = 80°$

A16 (a) Corresponding angles
(b) Alternate angles
(c) Vertically opposite angles
(d) Supplementary angles on a straight line
(e) Supplementary angles between parallel lines
(f) Alternate angles
(g) Corresponding angles
(h) Vertically opposite angles
(i) Supplementary angles on a straight line

A17 $a = 40°$ (corresponding angles)
$b = 50°$ (vertically opposite angles)
$c = 115°$ (corresponding angles)
$d = 100°$ (supplementary angles between parallel lines)
$e = 138°$ (vertically opposite angles)
$f = 125°$ (alternate angles)
$g = 48°$ (supplementary angles between parallel lines)
$h = 77°$ (alternate angles)

A18 $a = 93°$ (supplementary angles on a straight line)
$b = 87°$ (corresponding angles)
$c = 48°$ (alternate angles)

A19 $x = 103°$ (supplementary angles between parallel lines)
$y = 82°$ (corresponding angles)
$z = 131°$ (alternate angles)

A20 (a) $112°$ (corresponding angles)   (b) $50°$

A21 (a) $45°$ (b) $20°$

A22 $p = 105°$, $q = 75°$, $r = 92°$, $s = 118°$

B Finding angles in two or more steps (p 43)

In most cases there is at least one other explanation besides what is given here.

B1 (a) $\angle$KLN $= 105°$ (corresponding angles)
$x = 180° - 105° = 75°$ (angles on straight line)
(b) $\angle$BDE $= 81°$ (corresponding angles)
$p = 180° - 81° = 99°$ (angles on straight line)
(c) $\angle$GJK $= 115°$ (corresponding angles)
$w = 115°$ (vertically opposite angles)
(d) $\angle$DCF $= 59°$ (corresponding angles)
$u = 59°$ (vertically opposite angles)
(e) $\angle$MKN $= 74°$ (corresponding angles)
$r = 180° - 74° = 106°$ (angles on straight line)
(f) $\angle$RSU $= 110°$ (corresponding angles)
$y = 180° - 110° = 70°$ (angles on straight line)

B2 $a = 50°$, $b = 70°$

B3 $x = 180° - 119° = 61°$ (supplementary angles between parallel lines)
$\angle$A $= 180° - 131° = 49°$ (supplementary angles between parallel lines)
$y = 180° - \angle$A $- \angle$B (angles of $\triangle$ABC)
$= 180° - 49° - 61° = 70°$

B4 $p = 180° - 56° - 65° = 59°$ (angles of $\triangle$JFI)
$\angle$JFG $= 180° - 65° = 115°$ (supplementary angles between parallel lines)
$q = 115° - 56° - 35° = 24°$ (angles making up $\angle$JFG)
$r = 35°$ ($= \angle$GFH, alternate angles)

B5 (a) $\angle$STR $= 50°$ ($= \angle$UTV, vertically opposite angles)
$\angle$STQ $= \angle$STR $- \angle$QTR $= 50° - 20° = 30°$
$a = 180° - 30° = 150°$ ($\angle$PST and $\angle$STQ are supplementary angles between parallel lines)
(b) $\angle$BCF $= 70°$ ($= \angle$ABE, corresponding angles)
$p = 360° - 70° - 130° = 160°$
(angles round a point add up to $360°$)
(c) $\angle$HIL $= 57° + 42° = 99°$
$\angle$LIJ $= 180° - 99° = 81°$
(supplementary angles on a straight line)
$z = 81°$ ($= \angle$LIJ, alternate angles)

B6 $p = 280°$ (An extra parallel line needs to be drawn through C; the explanation can be in terms of alternate angles or of supplementary angles between parallel lines.)

$q = 150°$ (An extra line needs to be drawn through H; the simplest explanation is in terms of supplementary angles between parallel lines.)

B7 $a = 60°$, $b = 110°$, $c = 130°$

B8 (a) $112°$

(b) $068°$ (bearings are usually given as three digits)

B9

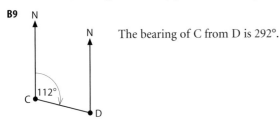

The bearing of C from D is 292°.

B10 (a) $x°$ (b) $(x + 180)°$

(c) If x is greater than 180, the expression $(x - 180°)$ has to be used, otherwise the result is a bearing greater than 360°.

Test yourself (p 46)

T1 c and j, d and i, e and h, f and g

T2 $a = 60°$ (vertically opposite angles)
$b = 108°$ (supplementary angles between parallel lines)
$c = 113°$ (corresponding angles)

T3 $\angle EBC = 117°$ (corresponding angles)
$x = 117° - 38° = 79°$

T4 30

T5 (a) (i) $109°$

(ii) $x = 180° - 47° - 24°$ (angles on the straight line PST)

(b) (i) $24°$

(ii) $\angle PQS = \angle RSQ$ (alternate angles) and $\angle RSQ = 24°$

6 Percentages

A Percentages, decimals and fractions (p 47)

A1 (a) S, E, E, T, R, V gives EVEREST

(b) N, W, N, D, S, O, O gives SNOWDON

(c) N, M, I, K, A, I, L, J, A, R, O gives KILIMANJARO

A2 (a) 0.99   (b) 0.03   (c) 0.7 or 0.70
(d) 0.495   (e) 0.125

A3 (a) $\frac{3}{5}$ (b) $\frac{7}{20}$ (c) $\frac{12}{25}$ (d) $\frac{2}{25}$ (e) $\frac{33}{100}$

A4 (a) 44%   (b) 85%   (c) 45%   (d) 90%   (e) 32%
(f) 12.5% or $12\frac{1}{2}$%

A5 (a) 55%   (b) 7%   (c) 80%   (d) 37.5% (e) 1.5%

A6 (a) $\frac{1}{10}$, 20%, $\frac{1}{4}$, 49%, 0.5   (b) 5%, 0.08, 76%, $\frac{4}{5}$, 0.9
(c) 0.03, 33%, $\frac{1}{3}$, $\frac{2}{5}$, 45%   (d) 4%, 5%, $\frac{1}{5}$, 0.4, 51%

B Percentage of a quantity (p 48)

B1 (a) 29.24   (b) 86.8   (c) 131.1
(d) 360   (e) 3.9   (f) 3352.5

B2 (a) 148 (or 150)   (b) 94 (or 90)

B3 (a) 250 000

(b) Botswana, with an explanation

(c) Senegal   (d) Senegal

B4 (a) 0.014   (b) 210

B5 (a) £149.60   (b) 364.8 kg   (c) £175

B6 £303.75

C One number as a percentage of another (p 49)

C1 90%

C2 60%

C3 (a) (i) 20%   (ii) 30%   (iii) 5%
(b) 50%   (c) 75%   (d) 45%

C4 46%

C5 7.6%

C6 (a) 24 792 000   (b) 85.4%

C7 (a) 1690 thousand or 1 690 000
(b) 54.8%   (c) 7.5%   (d) No, it's 1.8

D Percentage increase and decrease (p 50)

D1 £54

D2 5 kg

D3 230 g

D4 64 kg

D5 5750

D6 (a) 12 (b) 35p

E Increasing using a multiplier (p 51)

E1 (a) £48.30 (b) £29.44 (c) £42.32
(d) £17.25 (e) £20.47

E2 1.12

E3 (a) £3.25 (b) £43.23 (c) £67.20
(d) £17.81 (e) £41.16

E4 £3.88

E5 189

E6 (a) Tim (b) 60 480

E7 1590

E8 £329.60

E9 £336.05

E10 £1445

E11 £314.40

E12 (a) £605.88 (b) £1010.40 (c) £15.38 (d) £3.84

F Decreasing using a multiplier (p 52)

F1 (a) £12.60 (b) £4.20 (c) £67.50
(d) £2.55 (e) £0.15

F2 0.65

F3 (a) £16.25 (b) £19.24 (c) £32.50
(d) £11.04 (e) £25.99

F4 (a) £4.03 (b) £5.29 (c) £16.79
(d) £29.82 (e) £235.20

F5 0.91

F6 (a) £1128.40 (b) £618.80 (c) £8.65
(d) £0.58 (e) £13.38

F7 (a) 0.28 (b) 0.77 (c) 0.7 (d) 0.95 (e) 0.98

F8 (a) £208.80 (b) £111.60 (c) £2.30 (d) £395.60

F9 £5766

F10 A × 1.76 B × 0.76 C × 1.24 D × 0.24 E × 1.2 F × 0.8

F11 £119 900

F12 £3690

F13 30 kg

F14 7360

G Finding an increase as a percentage (p 54)

G1 8%

G2 (a) 14% (b) 65% (c) 70% (d) 7%

G3 30%

G4 85%

G5 21%

G6 32%

G7 (a) 92% (b) 9%

G8 England 29%, Scotland 5%

G9 23.9%

H Finding a decrease as a percentage (p 55)

H1 35%

H2 (a) 24% (b) 62% (c) 30% (d) 4%

H3 7%

H4 12%

H5 35%

H6 (a) 15% decrease (b) 43% increase
(c) 30% increase (d) 27% decrease
(e) 40% decrease (f) 9% increase
(g) 2% decrease (h) 7% increase

H7 (a) 21% decrease (b) 28% increase

H8

	% change
Cheese	16% increase
Beef and veal	**43% decrease**
Fish	**12% decrease**
Fresh green veg	**40% decrease**
Fresh fruit	**21% increase**
Instant coffee	**86% increase**

I Mixed questions (p 56)

I1 (a) 3 458 000 or 3458 thousand
(b) 55% (c) 18% (d) 13%

I2 (a) £39.24 (b) £50.74
(c) The VAT is £2.54, so Ann has to pay £53.28

I3 It has gone up by 3.1%, which is more than inflation.
If the subscription had gone up by 2.8% it would have
been £493.44.

I4 (a) £247.50 (b) £256 (c) £246.75

I5 £77.35

I6 (a) £87.80 (b) 119.5%

I7 49%

I8 £253.80

I9 27.75%

Test yourself (p 58)

T1 32

T2 45

T3 15%

T4 60%

T5 1.7%

T6 91 000

T7 2.17 m

T8 132

T9 3 253 000

T10 35%

T11 £694.50

7 Pie charts

A Interpreting pie charts (p 59)

A1 **(a)** 26 **(b)** 9 **(c)** 43 **(d)** $\frac{1}{3}$

A2 **(a)** 40% **(b)** 15% of 55 = 8.25 so 8 people

(c) $\frac{1}{5}$

A3 **(a)** **(i)** 40.8% **(ii)** 36.7% **(iii)** 22.5%

(b) 44

B Drawing a pie chart using angles (p 60)

B1

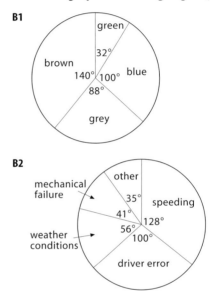

B2

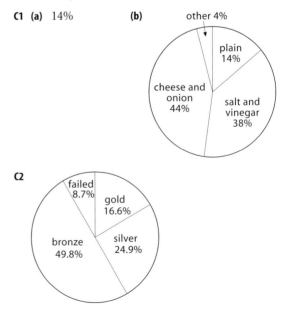

C Drawing a pie chart using a percentage scale (p 61)

C1 **(a)** 14% **(b)**

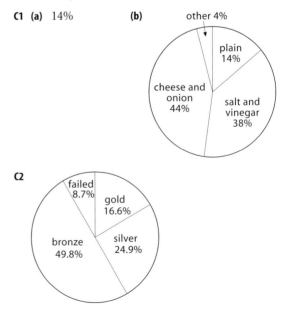

C2

D Mixed questions (p 62)

Here, and in 'Test yourself', the angles and percentages are given in a table for reference. They are not required for a full answer. The pie charts may or may not be marked with the percentages.

D1 (a)

Main carers	Angle	Percentage	Percentage (to 1 d.p.)
Couple	285°	79%	79.1%
Widow etc.	43°	12%	12.0%
Single mother	25°	7%	7.0%
Lone father	7°	2%	1.9%
	360°	**100%**	**100.0%**

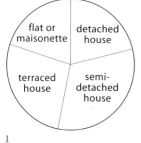

(b) $\frac{4}{5}$

D2 (a)

Type of home	Angle	Percentage	Percentage (to 1 d.p.)
Detached house	76°	21%	21.1%
Semi-detached house	115°	32%	32.1%
Terraced house	97°	27%	26.9%
Flat or maisonette	72°	20%	19.9%
	360°	**100%**	**100.0%**

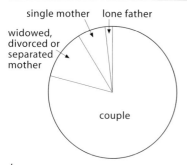

(b) $\frac{1}{2}$

D3 Comments such as:
'The sum of the weights is not a meaningful whole. The data is for a period of time and the changes over time would be much clearer in a line graph.'

D4 (a) 1950

	Angle	Percentage	Percentage (to 1 d.p.)
Pedestrians	162°	45%	44.9%
Cyclists	58°	16%	16.1%
Motor cyclists	81°	23%	22.5%
All other road users	59°	17%	16.5%
	360°	**101%**	**100.0%**

2000

	Angle	Percentage	Percentage (to 1 d.p.)
Pedestrians	91°	25%	25.1%
Cyclists	13°	4%	3.7%
Motor cyclists	64°	18%	17.7%
All other road users	192°	53%	53.4%
	360°	**100%**	**99.9%**

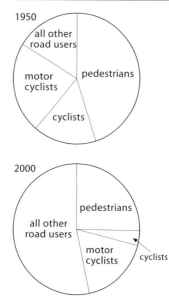

(b) The conclusion may be true but it cannot be drawn on the basis of this data. We would need to know, for example, how many cyclists and motorists used the roads in 1950 and 2000. It is likely that the number of people who regularly travelled on a bicycle was far more in 1950 (when few owned cars) than it was in 2000.

Test yourself (p 63)

T1 (a) 700 **(b)** 4550 **(c)** 4900

T2 (a) 1930

	Angle	Percentage	Percentage (to 1 d.p.)
Defence	38°	10%	10.4%
Education	34°	10%	9.6%
Health and social services	100°	28%	27.8%
Debt interest	91°	25%	25.2%
Other	97°	27%	27.0%
	360°	**100%**	**100.0%**

1990

	Angle	Percentage	Percentage (to 1 d.p.)
Defence	38°	11%	10.6%
Education	45°	12%	12.4%
Health and social services	153°	43%	42.5%
Debt interest	31°	9%	8.7%
Other	93°	26%	25.8%
	360°	**101%**	**100.0%**

1930   1990

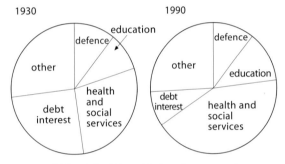

(b) He would be right if he said that the proportion or fraction of money spent on defence was about the same. Clearly the **amounts** are not the same.

(c) Comments such as:
'The proportion spent on defence was about the same. The proportion spent on education has gone up slightly. A much larger proportion was spent on health and social services in 1990 than in 1930 and a much lower proportion spent on debt interest.'

Review 1 (p 64)

1 30%

2 $\frac{9}{16}$

3 (a) $0.12\,\text{m}^2$ **(b)** $0.69\,\text{m}^2$

4 $0.555\ldots$ or $0.5\dot{}$

5 40

6 (a) 63   **(b)** $11\frac{1}{3}$ or $\frac{34}{3}$ **(c)** $\frac{1}{24}$ **(d)** $\frac{1}{12}$

   (e) $\frac{1}{2}$ **(f)** $1\frac{7}{15}$ or $\frac{22}{15}$ **(g)** $\frac{17}{36}$ **(h)** $2\frac{1}{2}$ or $\frac{5}{2}$

   (i) $3\frac{2}{11}$ or $\frac{35}{11}$ **(j)** $\frac{5}{6}$

7 (a) 2.76   **(b)** 2.76   **(c)** 23   **(d)** 1200

8 $\frac{2}{3}$

9 (a) (i) $200 \div 20 = 10$ so an estimate is £10 per hour
     (ii) It must be less as rounding has produced slightly less money for slightly more time.
   (b) £258.00

10 £293.75

11 1300 g or 1.30 kg

12 19.0%

13 (a) Angles a and c are alternate angles.
   (b) $a = 50°$ (vertically opposite angles)
     $b = 130°$ (supplementary angles on a straight line)
     $c = 50°$ (alternate angles or supplementary angles between parallel lines)
     $d = 50°$ (vertically opposite or corresponding angles)
     $e = 40°$ (supplementary angles on a straight line)

14 (a)

Week	1	2	3	4	5	6
Percentage faulty	6.1	4.8	3.9	2.1	1.5	1.5

   Quality is improving.
   (b) 3663

15 The following is one possible series of steps; there are others.
   $\angle AED = 180 - (109 + 35) = 36°$ (angles of triangle add up to 180°)
   $\angle AEB = 180 - (94 + 36) = 50°$ (supplementary angles on a straight line)
   $\angle ABE = 180 - 75 = 105°$ (supplementary angles between parallels)
   So $x = 180 - (105 + 50) = 25°$ (angles of triangle add up to 180°)

16 68p (to the nearest 1p) or 68.4p (to the nearest 0.1p)

17 (a) 10 000 000 or 10 million

(b) 40 200 000

(c) 17.7% (to 1 d.p.)

(d)

Age range	Angle	Percentage	Percentage (to 1 d.p.)
0–14	64°	18%	17.7%
15–64	239°	66%	66.5%
65+	57°	16%	15.8%
	360°	100%	100.0%

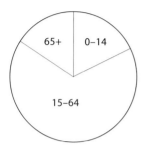

8 Pythagoras's theorem

A The area of a tilted square (p 66)

A1 (a) Diagram   **(b)** 20 sq units

A2 Diagrams

    (a) 26 sq units   **(b)** 18 sq units   **(c)** 34 sq units

B Squares on right-angled triangles (p 67)

B1 (a) $12\,cm^2$ **(b)** $12\,cm^2$ **(c)** $8\,cm^2$ **(d)** $13\,cm^2$

    (e) $33\,cm^2$ **(f)** $26\,cm^2$

B2 (a) $64\,cm^2$ **(b)** 8 cm

B3 $32\,cm^2$

B4 (a) 6 cm   **(b)** $33\,cm^2$ **(c)** $185\,cm^2$ **(d)** 7 cm

    (e) 4 cm   **(f)** 5 cm

B5 (a) $52\,m^2$ **(b)** 7 m   **(c)** 5 m   **(d)** $77\,m^2$

B6 (a) 17 cm   **(b)** A drawing and measuring check

B7 (a) 9 cm   **(b)** 12 cm   **(c)** 10 cm   **(d)** 5 cm

    (e) 13 cm   **(f)** 26 cm

B8 $3^2 + 4^2 = 25$, which is 5^2, so this is a right-angled triangle.

C Square roots – a reminder (p 70)

C1

Number	Square root
1	**1**
4	**2**
9	3
16	4
25	**5**
36	**6**
49	7

C2 (a) 9   **(b)** 10   **(c)** 11   **(d)** 20

C3 (a) 7   **(b)** 3   **(c)** 12   **(d)** 13

C4 For each of these, an estimate should be given, followed by the 2 d.p. answer.

    (a) 3.16   **(b)** 1.58   **(c)** 12.25   **(d)** 3.87

    (e) 14.14   **(f)** 4.47   **(g)** 6.48   **(h)** 20.49

    (i) 9.22   **(j)** 2.92   **(k)** 28.37   **(l)** 7.07

    (m) 22.36   **(n)** 2.24   **(o)** 0.71   **(p)** 70.71

C5 (a) 23.0 cm   **(b)** 17.3 cm   **(c)** 20.8 cm   **(d)** 22.8 cm

    (e) 30.5 cm   **(f)** 15.8 cm

C6 (a) 14.9 cm   **(b)** A drawing and measuring check

D Using Pythagoras (p 71)

D1 (a) 24.4 cm, to the nearest 0.1 cm

    (b) 34.4 cm, to the nearest 0.1 cm

D2 Results for the exercise book used

D3 About 26 metres shorter

D4 (a) 5.83 cm $\left(\sqrt{34}\ \text{cm}\right)$ (b) 13 cm

D5 (a) All sides are 7.07 units $\left(\sqrt{50}\ \text{units}\right)$

   (b) It is a rhombus.

D6 32.2 km

D7 (a) 5.7 cm   (b) 6.7 cm   (c) 3.6 cm   (d) 2.8 cm

   (e) 4.5 cm   (f) 9.5 cm   (g) 8.1 cm   (h) 5.0 cm

   (i) 10.4 cm

D8 20.5 km

D9 $a = 17$ cm, $b = 6.3$ cm, $c = 4.0$ cm

D10 $p = 25$ cm, $q = 65$ cm, $r = 12$ cm, $s = 37$ cm, $t = 7.7$ cm

D11 9.6 cm

Test yourself (p 74)

T1 (a) 16 cm^2 (b) 17 cm^2 (c) 8 cm^2

T2 (a) 10.4 m   (b) 5.9 m   (c) 12.7 m

T3 61.4 km (to 1 d.p.)

T4 (a)   (b) 2.9 m (to 1 d.p.)

T5 (a) 5.0 cm   (b) 7.2 cm and 9.8 cm

9 Working with linear expressions

A Substitution (p 75)

A1 (a) P: 10;   Q: 13;   R: 8;   S: 3;   T: 8;   U: 2.5;   V: 3;   W: 2

   (b) S and W   (c) Q   (d) U

A2 (a) 17   (b) 5   (c) 10   (d) 34

   (e) 45   (f) 5   (g) 4   (h) 4

A3 (a) 9 cm

   (b) (i)   (ii) 24 cm

   (c) 48 cm

B Simplifying (p 76)

B1 (a) $10n$ (b) $6y$ (c) $30a$ (d) $28b$ (e) $36x$

   (f) $2n$ (g) $2a$ (h) $3y$ (i) $5x$ (j) $4b$

B2 $8a$

B3 (a) $10t$ (b) $9b$

B4 (a) $7 + p$ (b) $8q$ (c) $2w + 2$ (d) $2k + 5$

   (e) $2h - 8$ (f) $2m$ (g) $7n - 4$ (h) 6

   (i) 1

B5 (a) (i) $4n + 2$ (ii) $4n + 6$

   (b) Triangle: 22, rectangle: 26

B6 (a) $7 - 2m$ (b) $3n - 4$ (c) $14 - 5p$ (d) $12 - 4$

   (e) $1 - 5v$ (f) $5 - 3w$ (g) $7 - 11g$ (h) $1 - 3h$

   (i) $9 - 9k$

B7 (a) $9 + x$ (b) 16

B8 (a) $100 - 4x$ (b) $80 - 2x$

C Brackets (p 78)

C1 A and H ($4a + 32$), B and D ($4a + 2$), C and E ($4a + 8$)
   F and G ($4a + 16$)

C2 (a) $6n + 6$ (b) $5m - 20$ (c) $15 + 3k$ (d) $10c +$

   (e) $12h - 8$ (f) $10a + 6$ (g) $12w - 18$ (h) $15 - 5$

   (i) $12 - 32x$ (j) $21c + 28$

C3 (a) $8 + 4f$ (b) $14x - 21$

C4 (a) 3 (b) $5b - 2$

C5 (a) $3(2n + 5) = 6n + 15$ (b) $4(2 - p) = 8 - 4p$

   (c) $5(4m - 3) = 20m - 15$ (d) $2(5x + 10) = 10x + 20$

C6 $2(x + 5)$, $2x + 10$

C7 $3(n - 2)$ or $3n - 6$

C8 (a)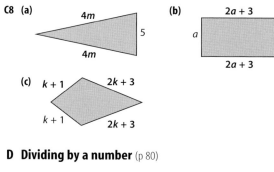

(b) rectangle with sides $2a + 3$ (top and bottom) and a (left and right)

(c) quadrilateral with sides $k + 1$, $2k + 3$, $k + 1$, $2k + 3$

D Dividing by a number (p 80)

D1 $2n + 5$

D2 (a) $3n + 2$ **(b)** $m + 3$ **(c)** $4 + 3k$ **(d)** $4h + 2$
(e) $p + 2$ **(f)** $2c + 3$ **(g)** $3y + 7$ **(h)** $6 + 4w$

D3 $2n - 6$

D4 (a) $a - 2$ **(b)** $3b - 4$ **(c)** $k - 10$ **(d)** $2h - 1$
(e) $2d - 3$ **(f)** $2g - 3$ **(g)** $3 - m$ **(h)** $12 - 5n$

D5 (a) $\dfrac{2m + 14}{2} = m + 7$ **(b)** $\dfrac{6c - 9}{3} = 2c - 3$

(c) $\dfrac{24 + 18y}{6} = 4 + 3y$

D6 $\frac{1}{3}(6n + 12) = \dfrac{6n + 12}{3} = 2n + 4$

D7 (a) $3n + 6$ **(b)** $3x - 2$ **(c)** $2k + 5$ **(d)** $p - 2$

D8

$\dfrac{10a}{2} - 1$ (**F**) $4(a+3)$ $\dfrac{4a}{2} + 3$ $\dfrac{6a}{2} + 4$	$2a + 2$ (**I**) $5 \times 2a$ $2(2a + 6)$ $\frac{1}{3}(12 - 3a)$	$\dfrac{5a - 5}{5}$ (**G**) $\dfrac{20a}{10}$ $\dfrac{30a}{3}$ $\frac{1}{5}(5 - 5a)$
$\dfrac{21a + 28}{7}$ (**D**) $2(5a + 1)$ $\dfrac{12a}{3} + 18$ $2(a + 2)$	$\dfrac{16 - 4a}{4}$ (**E**) $\dfrac{8a + 12}{2}$ $\dfrac{20a}{2} + 4$ $\dfrac{10a}{5} + 3$	$\dfrac{6 - 6a}{6}$ (**B**) $2(a + 4)$ $2(2a + 3)$ $\dfrac{9a}{3} - 4$
$\dfrac{20a + 40}{10}$ (**C**) $\frac{1}{2}(8a - 6)$ $\frac{1}{2}(8 - 6a)$ $3(a - 4)$	$\dfrac{8a + 12}{4}$ (**H**) $\dfrac{8a - 8}{8}$ $4a - 3$ $\dfrac{8a}{2} + 6$	$\frac{1}{2}(6a - 8)$ (**A**) $2(2a - 3)$ $\frac{1}{7}(7a - 7)$ $4(a + 6)$

D9 (a) $6y$ **(b)** $3x + 12$ **(c)** $12x - 4$

D10 (a) $10p + 8$ **(b)** $6a + 18$ **(c)** $10n$

E Justifying number puzzles (p 81)

E1 (a) The result is always the number first thought of.
(b) Working with $2n$ and n in the next two lines.

E2 (a) The result is always 2.
(b) Working with $3n + 6$, $n + 2$ and 2 in the next three lines.

E3 Puzzle A
(a) The result is always the number first thought of.
(b) An explanation using the expressions n, $n + 1$, $3n + 3$, $3n - 6$, $n - 2$ and n.

Puzzle B
(a) The result is always 0.
(b) An explanation using the expressions n, $n - 2$, $4n - 8$, $4n$, n and 0.

Puzzle C
(a) The result is always 5.
(b) An explanation using the expressions n, $6n$, $6n + 15$, $6n + 12$, $2n + 4$, $2n + 10$, $n + 5$ and 5.

E4 Made-up puzzles

Test yourself (p 83)

T1 (a) 19 **(b)** 20 **(c)** 39 **(d)** 3 **(e)** 7

T2 (a) $3b + 18$ **(b)** $10 - 2h$
(c) $10a - 15$ **(d)** $12x + 40$

T3 $2(n + 3)$, $2n + 6$

T4 $3p + 7$

T5 $2x + 4$

T6 (a) $3 - 2h$ **(b)** $3m + 5$ **(c)** $4k - 5$ **(d)** $2m - 7$

T7 (a) The result is always the number first thought of.
(b) An explanation using the expressions n, $n - 3$, $6n - 18$, $6n - 12$, $n - 2$ and n.

T8 $2x - 3$

T9 $8(3x + 5)$ or $24x + 40$

10 Representing 3-D objects

A The Soma cube (p 84)

A1 D needs 3; the rest need 4.

A2 A, B, C, E, F, G

A3 Drawings of A, B, C, D, F, G

B Nets (p 85)

B1 Only A

B2 Four of the following (or reflections or rotations of them)

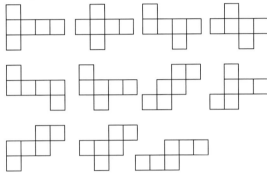

B3 There are only two nets for a regular tetrahedron (other than a reflection of the one on the right).

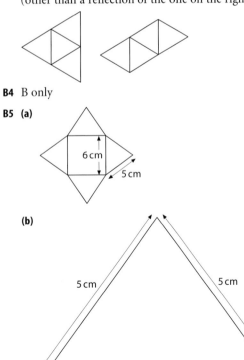

B4 B only

B5 (a)

6 cm

5 cm

(b)

5 cm   5 cm

6 cm

C Plan and elevations (p 86)

C1 B or C

C2

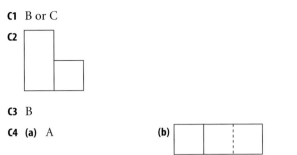

C3 B

C4 (a) A   (b)

C5 A plan, front and side view of another Soma cube piece

C6 Other orientations may be used.

(a)   (b)

(c)

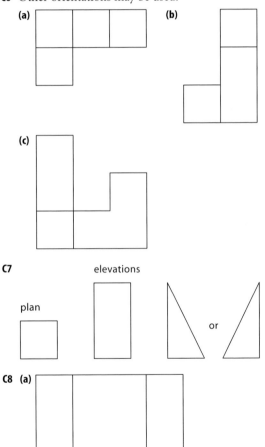

C7   elevations

plan   or

C8 (a)

(b)

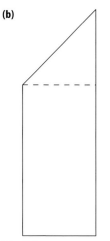

(c) 2.8 cm

(d) The edge AB is the hypotenuse of a triangle whose other two sides are both 2 cm.
So the length of AB is $\sqrt{8} = 2.8$ cm (to 1 d.p.)

D Reflection symmetry (p 88)

D1 D

D2 A and G, B and H, C and E, D and F

D3

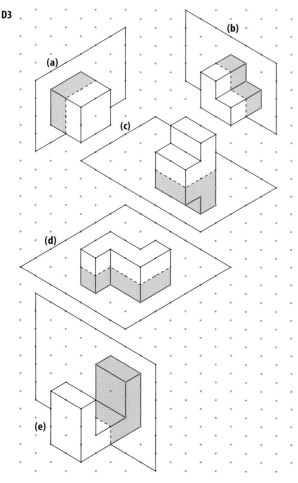

D4 (a) 2   **(b)** None   **(c)** 3   **(d)** 1

D5

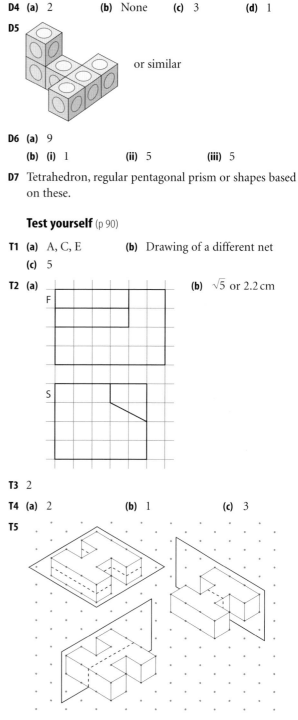

or similar

D6 (a) 9

   (b) (i) 1   **(ii)** 5   **(iii)** 5

D7 Tetrahedron, regular pentagonal prism or shapes based on these.

Test yourself (p 90)

T1 (a) A, C, E   **(b)** Drawing of a different net

   (c) 5

T2 (a)   **(b)** √5 or 2.2 cm

T3 2

T4 (a) 2   **(b)** 1   **(c)** 3

T5

(Drawing dotted lines on the surface of a shape is sufficient to define a plane of symmetry.)

11 Linear equations

A Solving equations (p 92)

A1 (a) $x = 7$ (b) $z = 3$ (c) $h = 5$
(d) $y = 10$ (e) $g = 2$ (f) $n = 3$
(g) $m = 0.5$ (h) $p = 1.5$ (i) $t = 1.5$

A2 (a) $x = 3$ (b) $x = 1$ (c) $x = 5$
(d) $x = 2$ (e) $x = 3$ (f) $x = 4$
(g) $x = 1.5$ (h) $x = 0.5$ (i) $x = 2.5$

A3 (a) $n = 1$ (b) $n = 2$ (c) $n = 3$
(d) $n = 4$ (e) $n = 7$ (f) $n = 5$
(g) $n = 1.5$ (h) $n = 2.5$ (i) $n = 0.5$

A4 (a) $k = 6.75$ (b) $k = 4.6$ (c) $k = 1.625$
(d) $k = 3.4$ (e) $k = 0.1875$ (f) $k = 1.75$
(g) $k = 3.75$ (h) $k = 1.875$ (i) $k = 0.4$
(j) $k = 0.4$ (k) $k = 0.1$ (l) $k = 0.1375$

B Forming equations from shapes (p 93)

B1 (a) (i)

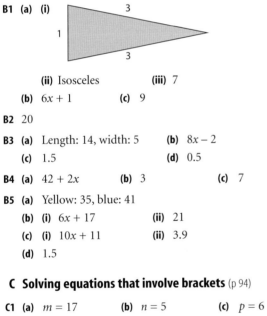

(ii) Isosceles   (iii) 7
(b) $6x + 1$ (c) 9

B2 20

B3 (a) Length: 14, width: 5   (b) $8x - 2$
(c) 1.5   (d) 0.5

B4 (a) $42 + 2x$ (b) 3   (c) 7

B5 (a) Yellow: 35, blue: 41
(b) (i) $6x + 17$ (ii) 21
(c) (i) $10x + 11$ (ii) 3.9
(d) 1.5

C Solving equations that involve brackets (p 94)

C1 (a) $m = 17$ (b) $n = 5$ (c) $p = 6$
(d) $g = 4.5$ (e) $h = 5$ (f) $k = 4$
(g) $x = 27$ (h) $y = 5$ (i) $z = 10$
(j) $a = 1.5$ (k) $b = 2.5$ (l) $c = 4.5$

C2 (a) $n = 4$ (b) $p = 5$ (c) $q = 6$
(d) $h = 5$ (e) $a = 2$ (f) $w = 1.5$
(g) $v = 1$ (h) $z = 7$ (i) $h = 4$

C3 (a) $k = 1.75$ (b) $k = 0.6$ (c) $k = 2.25$
(d) $k = 4$ (e) $k = 4.375$ (f) $k = 0.75$
(g) $k = 2.6875$ (h) $k = 1.25$ (i) $k = 2.5$
(j) $k = 0.4$ (k) $k = 2$ (l) $k = 1.4$

D Solving number puzzles (p 95)

D1 (a) 4   (b) 0.5

D2 (a) $2n + 12 = 3n$ (b) $n = 12$ with check

D3 (a) 20   (b) 7   (c) 1.5

D4 8

D5 $3(n - 5) = 21; n = 12$

D6 (a) 13   (b) 27   (c) 8

Test yourself (p 96)

T1 (a) $x = 3$ (b) $x = 5.5$

T2 (a) $x = 2$ (b) $x = 1.5$ (c) $x = 2$

T3 $x = 2$

T4 (a) $a = 1.5$ (b) $b = 4$ (c) $c = 5.6$

T5 (a) $2n + 30$ (b) $n = 5.5$

T6 (a) $k = 1$ (b) $k = 4$ (c) $k = 3$
(d) $k = 1.5$ (e) $k = 5$ (f) $k = 0.5$

T7 4

12 Multiples, factors and powers

A Multiples, factors and primes (p 97)

A1 (a) Five multiples of 4.   (b) Five multiples of 3.
  (c) A multiple of 12.

A2 (a) A multiple of 42 greater than 50; no, it is not the lowest common multiple.
  (b) 8; yes, it is the lowest common multiple.

A3 (a) 10   (b) 8   (c) 24   (d) 36

A4 1, 2, 3, 4, 5, 6, 10, 12, 15, 20, 30, 60

A5 Two factors from 1, 2 and 4

A6 (a) 1, 3, 9   (b) 9

A7 (a) 5   (b) 1   (c) 10   (d) 6

A8 6, 14, 9, 21, 10, 15

A9 23, 29, 31, 37

A10 Highest common factor 1
  Lowest common multiple 33
  For any two prime numbers, the highest common factor is always 1 and the lowest common multiple is the product of the two numbers.

A11 For any pair of numbers, the product of those numbers is equal to the product of the highest common factor and the lowest common multiple.

B Powers (p 99)

B1 (a) 2^8 (b) 4^{11}

B2 (a) 16   (b) 64   (c) 243   (d) 49   (e) 125

B3 (a) 16, 32 or 2^4, 2^5 (b) 9

B4 (a) 2^8 or 256   (b) 2 hours and 30 minutes

B5 (a) F   (b) T   (c) F   (d) F

B6 (a) <   (b) <   (c) >   (d) >

B7 (a) 6   (b) 1   (c) 2   (d) 1

B8 (a) (i) 8   (ii) 10 000   (iii) 729
  (b) 100^2, 16^6, 7^{10}, 2^{31}, 3^{20}

B9 2^{25}

B10 7

B11 2^{20} or 1 048 576

B12 (a) $x = 7$ (b) $x = 3$ (c) $x = 4$ (d) $x = 9$

B13
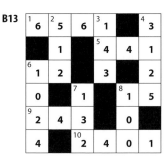

¹6	²5	6	³1		⁴3
	1		⁵4	4	1
⁶1	2		3		2
0		⁷1		⁸1	5
⁹2	4	3		0	
4		¹⁰2	4	0	1

B14 235 298 (or 2×7^6)

B15 (a) The numbers in the second row of the table are 3, 9, **7**, 1, **3**, **9**, 7, **1**, **3**, **9**
  (b) (i) 1   (ii) 3   (iii) 7

B16 (a) Investigations and conclusions
  (b) (i) 9   (ii) 5   (iii) 1

B17 (a) 6 as 2^n ends in a 6 when n is a multiple of 4
  (b) 9 as 9^n ends in a 9 when n is odd
  (c) 5 as all powers of 5 end in a 5
  (d) 6 as 4^n ends in a 6 when n is even
  (e) 6 as all powers of 6 end in a 6

C Multiplying powers (p 101)

C1 (a) 5   (b) 9   (c) 9   (d) 6

C2 (a) 5   (b) 6   (c) 8   (d) 12   (e) 6   (f) 1

C3 (a) A description of the rule, for example: 'To multiply powers of the same number, you need to **add** the indices', together with an explanation
  (b) $2^{12} \times 2^5 = 2^{17}$

C4 A and D, B and F, C and E

C5 (a) 3^7 (b) 10^{11} (c) 4^{12} (d) 8^5
  (e) 2^9 (f) 7^{12} (g) 10^{11} (h) 9^{30}

C6 (a) $2^8 \times 2^4 = 2^{12}$ (b) $5^2 \times 5^6 = 5^8$
  (c) $3^9 \times 3 = 3^{10}$ (d) $4^3 \times 4^2 \times 4^5 = 4^{10}$

C7 B and D

C8 (a) $3^2 \times 5^3 \times 5^4 \times 3^6 = 3^8 \times 5^7$
  (b) $2 \times 9^2 \times 2^5 \times 9^3 = 2^6 \times 9^5$
  (c) $4^7 \times 3^8 \times 4 \times 3^2 = 3^{10} \times 4^8$
  (d) $3^4 \times 11^3 \times 3^1 \times 11^5 = 3^5 \times 11^8$

C9 (a) $10^5 \times 3^9$ (b) $2^{11} \times 5^3$ (c) $5^{10} \times 7^7$

D Prime factorisation (p 102)

D1 A and H, B and F, C and G, D and E

D2 (a) $3^2 \times 5$ (b) $2 \times 3 \times 5^2$ (c) $2^4 \times 3$
  (d) $2 \times 3^2 \times 7$ (e) 3^5

D3 (a) 2, 3, 7, 6, 14 with an explanation
(b) Checks by calculation

D4 (a) 5, 7, 25, 35, 125 with an explanation.
(b) Checks by calculation

D5 Yes, 3465 is a multiple of 315; an explanation such as 'It just has the extra factor 11'.

D6 No, 5005 is not a multiple of 1155; an explanation such as 'You cannot get it just by multiplying by one or more extra factors'.

D7 (a) $2^3 \times 3 \times 5$, $2^3 \times 3 \times 7^2$, $2^4 \times 3$, $2^3 \times 3^2$
(b) Checks by calculation

D8 (a) 7, 3×7, $3^2 \times 7$
(b) Checks by calculation

D9 5, 11, 5×11

D10 $2^3 \times 3^2 \times 7$ $2^2 \times 3^7 \times 7$ $2^2 \times 3^2 \times 7 \times 13$

E Highest common factor and lowest common multiple
(p 104)

E1 (a) (i) $2 \times 2 \times 2 \times 2 \times 2 \times 2$ (or 2^6)
(ii) $2 \times 2 \times 2 \times 3 \times 7$ (or $2^3 \times 3 \times 7$)
(b) 8 (= $2 \times 2 \times 2$)

E2 (a) 36　(b) 15　(c) 11　(d) 26

E3 (a) $18 = 2 \times 3 \times 3$ (or 2×3^2)
$42 = 2 \times 3 \times 7$
(b) 126 (= $2 \times 3 \times 3 \times 7$)

E4 (a) 60　(b) 210　(c) 495　(d) 1050

E5 34 cm by 34 cm

E6 2520

E7 60, 140

Test yourself (p 105)

T1 (a) 1, 2, 3, 5, 6, 9, 10, 15, 18, 30, 45, 90
(b) 11, 13, 17, 19, 23, 29
(c) 27, 81　(d) 1　(e) 14

T2 (a) 2187　(b) 169　(c) 10

T3 (a) $x = 1$　(b) $x = 7$　(c) $x = 1$

T4 (a) 2^{14}　(b) 3^9　(c) 5^7

T5 $2^6 \times 3^9$

T6 $2 \times 3^2 \times 13$

T7 (a) 60　(b) 42

T8 165 seconds

13 Negative numbers

A Calculating with positive and negative numbers
(p 106)

A1 (a) An addition
(b) Seven different additions are possible:
$^-3 + 1 = ^-2$,　$^-3 + 2 = ^-1$,　$^-2 + ^-1 = ^-3$,　$^-2 + 1 = ^-$
$^-2 + 2 = 0$,　$^-1 + 1 = 0$,　$^-1 + 2 = 1$
(c) A subtraction
(d) Eight subtractions; fourteen different subtractions are possible:
$^-3 - ^-2 = ^-1$,　$^-3 - ^-1 = ^-2$,　$^-2 - ^-3 = 1$,　$^-2 - 1 = ^-$
$^-1 - ^-3 = 2$,　$^-1 - ^-2 = 1$,　$^-1 - 1 = ^-2$,　$^-1 - 2 = ^-$
$0 - ^-2 = 2$,　$0 - ^-1 = 1$,　$0 - 1 = ^-1$,　$0 - 2 = ^-2$,
$1 - ^-1 = 2$,　$1 - 2 = ^-1$

A2 (a)

×	3	⁻2
⁻5	⁻15	10
4	12	⁻8

(b)

×	5	⁻3
⁻1	⁻5	3
6	30	⁻18

(c)

×	⁻2	⁻7
⁻4	8	28
6	⁻12	⁻42

A3 (a)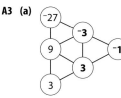

(b)

(c)

A4 (a)

⁻2	5	0
3	1	⁻1
2	⁻3	4

(b)

⁻4	1	0
3	⁻1	⁻5
⁻2	⁻3	2

(c)

⁻5	5	⁻9
⁻7	⁻3	1
3	⁻11	⁻1

A5 (a) 1, ⁻1　(b) 1, 4　(c) ⁻1, ⁻2.5　(d) ⁻32, 6

A6 (a) 4　(b) 21　(c) ⁻16　(d) 5　(e) ⁻2
(f) 11　(g) ⁻3　(h) ⁻1　(i) ⁻2　(j) 1
(k) ⁻1　(l) 1

A7 (a) ⁻2　(b) ⁻1　(c) 2　(d) 5　(e) 2
(f) 2　(g) ⁻2　(h) ⁻24　(i) ⁻2

B Substitution (p 108)

B1 (a) $^-1$ (b) $^-5$ (c) $^-6$ (d) 6

B2 (a) $^-5$ (b) 14 (c) 11 (d) 1

B3 (a) $^-20$ (b) $^-2$ (c) 13 (d) 27
(e) $^-3$ (f) 9 (g) $^-4$ (h) $^-216$

B4 (a) $^-5$ (b) $^-4$ (c) $^-45$ (d) $^-7$

B5 (a) 33 (b) $^-9$ (c) 70 (d) 7
(e) 2 (f) $^-8$ (g) 4 (h) $^-3$

B6 (a) $\dfrac{3n-17}{2}$, $5 - n^2$, $2(n-5)$

(b) $5 - n^2$, $3n^2 - 11$, $\dfrac{4n+3}{-5}$

B7 (a) Each expression has value 16.
They all have the same value.

(b) $n - 1$, $\dfrac{6-n}{4}$, $\dfrac{n^2}{4}$, $\dfrac{4n-3}{5}$

(c) $\dfrac{n-3}{2}$, $2n$, $n^2 - 3$, $n - 1$

(d) (i) $4n + 9$, $\dfrac{n^2}{4}$, $\dfrac{5-n}{7}$, $2n + 5$

(ii) $\dfrac{n-3}{2}$, $\dfrac{2n^2}{-6}$, $4n + 9$, $\dfrac{4n-3}{5}$

(iii) $n - 1$, $3n + 11$, $2n + 5$, $\dfrac{n^2}{2} - 25$

B8 (a) (i) 1 (ii) $^-3$ (iii) $^-11$
(b) (i) $^-15$ (ii) $^-18$ (iii) $^-24$
(c) (i) $n = ^-15$ (ii) A check by substitution

C Equations with negative solutions (p 110)

C1 (a) $n = ^-3$ (b) A check by substitution

C2 (a) $k = ^-1$ (b) $n = ^-1.5$ (c) $p = ^-2.5$

C3 $m = ^-5$

C4 (a) $k = ^-4$ (b) $g = ^-2$ (c) $n = ^-3$
(d) $b = ^-3$ (e) $t = ^-1$ (f) $x = ^-2$

C5 (a) $n = ^-2$ (b) $t = ^-3$ (c) $b = ^-4$

C6 (a) $m = ^-2$ (b) $d = ^-0.5$ (c) $h = ^-0.2$

C7 (a) $q = ^-2$ (b) $r = ^-1$ (c) $t = ^-4$
(d) $v = ^-9$ (e) $w = ^-0.5$ (f) $x = ^-2.5$

Test yourself (p 110)

T1 (a) $^-9$ (b) 12 (c) $^-4$ (d) 21
(e) 3 (f) 9

T2 (a) $^-26$ (b) $^-35$ (c) 6 (d) 13
(e) 45 (f) 28 (g) $^-4$ (h) 5

T3 (a) $x = ^-2$ (b) $m = ^-5$ (c) $w = ^-2$ (d) $n = ^-3$
(e) $d = ^-5$ (f) $y = ^-3$

14 Drawing and using linear graphs

A Drawing straight-line graphs (p 111)

A1 A, C and E

A2 (a)

x	$^-2$	0	2
$2x + 3$	$^-1$	3	7

(b)

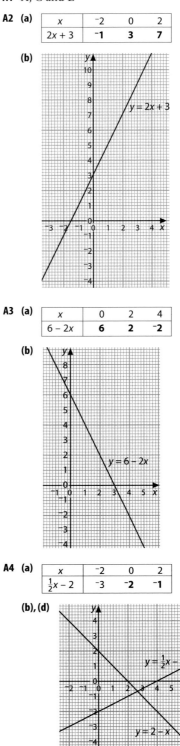

A3 (a)

x	0	2	4
$6 - 2x$	6	2	$^-2$

(b)

A4 (a)

x	$^-2$	0	2
$\frac{1}{2}x - 2$	$^-3$	$^-2$	$^-1$

(b), (d)

(c)

x	$^-2$	0	2
$2 - x$	$^-4$	**2**	**0**

(e) $(2.7, ^-0.7)$

A5 (a)

x	$^-3$	$^-2$	$^-1$	0	1	2	3
y	3	3	3	**3**	**3**	**3**	**3**

(b)

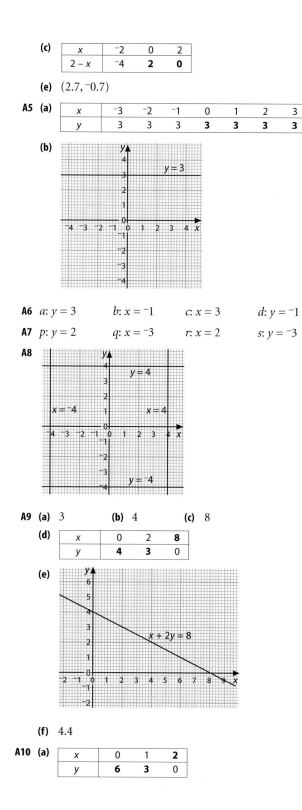

A6 a: $y = 3$ b: $x = ^-1$ c: $x = 3$ d: $y = ^-1$

A7 p: $y = 2$ q: $x = ^-3$ r: $x = 2$ s: $y = ^-3$

A8

A9 (a) 3   **(b)** 4   **(c)** 8

(d)

x	0	2	**8**
y	**4**	**3**	0

(e)

(f) 4.4

A10 (a)

x	0	1	**2**
y	**6**	**3**	0

(b)

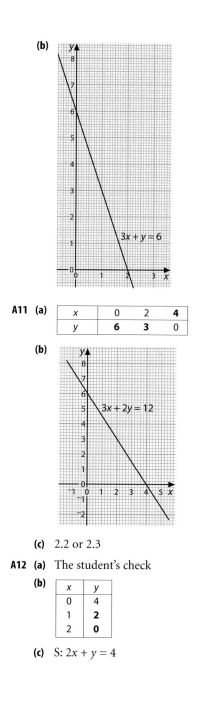

A11 (a)

x	0	2	**4**
y	**6**	**3**	0

(b)

(c) 2.2 or 2.3

A12 (a) The student's check

(b)

x	y
0	4
1	**2**
2	**0**

(c) S: $2x + y = 4$

A13

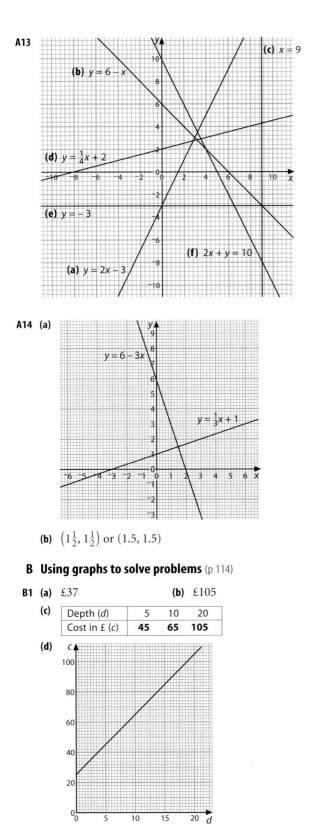

(c) $x = 9$

(b) $y = 6 - x$

(d) $y = \frac{1}{4}x + 2$

(e) $y = -3$

(f) $2x + y = 10$

(a) $y = 2x - 3$

A14 (a)

$y = 6 - 3x$

$y = \frac{1}{3}x + 1$

(b) $\left(1\frac{1}{2}, 1\frac{1}{2}\right)$ or (1.5, 1.5)

B Using graphs to solve problems (p 114)

B1 (a) £37
(b) £105

(c)

Depth (d)	5	10	20
Cost in £ (c)	45	65	105

(d)

(e) 12.5 cm

B2 (a) £59
(b) £41

(c)

Weight (w)	1	4	6
Cost in £ (c)	41	59	71

(d) See answer to B3 (d)

(e) 3.3 tonnes
(f) $c = 35 + 6w$

B3 (a)

Weight (w)	1	4	7
Cost in £ (c)	20	50	80

(b) See graph below
(c) £65

(d) Mendip Mushrooms is cheaper; the student's explanation

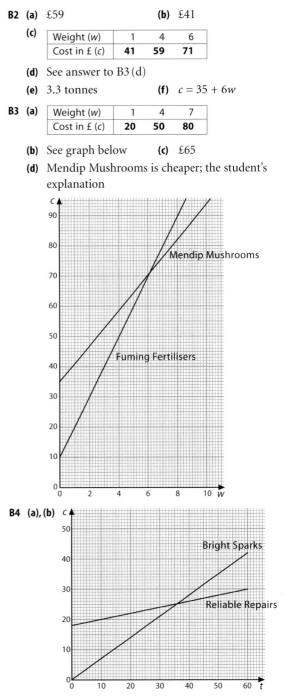

B4 (a), (b)

(c) A decision and explanation such as:
'I would advise her to take it to Reliable Repairs as any repair that takes longer than 36 minutes will be cheaper than Bright Sparks.'

Test yourself (p 115)

T1 (a)

x	$^-1$	0	3
$2x - 2$	**$^-4$**	**$^-2$**	**4**

(b)

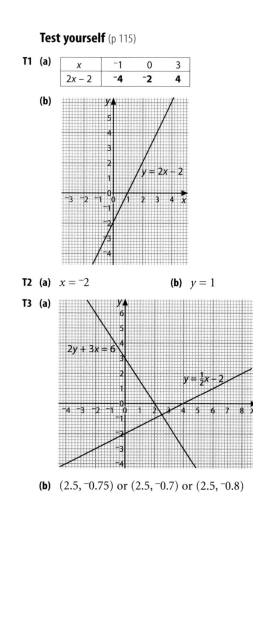

$y = 2x - 2$

T2 (a) $x = {}^-2$ **(b)** $y = 1$

T3 (a)

$2y + 3x = 6$

$y = \frac{1}{2}x - 2$

(b) $(2.5, {}^-0.75)$ or $(2.5, {}^-0.7)$ or $(2.5, {}^-0.8)$

15 Using a calculator

A Brackets and order of operations (p 116)

A1 (a) 27   **(b)** 20   **(c)** 16   **(d)** 68
     (e) 33   **(f)** 43   **(g)** 200   **(h)** 23

A2 (a) 50.44   **(b)** 23.93   **(c)** 8.85   **(d)** 11.60
     (e) 8.53   **(f)** 1.47   **(g)** 15.51

A3 (a) 20.2   **(b)** 16.9   **(c)** 341   **(d)** 452
     (e) 10.1   **(f)** 4.92   **(g)** 1.68

B Division (p 117)

B1 (a) 3   **(b)** 12   **(c)** 18   **(d)** 10   **(e)** 4
     (f) 18   **(g)** 4   **(h)** 16   **(i)** 5

B2 A: V, B: U, C: Y, D: X, E: Z, F: T, G: W

B3 (a) 1.81   **(b)** 3.44   **(c)** 3.26   **(d)** 0.58
     (e) 18.55   **(f)** 5.02

C Checking by rough estimates (p 118)

C1 (a) 12   **(b)** 12.2

C2 (a) $\dfrac{0.5 \times 200}{4}$ **(b)** 25   **(c)** 27.278…

C3 (a) (i) 10   **(ii)** 9.01
    (b) (i) 80   **(ii)** 81.4
    (c) (i) 5   **(ii)** 5.41
    (d) (i) 5   **(ii)** 5.32
    (e) (i) 2   **(ii)** 2.03
    (f) (i) 4   **(ii)** 4.01

D Other keys (p 118)

D1 (a) 5   **(b)** 0   **(c)** 12   **(d)** $^-5$ **(e)** $^-3.5$

D2 (a) 9
    (b) (i) 18.49   **(ii)** 2.95   **(iii)** 7.6729
        (iv) $^-12.3464$ **(v)** 12.25

D3 (a) 4.36   **(b)** 26.15   **(c)** 10.68   **(d)** 0.73   **(e)** 1.78

D4 (a) 13.72   **(b)** 1.42   **(c)** 5.31   **(d)** 0.68   **(e)** 5.90
    (f) 3.83   **(g)** 4.79   **(h)** 15.58   **(i)** 2.27

Test yourself (p 119)

T1 49.7

T2 (a) $\dfrac{700 \times 20}{600 + 400} = \dfrac{14000}{1000} = 14$
    (b) (i) 14.235 532 99…   **(ii)** 14.2

T3 41.2

T4 (a) 2.40   **(b)** $\dfrac{5^2 + \sqrt{9}}{2 \times 7} = \dfrac{28}{14} = 2$

16 Changing the subject

A Forming and using formulas (p 120)

A1 (a) 104   (b) 154   (c) 34

A2 $80 = 2a + 4$, so $a = 38$; 38 artichoke plants are needed.

A3 (a)

b	1	2	3	4	5	10	100
c	6	10	14	18	22	42	402

   (b) $c = 4b + 2$

   (c) (i) 62   (ii) 102

   (d) $90 = 4b + 2$, $b = 22$

   (e) She needs 22 broccoli plants.

A4 (a) An explanation   (b) 304   (c) 16

B Changing the subject of a formula (p 122)

B1 (a) 26   (b) 66   (c) 13

B2 (a) An explanation   (b) 62

   (c)
$$w = 3r + 2$$
$$w - 2 = 3r$$
$$\frac{w - 2}{3} = r$$

   (d) 16   (e) 22 (and check)

B3 (a) $r = \dfrac{w - 4}{2}$ (b) 42   (c) 62

B4 (a) 32   (b) $g = \dfrac{f - 2}{3}$ (c) A check

B5 (a) $t = \dfrac{s - 1}{5}$ (b) A check

B6 (a) $w = \dfrac{b - 7}{8}$ (b) $v = \dfrac{u - 2}{5}$ (c) $d = \dfrac{g}{6}$

   (d) $x = \dfrac{y - 12}{3}$ (e) $b = \dfrac{t - 5}{3}$ (f) $d = \dfrac{f - 8}{3}$

   (g) $k = h - 5$ (h) $d = \dfrac{w - 1}{7}$

B7 (a)
$$y = 5x - 6$$
$$y + 6 = 5x$$
$$\frac{y + 6}{5} = x$$

   (b) $x = 27$ (c) A check

B8 B, C and F

B9 (a) $w = \dfrac{a + 6}{8}$ (b) $h = \dfrac{b + 1}{4}$ (c) $f = \dfrac{h + 2}{2}$

   (d) $x = y + 15$ (e) $r = \dfrac{z + 15}{2}$ (f) $d = \dfrac{k + 3}{2}$

   (g) $g = b + 5$ (h) $m = \dfrac{l + 1}{2}$

B10 A and F, B and E, C and H, D and G

B11 (a) $b = \dfrac{a - 30}{3}$ (b) $t = \dfrac{s + 40}{2}$ (c) $g = \dfrac{t + 60}{12}$

   (d) $b = \dfrac{f - 12}{3}$ (e) $x = \dfrac{y - 12}{8}$ (f) $s = \dfrac{r + 20}{5}$

   (g) $b = \dfrac{a}{3}$ (h) $u = \dfrac{v + 10}{7}$ (i) $x = y - 35$

   (j) $j = \dfrac{d - 8}{4}$ (k) $j = \dfrac{k + 45}{8}$ (l) $z = \dfrac{w + 1}{7}$

Test yourself (p 124)

T1 (a) $r = \dfrac{a - 8}{6}$ (b) $s = \dfrac{b - 6}{4}$ (c) $t = \dfrac{c - 12}{5}$

   (d) $u = \dfrac{d - 8}{4}$

T2 (a)
$$n = 3m - 2$$
$$n + 2 = 3m$$
$$\frac{n + 2}{3} = m$$

   (b) A pair of values that fit $n = 3m - 2$

   (c) A check

T3 B and D

T4 (a) $v = \dfrac{e + 12}{4}$ (b) $w = \dfrac{f + 15}{2}$ (c) $x = g + 12$

   (d) $y = \dfrac{h + 10}{5}$

T5 (a) $t = \dfrac{n - 8}{5}$ (b) $t = \dfrac{s + 7}{4}$ (c) $x = \dfrac{y - 12}{2}$

   (d) $u = \dfrac{m + 5}{3}$ (e) $v = \dfrac{j - 12}{5}$ (f) $w = \dfrac{f - 15}{5}$

   (g) $x = \dfrac{k}{3}$ (h) $y = \dfrac{b - 4}{8}$

17 Grid totals

A Expressions from patterns on a number grid (p 125)

A1 (a) 47

(b) Other valid totals

(c) (i)

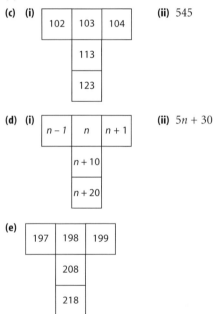

106	107
116	

(ii) 329

(d) (i)

n	$n+1$
$n+10$	

(ii) $3n + 11$

(e) 201, 202 and 211

(f) An explanation such as:
'$3n + 11 = 154$ leads to $n = 143 \div 3$ which is not a whole number. So this L-shape is impossible.'

A2 (a) 105

(b) Other valid totals

(c) (i)

102	103	104
	113	
	123	

(ii) 545

(d) (i)

$n-1$	n	$n+1$
	$n+10$	
	$n+20$	

(ii) $5n + 30$

(e)

197	198	199
	208	
	218	

(f) An explanation such as:
'$5n + 30 = 231$ leads to $n = 201 \div 5$ which is not a whole number. So this T-shape is impossible.'

A3 (a) (i)

$n-1$	n	$n+1$
	$n+6$	
	$n+12$	

(ii) $5n + 18$

(b) An investigation, perhaps leading to the total for a T-shape on a grid with m columns

A4 (a) 64

(b) Other valid totals

(c)

	$n-12$	
$n-1$	n	$n+1$

(d) An explanation such as:
'The total is $4n - 12$. The equation $4n - 12 = 84$ leads to $n = 24$. This gives a shape whose 'n' square would be at the right-hand edge of the grid, and which therefore cannot be drawn on the grid'.

(e) An explanation such as:
'The result of dividing $4n - 12$ by 4 is $\frac{4n - 12}{4} = n - 3$. As $n - 3$ is a whole number, the total must be a multiple of 4.'

Test yourself (p 127)

T1 (a) 52

(b) Other valid totals

(c)

n	$n+1$
$n+7$	$n+8$

(d)

46	47
53	54

(e) An explanation such as:
'The total is $4n + 16$. The equation $4n + 16 = 62$ leads to $n = 46 \div 4$ which is not a whole number. So this square is not possible.'

(f) An explanation such as:
'The total is $4n + 16$. $\frac{4n + 16}{2} = 2n + 8$ which is always a whole number so $4n + 16$ is always even. Hence there cannot be an odd total.'

(g) An explanation such as:
'The total is $4n + 16$. The equation $4n + 16 = 100$ leads to $n = 21$. This results in a shape where the top left-hand square is on the right-hand edge of the grid. So this shape is not possible on this grid.'

Review 2 (p 128)

1 (a) (i) P: 7; Q: 8; R: 4; S: 7; T: 0
(ii) P: 5; Q: 2; R: 3.5; S: 9; T: 1
(iii) P: ⁻5; Q: ⁻28; R: 1; S: 19; T: 36
(b) Q $(2(3n-5))$ has the smallest value.

2 3^4

3 (a) 10 **(b)** 7 **(c)** 3

4 $21p - 35$

5 31, 37

6 $2n - 4, 2(n-2)$

7 (a) $5 - 2p$ **(b)** $2b + 1$ **(c)** $2 - 3k$

8 4

9 (a) $x = 6$ **(b)** $x = 3$ **(c)** $x = {}^-4$ **(d)** $n = 6.5$
(e) $n = 1$ **(f)** $n = {}^-3$

10 (a) $2^2 \times 3 \times 5^2$ **(b)** $2 \times 3^2 \times 11$ **(c)** 6

11 (a) $120 - 2n$ **(b)** 100 **(c)** 12.5 **(d)** 20

12 20 cm

13 (a) $P = 2s + 6$ **(b)** $s = \dfrac{P-6}{2}$ **(c)** 4.5

14 7 cm

15 (a)

(b) Trapezium

16 (a) (i) Q **(ii)** P
(b) P: 1.95; Q: 6.95; R: 2.89

17 $h = \dfrac{v+9}{7}$

18 (a) 4.2 cm^2 **(b)** 2
(c)

19 (a) 63.85 **(b)** 1.87 **(c)** 8.30 **(d)** 9.67
(e) 22.09 **(f)** 4.08

20 24.2 cm (to the nearest 0.1 cm)

18 Ratio

A Writing a ratio in its simplest form (p 130)

A1 1:4, 20:80
6:10, 3:5
150:200, 3:4
25:75, 2:6

A2 (a) 5:2 **(b)** 2:5

A3 (a) 1:4 **(b)** 1:3 **(c)** 3:4 **(d)** 4:5 **(e)** 2:1
(f) 9:10 **(g)** 3:2 **(h)** 8:5 **(i)** 3:2 **(j)** 7:5
(k) 3:1 **(l)** 6:7 **(m)** 3:8 **(n)** 5:2 **(o)** 3:7

A4 (a) 2:5 **(b)** 2:5 **(c)** 2:5

A5 (a) One measurement is in cm and the other in m.
(b) 1:50

A6 (a) 1:5 **(b)** 3:10 **(c)** 1:5 **(d)** 4:15
(e) 12:1 **(f)** 10:1 **(g)** 20:1 **(h)** 12:1

A7 3:1:2

A8 20:4:5

A9 20:5:2

A10 30:5:2

A11 (a) 1:4:6 **(b)** 2:3:5 **(c)** 2:3:5 **(d)** 4:3:2

A12 (a) 6:3:2 **(b)** A, C

B Finding a value from a given ratio (p 132)

B1

Red (1 part)	White (3 parts)
2 litres	**6 litres**
3 litres	9 litres
0.5 litre	**1.5 litres**
4 litres	12 litres

B2

Red (2 parts)	White (3 parts)
6 litres	**9 litres**
10 litres	15 litres
8 litres	**12 litres**
1 litre	1.5 litres

B3 (a) 2.5 litres **(b)** 100 ml

B4 (a) 40 **(b)** 25

B5 6

B6 64

B7 (a) 25 kg **(b)** 12 kg

B8

Ratio	Quantities
1:5	15 kg:**75** kg
2:3	50 g:**75** g
5:4	20 m:**16** m
3:8	**120** g:320 g

B9 (a) £3.30   (b) £3.50

B10 (a) 80   (b) 15

B11 16

B12 7.5 litres

B13 12.5 litres

B14 (a) 48 ml mango juice, 72 ml fizzy water

     (b) 250 ml pineapple juice, 100 ml mango juice

B15 90 cows, 36 pigs

B16 168

C Dividing in a given ratio (p 134)

C1 Colin £50, Dilip £150

C2 Emma £60, Farnaz £100

C3 (a) 600 ml or 0.6 litre   (b) 400 ml or 0.4 litre

C4 (a) 45 g   (b) 5 g

C5 (a) £3, £9   (b) £10, £25   (c) 18 kg, 42 kg

     (d) £3.50, £1

C6 (a) 2:1   (b) 320

C7 1400 g

C8 Paul £4, Steph £8, Ronnie £12

C9 Blue 0.25 litre, yellow 0.75 litre, white 1 litre

C10 10 chocolate, 10 cream, 15 plain

C11 140 g copper, 140 g nickel, 70 g zinc

D Converting between ratios, fractions and percentages (p 135)

D1 $\frac{1}{5}$

D2 (a) $\frac{1}{8}$ (b) $\frac{7}{8}$

D3 (a) $\frac{3}{5}$ (b) 60%

D4 1:1

D5 1:2

D6 1:3

D7 1:5

D8 3:2

D9 A, H; B, D; C, E; F, G

D10 (a) $\frac{3}{4}$ (b) 75%

D11 A, E; B, C

A statement matching D, e.g. 'The ratio of boys to girls is 3:1'.

D12 4:1

E Writing in the form $k:1$ and $1:k$ (p 136)

E1 1.5 litres

E2 (a) 3.5:1   (b) 2.5:1   (c) 1.25:1   (d) 3.3:1   (e) 0.4:1

E3 1:5.5

E4 (a) 1:2.5   (b) 1:3.5   (c) 1:4.5   (d) 1:0.7   (e) 1:0.75

E5 1:19

E6 3.5:1

E7 (a) 11.5:1   (b) 575 g

Test yourself (p 137)

T1 20

T2 (a) 720 City fans, 480 United fans   (b) $\frac{1}{8}$

T3 (a) Sharon £234, Liam £126   (b) 65%

T4 (a) £735   (b) £196

19 Substitution

A Substitution review (p 138)

A1 (a) 32   (b) 84   (c) 5   (d) 4   (e) $^-3$

A2 (a) 50   (b) 4.78   (c) 4.05   (d) 5   (e) 8.1   (f) $^-9.45$

A3 (a) 12.6 cm   (b) 9.4 cm   (c) 15.7 cm

A4 (a) $12.6 \, \text{cm}^2$ (b) $7.1 \, \text{cm}^2$ (c) $19.6 \, \text{cm}^2$

A5 (a) $10(x + 3)$ (b) $2 - 4x^2$

A6 (a) 4   (b) 5, $^-5$ (c) 3.5   (d) 1, $^-1$

B Expressions with more than one letter (p 139)

B1 (a) 30   (b) 15   (c) 1   (d) 4.5   (e) 180

B2 (a) $^-22$ (b) $^-0.2$ (c) 16   (d) 360   (e) 20

B3 (a) 29.6   (b) 4.2   (c) 185.0   (d) 324.9   (e) 76.9

B4 (a) 0.23   (b) 5.22   (c) 20.39   (d) 0.58   (e) 20.18

B5 (a) 3.12   (b) 12.25   (c) 0.75   (d) 2.25   (e) 7.75

B6 (a) 1   (b) $\frac{1}{4}$ (c) $\frac{5}{6}$ (d) $1\frac{7}{12}$ (e) $\frac{1}{12}$

B7 (a) 12   (b) 18   (c) 36

C Units in formulas (p 140)

C1 (a) $125 \, \text{cm}^2$ (b) $0.54 \, \text{m}^2$ or $5400 \, \text{cm}^2$

C2 (a) $2800 \, \text{cm}^2$ (b) $9200 \, \text{cm}^2$ or $0.92 \, \text{m}^2$

C3 (a) (i) 1 amp (ii) 0.4 amp (iii) 0.3 amp (iv) 20 amp
     (b) 6.9 kilowatt

C4 (a) $8.4 \, \text{cm}^2$ (b) $0.51 \, \text{km}^2$

C5 (a) 640 m   (b) 210 cm   (c) 8.6 cm   (d) 3.9 m

C6 (a) $80\,000 \, \text{cm}^3$ or $0.08 \, \text{m}^3$ (b) $90\,000 \, \text{cm}^3$ or $0.09 \, \text{m}^3$

C7 (a) $192 \, \text{cm}^2$ (b) $4.73 \, \text{m}^2$ (to 2 d.p.)

D Mixed questions (p 142)

D1 (a) 32 °F   (b) 212 °F
     (c) About 22 °C   (d) 2.2 °C (to 2 s.f.)
     (e) About 1500 °C   (f) About 15 000 000 °C
     (g) $^-27$ °C (to 2 s.f.)   (h) $^-89$ °C (to 2 s.f.)
     (i) $^-38$ °F (to 2 s.f.)   (j) $^-40°$

D2 (a) 2000 kg   (b) 6750 kg   (c) 250 kg

D3 (a) 3.7 tonnes (to 1 d.p.)   (b) 8.8 tonnes (to 1 d.p.)
     (c) No (it weighs 425 kg)

D4 2700 kg

D5 (a) 35 m
     (b)

t	0	1	2	3	4
h	80	75	60	35	0

     (c) 80 m above the sea
     (d) It speeds up as it falls.
     (e) 4 seconds

D6

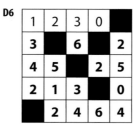

E Using formulas in a spreadsheet (p 144)

E1 (a) 55   (b) 97.02

E2 8.2

E3 6.4 cm

E4 (a) $66 \, \text{cm}^2$ (to 2 s.f.)   (b) $122 \, \text{cm}^2$ (to 3 s.f.)
     (c) $0.063 \, \text{km}^2$ (to 2 s.f.)   (d) $15\,700 \, \text{m}^2$ (to 3 s.f.)

E5 12.0 cm

E6 38.90 m

Test yourself (p 145)

T1 (a) 6   (b) 9   (c) $^-8$ (d) 3   (e) 32

T2 (a) $\frac{7}{12}$ (b) $\frac{3}{4}$ (c) $\frac{5}{12}$ (d) $1\frac{11}{24}$ (e) $\frac{3}{8}$

T3 (a) $5.5 \, \text{cm}^2$ (b) $1.275 \, \text{m}^2$

T4 (a) 1.005 m   (b) 1.02 m
     (c) 0.997 m   (d) 0.993 m (to 3 d.p.)

T5 (a) 10.28 (to 2 d.p.)   (b) 1028.32 (to 2 d.p.)
     (c) 5.78 (to 2 d.p.)

20 Scaling and ratio

A Scaling drawings (p 146)

A1 B (scale factor 2), C $\left(\text{scale factor } 1\frac{1}{2}\right)$, D $\left(\text{scale factor } \frac{1}{2}\right)$

A2 (a) A copy of the original and this enlargement. (b)

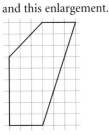 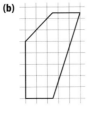

A3 (a)

Measurement	Original length	× ?	Length in copy
Height of building	**4.2 cm**	**1.5**	**6.3 cm**
Length of ladder	**3.2 cm**	**1.5**	**4.8 cm**
Height of door	**2.0 cm**	**1.5**	**3.0 cm**
Width of door	**1.0 cm**	**1.5**	**1.5 cm**

(b) 1.5   (c) Both 72°

A4

	Original length	Scale factor	Copy length
Width of picture	10 cm	**2.5**	25 cm
Height of picture	6 cm	**2.5**	**15 cm**
Height of house	3 cm	**2.5**	**7.5 cm**
Length of car	**2 cm**	**2.5**	5 cm
Length of hedge	**8 cm**	**2.5**	20 cm

A5 (a) 1.6   (b) 2.2   (c) 4.2

A6

	Original length	Scale factor	Copy length
Width of picture	15.0 cm	**3.6**	54.0 cm
Height of picture	10.0 cm	**3.6**	**36.0 cm**
Length of bike	13.5 cm	**3.6**	**48.6 cm**
Height of saddle	**7.5 cm**	**3.6**	27.0 cm
Diameter of wheel	**4.5 cm**	**3.6**	16.2 cm

A7 224 mm

B Scaling down (p 149)

B1 (a) $\frac{1}{2}$ (b) $\frac{1}{6}$ (c) $\frac{1}{3}$ (d) $\frac{2}{3}$

B2 (a) 0.45   (b) 0.65   (c) 0.36   (d) 0.83

B3

	Original length	Scale factor	Copy length
Width of picture	8 cm	**0.6**	4.8 cm
Height of picture	5 cm	**0.6**	**3 cm**
Height of tree	3 cm	**0.6**	1.8 cm
Length of pond	**7.5 cm**	**0.6**	4.5 cm
Length of fence	**9 cm**	**0.6**	5.4 cm

C Proportion within a shape (p 150)

C1 (a) (i) 3 cm   (ii) 7.5 cm   (b) 2.5

(c)

Copy	A	B	C	D
Length (cm)	5	10	2.5	12.5
Height (cm)	2	4	1	5
Ratio	2.5	2.5	2.5	2.5

(d) It is always the same.

(e) 17.5 cm   (f) 8 cm

C2 A and C (ratio 1.6), B and G (ratio 1.4)
D and H (ratio 1.25), E and F (ratio 1.75)

Test yourself (p 152)

T1 (a) 2   (b) 4   (c) $\frac{1}{2}$

T2 (a) 1.25   (b) 55 mm   (c) 12 m

21 Understanding inequalities

A Single inequalities (p 153)

A1 (a) T   (b) F   (c) T   (d) T
    (e) T   (f) F   (g) T   (h) F

A2 (a) $^-20, 1, \frac{2}{5}$ (b) $\sqrt{10}, \frac{13}{4}$

A3 (a) $x \geq {}^-5$ (b) $x < 0$ (c) $x \leq 2.5$ (d) $x > {}^-2$

A4 (a)

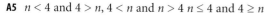

(b)

(c)

(d)

A5 $n < 4$ and $4 > n$, $4 < n$ and $n > 4$ $n \leq 4$ and $4 \geq n$

A6

A7 (a) Sometimes   (b) Always   (c) Always
    (d) Never   (e) Always   (f) Sometimes
    (g) Always   (h) Never

B Combined inequalities (p 154)

B1 A: $^-4 < x < 2$ B: $^-3 \leq x \leq 1$ C: $^-3 \leq x < 1$

B2 (a)

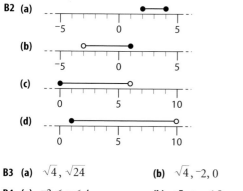

(b)

(c)

(d)

B3 (a) $\sqrt{4}, \sqrt{24}$ (b) $\sqrt{4}, {}^-2, 0$

B4 (a) $^-3 \leq x \leq 4$ (b) $^-5 < x \leq 0$
    (c) $0 < x < 5$ (d) $^-5 \leq x < {}^-1$

B5 $0, 1, {}^-1.5$

B6 $0, 1, 2, 3$

B7 Any five numbers between $^-1$ and 2 (they may include $^-1$, but not 2)

B8 23, 29

B9 12, 15 and 18

B10 9, yes

B11 25, no

B12 $9, {}^-7, 0$

B13 $^-4, {}^-3, {}^-2, {}^-1, 0, 1, 2, 3$ and 4

B14 $^-4$ and 4

B15 Any three of 2, 3, 4, 5 and 6

B16 Any three of 5, 6, 7, 8, 9, 10 and 11

B17 $^-1, 0$ and 1

C Converting between words and symbols (p 156)

C1 (a) $t \leq 4$ (b) $t < {}^-18$ (c) $t \geq 24$

C2 $w \leq 7$

C3 (a) $n \geq 20$ (b) $s \leq 35\,000$

C4 Appropriate sentences

Test yourself (p 157)

T1 (a) F   (b) T   (c) F   (d) T   (e) T

T2 (a) $x \geq 2$ (b) $x < 3$ (c) $x > 0$ (d) $x < {}^-2$

T3 (a)

(b)

(c)

(d)

T4 (a) $0 < x < 4$ (b) $^-3 \leq x \leq 4$
    (c) $1 \leq x < 5$ (d) $^-4 < x \leq 3$

T5 2, 3, 4 and 5

T6 $^-1, 0, 1, 2$ and 3

T7 1, 2, 3, 4 and 5

T8 Five from $^-3, {}^-2, {}^-1, 0, 1, 2$ and 3

T9 $3, 4, {}^-3, {}^-4$

T10 (a) $p \leq 25$ (b) $c > 20\,000\,000$
     (c) $x \geq 50\,000$ (d) $w < 5$

22 Sequences

A Sequences from shapes (p 158)

A1 (a) 36   (b) 400

A2 (a) The numbers in the second row are 1, **3**, **5**, **7**, **9**

(b) 11

(c) 29, with explanation

(d) Design 50

(e) No, with explanation

A3 (a)

triangle 5   triangle 6

(b) The numbers in the second row are
1, **3**, 6, **10**, **15**, **21**

(c) 1, 3, 6, 10, 15, 21, 28, 36, 45, 55

A4 (a) 27

(b) The numbers in the second row are **1**, 8, **27**

(c) $4 \times 4 \times 4 = 64$

(d) 1000

B Continuing linear sequences (p 159)

B1 (a) 17   (b) 33   (c) Yes

B2 (a) 33   (b) 129   (c) No

B3 (a) 19, 22   (b) Add 3

B4 30, 62

B5 (a) + 1, then + 2, then + 3 and so on

(b) 24   (c) No

B6 (a) Add 7   50

(b) Subtract 5   0

(c) Multiply by 2   192

(d) Divide by 2   6.25

(e) Multiply by 3   243

(f) Multiply by 3 and add 1   3280

B7 88, with explanation

B8 (a) 5, 7, 9, **11**, 13, **15**, 17, 19, …

(b) 1, 3, 7, 13, 21, 31, **43**, 57, **73**, …

(c) **0.25**, 0.5, 1, 2, 4, 8, **16**, 32, …

(d) 1, 1, 2, 3, 5, 8, 13, **21**, 34, 55, **89**, …

(e) 1, 5, 13, 29, **61**, 125, **253**, …

B9 (a) 4, 6, **8**, **10**, 12, 14, …

(b) 25, **22**, 19, **16**, 13, 10, …

C The nth term (p 161)

C1 (a)

4, 14, 24, 34, 44, **54**	(b) $10n - 6$
3, 6, 9, 12, **15**	$3n$
2, 9, 16, 23, 30, 37, 44, **51**	$7n - 5$
4, 10, 16, 22, 28, 34, 40, **46**	$6n - 2$
3, 4, 5, 6, 7, 8, 9, **10**	$n + 2$
6, 11, 16, 21, 26, 31, 36, **41**	$5n + 1$
3, 5, 7, 9, **11**	$2n + 1$
4, 8, 12, 16, 20, 24, **28**	$4n$
4, 7, 10, 13, **16**	$3n + 1$

C2 13, 17

C3 (a) 5, 7, 9, 11, 13, 15   (b) 203

C4 (a) A: 5, 12, 19, 26, 33   B: 9, 8, 7, 6, 5

C: $-2\frac{1}{2}, -2, -1\frac{1}{2}, -1, -\frac{1}{2}$ D: 2, 5, 10, 17, 26

E: 60, 30, 20, 15, 12   F: 2, 4, 8, 16, 32

(b) A: 138   B: -10 C: 7

D: 401   E: 3   F: 1 048 576

(c) A, B, C

D The nth term of a linear sequence (p 162)

D1 (a) $3n + 1$; 151   (b) $9n - 8$; 442   (c) $5n - 3$; 247

(d) $5n - 1$; 249   (e) $2n + 1$; 101

D2 (a) 30   (b) $2n$ (c) 19   (d) $2n - 1$

(e) 100 (North St), 99 (South St)

D3 (a) The numbers in the middle row are
$-2, -4, -6, -8, -10$ …
The amount added is 42 each time.

(b) $42 - 2n$ (c) 2

D4 (a) $32 - 2n$ (b) $43 - 3n$ (c) $38 - 5n$ (d) $66 - 6$

E The nth term of other sequences (p 163)

E1 (a) 50

(b) It does not go up or down by equal amounts.

(c) $n^2 + 1$

E2 (a) $n^2 + 3$ (b) 228

E3 (a) $3n^2$ (b) 300

E4 (a) $2n^2$ (b) $2n^2 + 1$

E5 (a) $n^2 - 1$ (b) $n^2 + 10$ (c) $4n^2$ (d) $4n^2 +$

B10
(a) $x, x + 4, x + 8, x + 12, …$

(b) $a, a + b, a + 2b, a + 3b, …$

(c) $n - 5, n - 3, n - 1, n + 1, …$

(d) $x, x - y, x - 2y, x - 3y, …$

(c) 1, 6, 11, **16**, 21, **26**, …

(d) 7, 10, **13**, **16**, 19, **22**, …

F Ways of seeing (p 164)

F1 (a)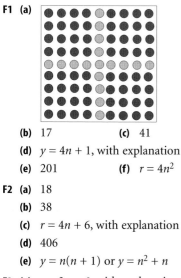

(b) 17   **(c)** 41

(d) $y = 4n + 1$, with explanation

(e) 201   **(f)** $r = 4n^2$

F2 (a) 18

(b) 38

(c) $r = 4n + 6$, with explanation

(d) 406

(e) $y = n(n + 1)$ or $y = n^2 + n$

F3 (a) $r = 3n + 6$, with explanation

(b) 306

G Ways of seeing further (p 166)

G1 (a) 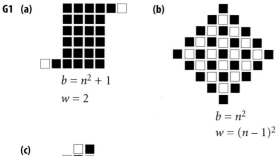 **(b)**

$b = n^2 + 1$
$w = 2$

$b = n^2$
$w = (n - 1)^2$

(c)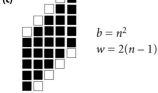

$b = n^2$
$w = 2(n - 1)$

G2 (a) Drawings of mystic roses

(b) 190   **(c)** $\dfrac{n(n-1)}{2}$

Test yourself (p 167)

T1 25, 31

T2 (a) 31   **(b)** $6n - 4$

T3 (a) 13   **(b)** 23

(c) $2n + 3$, with explanation

(d) 203

T4 (a) 53, 68   **(b)** $n^2 + 4$ **(c)** 404

23 Paired data

A Scatter diagrams and correlation (p 168)

A1 (a)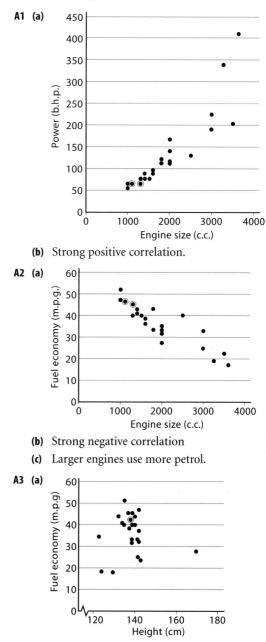

(b) Strong positive correlation.

A2 (a)

(b) Strong negative correlation

(c) Larger engines use more petrol.

A3 (a)

(b) There is no apparent connection between height and fuel economy.

A4 (a)

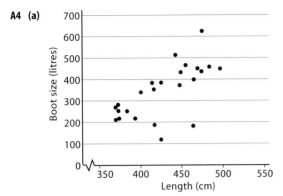

(b) Weak positive correlation

(c) The data gives some support to the statement.

B Line of best fit (p 170)

All answers in this section are approximate.

B1 (a), (b)

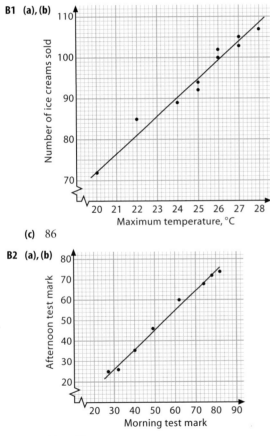

(c) 86

B2 (a), (b)

(c) 50 or 51

B3 (a)

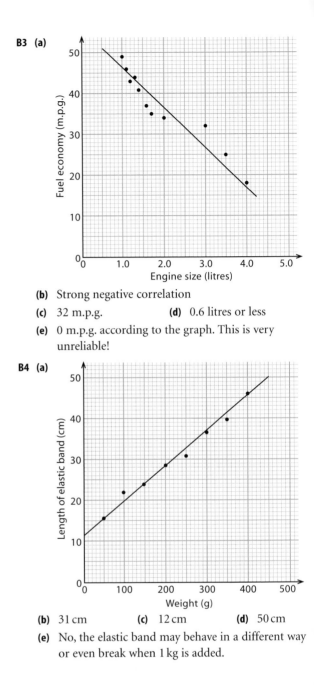

(b) Strong negative correlation

(c) 32 m.p.g.   **(d)** 0.6 litres or less

(e) 0 m.p.g. according to the graph. This is very unreliable!

B4 (a)

(b) 31 cm   **(c)** 12 cm   **(d)** 50 cm

(e) No, the elastic band may behave in a different way or even break when 1 kg is added.

C Interpreting scatter diagrams (p 173)

C1 (a)

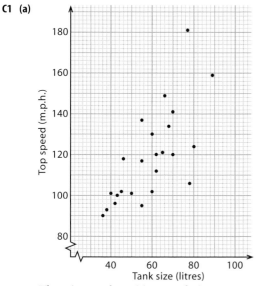

(b) There is a weak positive correlation.
Cars that go faster generally have larger engines and lower m.p.g. so need larger tanks.

C2 (a)

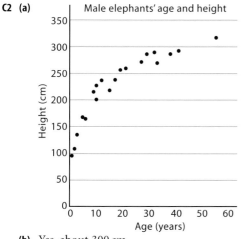

Male elephants' age and height

(b) Yes, about 300 cm

(c) The connection between height and age is not linear and it would be unreasonable to draw a straight line of best fit.

Test yourself (p 174)

T1 (a), (c)

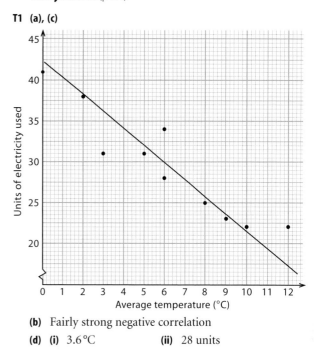

(b) Fairly strong negative correlation

(d) (i) 3.6 °C   **(ii)** 28 units

24 Working with coordinates

A Shapes on a coordinate grid (p 175)

A1

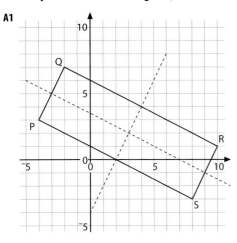

(a) See diagram above for P, Q R

(b) See diagram for S; it has coordinates $(8, ^-3)$

(c) See diagram for lines of symmetry; intersection point has coordinates $(3, 2)$

A2

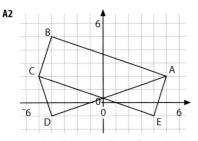

(a) See diagram above for A, B, C

(b) See diagram for D; it has coordinates $(^-4, ^-1)$

(c) $30\,cm^2$

(d) See diagram for E; it has coordinates $(4, ^-1)$

(e) $30\,cm^2$

A3

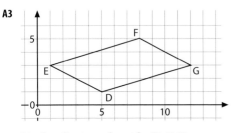

(a) See diagram above for D, E, F

(b) See diagram for G at $(12, 3)$

(c) Rotation symmetry of order 2, centre $(6.5, 3)$.

A4

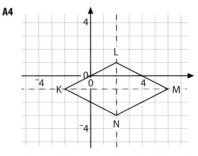

(a) See diagram above for K, L, M

(b) See diagram for N; it has coordinates $(2, ^-3)$

(c) See diagram for lines of symmetry; equations are $x = 2$ and $y = ^-1$

B Mid-point of a line segment (p 176)

B1 **(a)** 10   **(b)** 7   **(c)** $4\frac{1}{2}$ **(d)** 2

     (e) $4\frac{1}{2}$ **(f)** 3   **(g)** $^-3$ **(h)** $^-6$

B2 13

B3 $(4, 2\frac{1}{2})$

B4 **(a)** $(3, 5)$ **(b)** $(6, 6)$ **(c)** $(1, 3)$ **(d)** $(0, 4)$

     (e) $(4\frac{1}{2}, 5)$ **(f)** $(4, 8\frac{1}{2})$

B5 $(^-1, 7)$

C Mixed questions (p 177)

C1 **(a)**

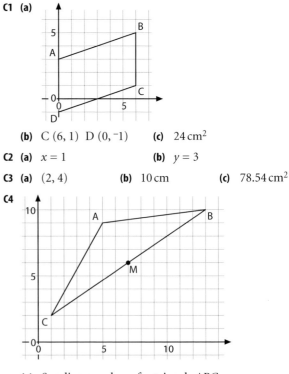

(b) C $(6, 1)$ D $(0, ^-1)$ **(c)** $24\,cm^2$

C2 **(a)** $x = 1$ **(b)** $y = 3$

C3 **(a)** $(2, 4)$ **(b)** $10\,cm$ **(c)** $78.54\,cm^2$

C4

(a) See diagram above for triangle ABC

(b) (i) $\sqrt{65} \approx 8.06\,\text{cm}$ **(ii)** $\sqrt{65} \approx 8.06\,\text{cm}$

(iii) Isosceles

(c) (i) See diagram for M; it has coordinates (7, 6)

(ii) An explanation, for example: AB = AC and M is the mid-point of BC so AM is the perpendicular bisector of BC and hence $\angle$AMB = 90°.

(d) (9, 3)

C5 (a) 5 cm **(b)** 7.5 cm **(c)** 18.75 cm^2

C6

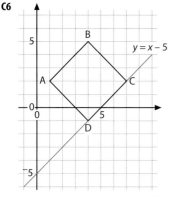
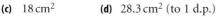

(a) See diagram above for line segment AB

(b) See diagram for line $y = x - 5$ and the points C (7, 2) and D (4, $^-$1)

(c) 18 cm^2 **(d)** 28.3 cm^2 (to 1 d.p.)

C7

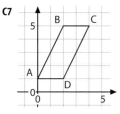

Test yourself (p 179)

T1

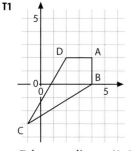
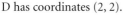

D has coordinates (2, 2).

T2 (a) 9 cm^2

(b) D has coordinates (1, $^-$2).

(c)

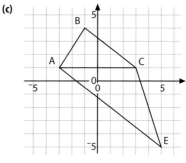

ABCE is a trapezium.

T3 (a) Drawing with A ($^-$5, 6) and B (10, $^-$2) shown

(b) (2.5, 2) **(c)** 17 units

25 Brackets and equations

A Adding and subtracting expressions in brackets

A1 (a) $8z - 3$ **(b)** $3y + 4$ **(c)** $4x - 4$

(d) $15 - w$ **(e)** $7v - 4$ **(f)** $8 - 4u$

A2 (a) $5t - 9$ **(b)** $11 - s$ **(c)** $r - 5$

(d) $12q - 3$ **(e)** $5p + 1$ **(f)** $4n - 8$

A3 A and H $(3a - 6)$, B and D $(a - 6)$, C and G $(3a - 8)$, E and F $(7a - 6)$

A4 (a) $6m - 6$ **(b)** $7k + 8$ **(c)** $2j + 4$ **(d)** $5h + 2$

(e) $9g - 8$ **(f)** $2f - 3$ **(g)** $2 - 11e$ **(h)** $2d - 1$

(i) $8c - 11$ **(j)** $12 - 8b$ **(k)** $8 - 2a$ **(l)** $2 - x$

A5 The words are COMPUTER, SYMMETRY and GRAPH.

A6 (a) The result is always 25.

(b) The missing expression simplifies to 25.

A7 (a) (i) The result is always 1.

(ii) An explanation using the expressions n, $3n$, $3n + 9$, $3 - 3n$, $1 - n$ and 1.

(b) (i) The result is always the number first thought of.

(ii) An explanation using the expressions n, $20 - n$, $40 - 2n$, $60 + 2n$, $30 + n$ and n.

(c) (i) The result is always 11.

(ii) An explanation using the expressions n, $n - 1$, $4n - 4$, $44 - 4n$, $11 - n$ and 11.

B Further simplifying (p 182)

B1 (a) $13n + 7$ (b) $7n + 3$ (c) $14n - 12$
    (d) $4n - 12$ (e) 14 (f) $9n$

B2 (a) $8n + 11$ (b) $20n - 2$ (c) 13

B3 (a) $6 - 2x$ (b) $4x + 2$ (c) $7x + 27$
    (d) $4x - 30$ (e) $4x + 15$ (f) $14x$

B4 (a) $2x - 4$ (b) $8x - 15$ (c) $7x - 17$

B5 (a) $10 - 3p$ (b) $4p - 15$ (c) $p + 24$
    (d) 7 (e) $5p + 2$ (f) $11p$

B6 (a) $2(3x + 1) + 5(x - 3) = 11x - 13$
    (b) $10p - 3(2 - p) = 13p - 6$
    (c) $2(3m - 1) - 3(2m - 5) = 13$
    (d) $\dfrac{8h - 12}{4} - 3(1 - h) = 5h - 6$

C Simplifying to solve an equation (p 183)

C1 (a) $8n - 15$ (b) $8n - 15 = 1$ so $n = 2$

C2 (a) $5 + c$ (b) $5 + c = 20$ so $c = 15$

C3 (a) $9 - 3e$ (b) $9 - 3e = 21$ so $e = {}^-4$

C4 (a) $c = 10$ (b) $d = 1.5$ (c) $f = 2$ (d) $g = 10$
    (e) $h = 1.5$ (f) $k = {}^-1$ (g) $m = 2.5$ (h) $n = {}^-3$
    (i) $p = 3$

C5 (a) $q = 5$ (b) $r = {}^-1$ (c) $s = 4.5$ (d) $t = 1$

Test yourself (p 183)

T1 (a) $6 - 5x$ (b) $7n - 24$ (c) $18m - 11$ (d) $4 - 2n$
    (e) $16k - 3$ (f) $x + 15$

T2 (a) $m = 8$ (b) $c = {}^-1$ (c) $n = 2.5$ (d) $k = 9$

T3 (a) $s = 6$ (b) $x = {}^-3$

26 Roots

A Squares and cubes (p 184)

A1 $4, 121, 49, 1$

A2 (a) 169 (b) No

A3 $27, 1, 64, 1000$

A4 125

A5 (a) 9 (b) 64 (c) 25 (d) 27

A6 $4, 25$

A7 (a) 121 (b) 1 (c) 225 (d) 1000

A8 (a) 144 (b) $240\,\text{cm}$ or $2.4\,\text{m}$

A9 25

A10 (a), (b)

The square numbers form two diagonal lines from the centre (with explanation).

B Square and cube roots (p 185)

B1 (a) 25 (b) 25 (c) 100 (d) 8 (e) ${}^-8$

B2 (a) 10 (b) ${}^-10$

B3 ${}^-6$

B4 (a) $7, {}^-7$ (b) $2, {}^-2$ (c) $1, {}^-1$ (d) $9, {}^-9$

B5 $11, {}^-11$

B6 (a) 2 (b) 3 (c) 1 (d) 4 (e) ${}^-3$

B7 (a) $5\,\text{cm}$ (b) 5

B8 (a) $n = 4$ or ${}^-4$ (b) $m = 12$ or ${}^-12$ (c) $x = 6$
    (d) $n = 4$ or ${}^-4$ (e) $k = 2$ (f) $n = 1$

B9 An explanation

C Approximating a square root or cube root from a graph (p 186)

C1 (a) (i) Estimate such as 6.2 or 6.3
      (ii) Estimate such as 1.9 or 2
      (iii) Estimate such as 7.8 or 8
   (b) Checks on a calculator

C2 (a) (i) Estimate such as 1.7
      (ii) Estimate such as ${}^-2.6$, ${}^-2.7$ or ${}^-2.65$
   (b) Checks on a calculator

C3 (a) Estimate such as 3.2   (b) 3.16   (c) ${}^-3.16$

C4 (a) (i) Estimate such as 3 or 3.3
      (ii) Estimate such as ${}^-5.8$, ${}^-5.9$ or ${}^-6$
      (iii) Estimate such as 12, 12.1 or 12.2
   (b) Checks on a calculator

C5 (a) Estimate such as 2.1, 2.15 or 2.2
   (b) Estimate such as ${}^-2.1$, ${}^-2.15$ or ${}^-2.2$
   (c) Estimate such as 1.7
   (d) Estimate such as ${}^-1.7$
   (e) Estimate such as 1.9, 1.95 or 2

D Cube roots on a calculator (p 187)

D1 (a) 13   (b) ⁻14   (c) 1.5

D2 Checks of C5 on a calculator

D3 Estimate such as $x = 1.4$; $x = 1.442$ (to 3 d.p.)

D4 (a) 3.11   (b) 3.48   (c) 2.03   (d) 1.85
    (e) 5.26   (f) 4.88   (g) 2.78   (h) 1.56

D5 (a) $\sqrt[3]{10^2 + 5^2} = \sqrt[3]{125} = 5$ (b) 4.9

D6 (a) 5.76   (b) 6.2 cm

Test yourself (p 188)

T1 9, 25, 81

T2 (a) 64   (b) 125   (c) 15

T3 (a) 8   (b) 15

T4
$$1^3 = 1 = 1^2$$
$$1^3 + 2^3 = 9 = 3^2$$
$$1^3 + 2^3 + 3^3 = 36 = 6^2$$
$$1^3 + 2^3 + 3^3 + 4^3 = 100 = 10^2$$
$$1^3 + 2^3 + 3^3 + 4^3 + 5^3 = 225 = 15^2$$

T5 (a) 50.653   (b) 2.9

T6 2.88

Review 3 (p 189)

1 3:2

2 24

3 (a) 216   (b) ⁻4

4 $1\frac{4}{5}$

5 (a)

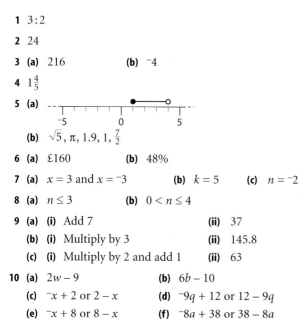

   (b) $\sqrt{5}$, π, 1.9, 1, $\frac{7}{2}$

6 (a) £160   (b) 48%

7 (a) $x = 3$ and $x = ⁻3$ (b) $k = 5$ (c) $n = ⁻2$

8 (a) $n \leq 3$ (b) $0 < n \leq 4$

9 (a) (i) Add 7   (ii) 37
   (b) (i) Multiply by 3   (ii) 145.8
   (c) (i) Multiply by 2 and add 1   (ii) 63

10 (a) $2w - 9$ (b) $6b - 10$
    (c) $⁻x + 2$ or $2 - x$ (d) $⁻9q + 12$ or $12 - 9q$
    (e) $⁻x + 8$ or $8 - x$ (f) $⁻8a + 38$ or $38 - 8a$

11 6, 4, 3, 2.4, 2, 1.71

12 (a) 300 ml   (b) 30 ml   (c) $\frac{6}{7}$

13 (a), (c)

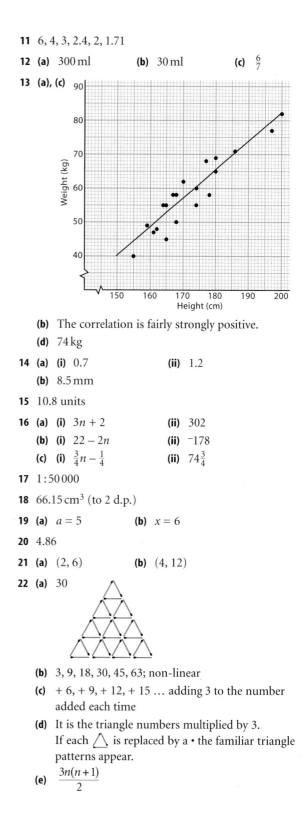

   (b) The correlation is fairly strongly positive.
   (d) 74 kg

14 (a) (i) 0.7   (ii) 1.2
    (b) 8.5 mm

15 10.8 units

16 (a) (i) $3n + 2$ (ii) 302
    (b) (i) $22 - 2n$ (ii) ⁻178
    (c) (i) $\frac{3}{4}n - \frac{1}{4}$ (ii) $74\frac{3}{4}$

17 1 : 50 000

18 66.15 cm³ (to 2 d.p.)

19 (a) $a = 5$ (b) $x = 6$

20 4.86

21 (a) (2, 6)   (b) (4, 12)

22 (a) 30

   (b) 3, 9, 18, 30, 45, 63; non-linear
   (c) + 6, + 9, + 12, + 15 … adding 3 to the number added each time
   (d) It is the triangle numbers multiplied by 3.
      If each △ is replaced by a • the familiar triangle patterns appear.
   (e) $\dfrac{3n(n+1)}{2}$

Index